D1479505

WORLD WAR II DATA BOOK

THE
LUFTWAFFE
1933–1945

WORLD WAR II DATA BOOK
THE
LUFTWAFFE
1933–1945

THE ESSENTIAL FACTS AND FIGURES
FOR GÖRING'S AIR FORCE

S. MIKE PAVELEC

SAYVILLE LIBRARY

amber
BOOKS

First published in 2010 by
Amber Books Ltd
Bradley's Close
74–77 White Lion Street
London N1 9PF
United Kingdom
www.amberbooks.co.uk

Copyright © 2010 Amber Books Ltd

All rights reserved. No part of this work may be reproduced, stored in a retrieval system, or transmitted in any form or by any means, electronic, mechanical, photocopying, recording, or otherwise, without the prior permission of the copyright holder.

ISBN: 978-1-907446-11-5

Project Editor: Michael Spilling
Design: Hawes Design
Picture Research: Terry Forshaw

Printed in Thailand

PICTURE CREDITS

Art-Tech/Aerospace: 2, 38, 40/41, 45, 49, 58/59, 77, 78/79, 94/95, 104, 115, 116/117, 128/129, 163, 166/167, 168

Cody Images: 6/7, 24/25, 62, 132, 136

All artwork profiles Art-Tech/Aerospace except for pages 119 top & bottom, 123 and 127 courtesy of Vincent Bourguignon

All other images © Amber Books

CONTENTS

CHAPTER 1

The German Air Force before World War II

In 1935, Adolf Hitler, Führer of Germany, made the momentous decision to rearm. In open defiance of the Treaty of Versailles which ended World War I, he gambled that he could reinvigorate the German economy with impunity by remilitarization. Hitler's former adversaries in Britain and France stood idly by while the new German empire, the Third Reich, began to rebuild its military might.

The Germans resurrected military industry, with aircraft, ships, tanks and military equipment produced on a massive scale to restore German pride and stabilize a fragile economic situation. The world powers refused to acknowledge that Hitler was preparing for an industrial war of conquest.

Dornier Do 17 bombers fly past the annual Nazi Party rally at

The Reich Air Ministry

In late February 1935, Adolf Hitler stood on the rostrum and announced the rearmament of Germany, beginning with the Luftwaffe, *in direct defiance of the Treaty of Versailles.*

In the treaty that ended World War I, Germany was forbidden from having a military of any significance and could not have weapons of any type. The treaty forbade Germany from having a military air force, which had been particularly effective in the previous war. Hitler, however, pronounced the birth of the new air force – which he called the *Luftwaffe* – for two reasons. First, a new air arm would rebuild the German economy, using government funds to put Germans back to work during troubling economic times. Second, and more importantly, it signified the rebirth of Germany as a power player in European politics, and would rebuild German prestige as a military

power. Two days later, on 1 March, the *Luftwaffe* came into being.

Hermann Göring – World War I ace, German hero and second only to Hitler in Nazi Germany – was named the first leader of the *Luftwaffe*. As the *Reichsminister* of Aviation, Göring was in charge of the *Luftwaffe*, its organization, procurement and staffing. He was also named *General der Flieger* (General of *Luftwaffe*; equivalent to an Allied lieutenant-general). With this inauspicious beginning, the *Luftwaffe* was born.

Early days
In March 1935, the *Luftwaffe* was small and underequipped. *Luftwaffe* strength stood at 16 squadrons of all

types – mostly training squadrons – and only 1833 aircraft. Almost all were already obsolete. Göring's first job was to rebuild the air force almost from the ground up.

According to the Treaty of Versailles, the Germans were severely restricted on types and power of aircraft engines as well as having a standing prohibition on military aircraft. However, in the intervening years (1919–35), the Germans had circumvented the restrictions by building training and transport aircraft. As well, they built aircraft in other countries which were friendly or at least sympathetic, such as Sweden. For a number of years, the Soviets allowed the Germans to train pilots in Soviet airspace; this went a long way to keeping up German pilot numbers. Thus German aircraft, although obsolete, and fully trained pilots were available for incorporation into the *Luftwaffe* in 1935.

Aircraft types
Advanced aircraft were already in the design phase when Hitler made his announcement. The ubiquitous Messerschmitt Bf 109 was being built and made its first flight in May. Early 109s carried the prefix 'Bf' for the company that produced them – Bayerische Flugzeugwerke. Its owner, an excellent aircraft designer

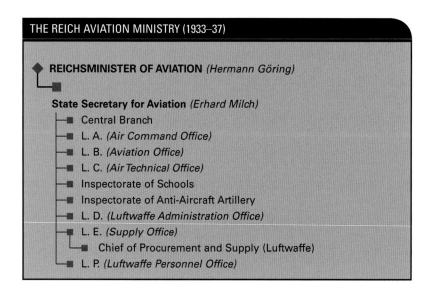

THE REICH AVIATION MINISTRY (1933–37)

◆ **REICHSMINISTER OF AVIATION** *(Hermann Göring)*
 ■
 State Secretary for Aviation *(Erhard Milch)*
 ├─■ Central Branch
 ├─■ L. A. *(Air Command Office)*
 ├─■ L. B. *(Aviation Office)*
 ├─■ L. C. *(Air Technical Office)*
 ├─■ Inspectorate of Schools
 ├─■ Inspectorate of Anti-Aircraft Artillery
 ├─■ L. D. *(Luftwaffe Administration Office)*
 ├─■ L. E. *(Supply Office)*
 │ └─■ Chief of Procurement and Supply (Luftwaffe)
 └─■ L. P. *(Luftwaffe Personnel Office)*

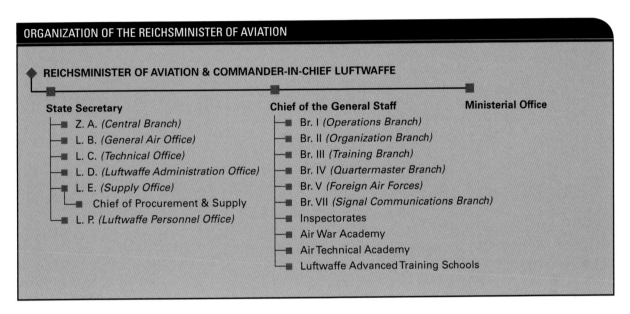

ORGANIZATION OF THE REICHSMINISTER OF AVIATION

◆ REICHSMINISTER OF AVIATION & COMMANDER-IN-CHIEF LUFTWAFFE

State Secretary
- Z. A. *(Central Branch)*
- L. B. *(General Air Office)*
- L. C. *(Technical Office)*
- L. D. *(Luftwaffe Administration Office)*
- L. E. *(Supply Office)*
  - Chief of Procurement & Supply
- L. P. *(Luftwaffe Personnel Office)*

Chief of the General Staff
- Br. I *(Operations Branch)*
- Br. II *(Organization Branch)*
- Br. III *(Training Branch)*
- Br. IV *(Quartermaster Branch)*
- Br. V *(Foreign Air Forces)*
- Br. VII *(Signal Communications Branch)*
- Inspectorates
- Air War Academy
- Air Technical Academy
- Luftwaffe Advanced Training Schools

Ministerial Office

himself, was Willi Messerschmitt. In 1938, the 'Bf' prefix was dropped for the better known 'Me'. The Bf 109 was the latest in fighter aircraft technology, incorporating a low-wing monoplane design together with heavy armament.

By the first production models, the 109 employed an inverted V, liquid-cooled, 12-cylinder Daimler-Benz DB 601 engine that was fuel-injected. This high-performance aircraft (in its early models) carried two 13mm (0.51in) machine guns as well as two 20mm (0.79in) aerial cannons for fighting. The finest design of the time, the 109 (in many variations) would go on to become the most-produced aircraft of all time, and would see action on every front during the war.

Messerschmitt's main rival for fighter contracts was Ernst Heinkel and his namesake company. The Heinkel He 100 (and later the He 112) were competitors for the coveted *Luftwaffe* contracts that were won by

the Bf 109. Heinkel, who figures prominently in the *Luftwaffe* story, was angered by the fighter contracts. But he stayed in the competition, building excellent medium bombers for the *Luftwaffe* such as the He 111. Existing fighter types such as the Arado Ar 64 and 65, as well as another Heinkel, the He 51, were quickly outclassed by the latest designs of the 1930s.

German bombers and transports were initially a mixed bag of aircraft. The existing Dornier models, the Do 11 and 23, were quickly replaced by the Do 17, introduced in 1937. The Heinkel He 111 also showed early promise and was put into serial production. Transport was a secondary mission for the *Luftwaffe*, and little effort was put into improvements to the Junkers Ju 52, which continued in production and use throughout the war. The Ju 52 was initially designed as a Lufthansa airliner; it was converted for wartime

as a transport and liaison aircraft. Over 4800 were eventually built, forming the backbone of the *Luftwaffe* transportation fleet. The Ju 52 was an early design (first flew 1930), and the *Luftwaffe* had 450 of them in 1935.

New military aircraft

Erhard Milch, State Secretary for Aviation at the Reich Aviation Ministry (*Reichsluftfahrtministerium* – RLM), in cooperation with Ernst Udet, head of the *Luftwaffe* Technical Department (*T-Amt*), set to work offering contracts for the procurement of new aircraft. They concentrated on military hardware: fighters, bombers, dive-bombers and transports. The competition was at times biased; Milch did not get along with Messerschmitt, and other frictions existed between the government and industry.

Both Milch and *Generalleutnant* Walter Wever, the *Luftwaffe*'s chief of staff, wanted a heavy, four-engine bomber. Wever perceived the need for such a bomber for wartime and pushed the Dornier and Junkers companies to design heavy bombers for the *Luftwaffe*. However, after his untimely death in an aircraft accident in 1936, and also for technical reasons, the Germans did not pursue the heavy bomber with much interest and prosecuted the war without the capability.

After 1935 and into the remaining years of 'peace', the *Luftwaffe* relied on a small number of companies for its equipment. Engines came primarily from Daimler-Benz and Bayerische Motoren Werke (BMW), and airframes were delivered by five companies: Messerschmitt, Heinkel, Junkers, Dornier, and a few from Arado. In this way, with the addition of a few more companies later, the *Luftwaffe* began its rebuilding period, awarding contracts and funding research and development. Concurrently, German military industry was recapitalized, stabilizing the turbulent economy.

International concern

There was some concern from other countries, but not enough to stop the Germans in their rearmament drive. The least concerned were the Soviets, who were actively helping the Germans throughout the 1920s and 1930s. Equally unconcerned were the Americans, who were dealing with their own Great Depression and ongoing economic crises. The Americans were uninterested in further European entanglements after the Wilson era; they wanted to be left alone in the Western Hemisphere.

Britain was somewhat concerned but was willing to allow a resurgent Germany in order to foster trade and economic exchange with a valuable partner. While Britain did not want an overwhelmingly strong Germany, foreign policy tolerated a somewhat stronger Germany to counter French hegemony on the continent.

The French were the most concerned, and rightly so. In many ways, the Germans were openly antagonistic towards the French, the 'victors' of World War I; the Germans wanted revenge for the harsh imposition of the Treaty of Versailles. Hitler's own writing, in his convoluted tome *Mein Kampf*, pointed to the French as an historic enemy. German foreign policy was aimed at rebuilding strength to counter France. However, regardless of French concern, there was little they could or would do about German rearmament. France was also in the midst of economic and political crises; France had an ever-changing sequence of political leaders in the 1930s, none of whom could sway the population to action.

France concentrated on defensive fortifications like the Maginot Line as well as a defensive foreign policy aimed at preserving the empire. France could not muster popular support, never mind international support, against the Germans. When Germany walked away from the League of Nations in 1933, there was little France could do. Overall, Germany was allowed to rearm to restore the balance of power in Europe and around the world. With a little foresight it should have been obvious that a resurgent Germany,

led by Hitler, could potentially upset the status quo.

Expansion

From its birth in 1935, the *Luftwaffe* proceeded from strength to strength. New models of fighters and bombers were tested and put into series production as the *Luftwaffe* expanded. Squadrons were formed; pilots were trained; the *Luftwaffe* became a viable military force. And unlike the other two branches of the *Wehrmacht* – the *Heer* (Army) and the *Kriegsmarine* (Navy) – the *Luftwaffe* was staffed and manned by ardent Nazis and patriots, who were loyal followers of Hitler for political and promotion reasons. The relative novelty of the service led to a political dedication that was not present in the army or navy, which were staffed primarily by multi-generational Junkers (German landed nobility). The *Luftwaffe* was founded by the Nazis and gathered like-minded politicos to its ranks.

Aircraft coming on stream

By 1935, the Bf 109 was ready for testing; the first production models rolled off the line in early 1937. Immediately it was the most advanced fighter design in the world; all others were obsolete. The Soviets had the nearest competition in the Polikarpov I-16, while Britain's Hawker Hurricane Mk I entered service in 1937. France was behind in fighter development: the Dewoitine D.520 was not ready before 1940. Initial Bf 109 tests were encouraging. It was immediately successful and it impressed during its first wartime trials, during the Spanish Civil War.

Concurrently, the Germans were successful in bomber design and manufacture, with a menu of bomber aircraft nearing operational status: the He 111 (introduced 1935), Do 17 (1937), Ju 87 (1936) and Ju 88 (1939). Thus, in the mid-1930s, the *Luftwaffe* was quickly emerging as the most powerful and modern air force in the world. Germany led the way in the technical development of air power.

Remilitarizing the Rhineland

In March 1936, in response to French and Soviet diplomatic actions, Hitler decided to remilitarize the Rhineland. This area of Germany was especially important for its industrial wealth,

raw materials and strategic geographical significance. The Rhineland contained a network of industries important to the German economy. The region also provided resources (coal, for example) for German industry and power. Furthermore a number of strategic rivers and bridges linked Germany and France in this area. After World War I, the area was still governed by Germany, and was part of the Reich, but was occupied by Allied forces until 1930. The Allies then withdrew but were allowed by treaty to reoccupy if they thought Germany was acting up. The Germans were not allowed to have any troops in the

Rhineland. The French fear was that the Germans would make the Rhineland a strategic staging point for a future invasion of France.

In February 1936, the French and Soviets agreed to a mutual assistance pact. Hitler was increasingly annoyed by the French and decided to take a gamble. On Saturday 7 March 1936, Hitler ordered a military marching band, flanked by bicycle-mounted military police, to march into the Rhineland. Another three battalions of light infantry supported. His orders were to retreat if resisted. No resistance emerged, the band played on, the German civilians welcomed the

LUFTWAFFE AIRCRAFT STRENGTH (MARCH 1935)

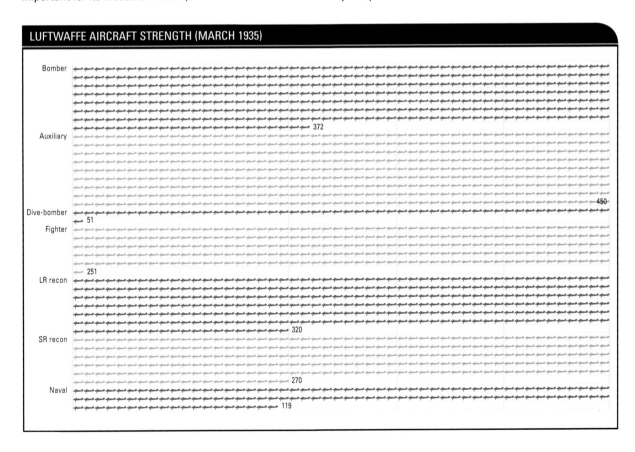

Bomber 372

Auxiliary 450

Dive-bomber 51

Fighter 251

LR recon 320

SR recon 270

Naval 119

troops with cheers. The French, although concerned, could not organize a protest; British government offices were closed for the weekend and they did not respond until the following Monday. Hitler's gamble worked.

Luftwaffe role

The *Luftwaffe* played an interesting role in the remilitarization of the Rhineland. Two understrength *Jagdgeschwader* (fighter groups) – JG 132 and JG 134 – flew overhead. According to one source, the aircraft had neither working guns nor ammunition; they could not have shot at anything if challenged. Another anecdote recounts that the fighters were painted with different squadron insignia every time they returned to base for fuel, thus giving the impression that there were dozens of aircraft in the inventory, rather than a handful. The ruse worked. With the impression of strength and without resistance from the French, Hitler had won his first gamble. Intent on rebuilding Germany economically and spiritually, he had remilitarized the Rhineland without opposition, making use of the newly proclaimed armed forces.

The Spanish Civil War, 1936–39

In 1936 the Luftwaffe *received an invitation to earn its wings. On 26 July, Captain Francisco Arranz gained an audience with Hitler to request assistance in the fascist uprising in Spain. The fascist Nationalists, led by Francisco Franco, had risen against the Republican government and started the Spanish Civil War.*

Unfortunately for Franco, his fighting force was in Spanish North Africa, and he had no means of sea transport. Franco, through Arranz, begged Hitler to consider the Spanish fascist plight and offer support in the form of transport aircraft. Hitler agreed immediately, for three main reasons: assisting Franco would help a fascist partner, prevent the spread of communism and provide a testing ground for the *Luftwaffe*. There were other reasons, but Hitler was convinced. He ordered Göring to send transport aircraft (Ju 52s) to Franco immediately, providing the vital air bridge to the Nationalist cause. Franco had asked for 10 aircraft; Hitler sent 30. Operation *Magic Fire* was under way.

Within two days, German aircraft were ferrying Spanish Nationalist troops across the Strait of Gibraltar. Over the course of a month, the unceasing transport moved more than 10,000 troops from North Africa to Spain, as well as needed military equipment and supplies. Impressively, this came without the loss of a single aircraft. Franco's army began its push from the south.

Franco was still in need. He had soldiers, he had equipment, but he had little in the way of air power. His forces could muster no more than a few obsolete aircraft, mostly of World War I vintage and hopelessly outclassed. Franco had 88 pilots and 50 aircraft on hand, against as many as 200 Republican aircraft, all of more modern design. Franco made another request from Hitler: this time for a proper air force to supplement his land army. In the War Ministry in Berlin, Special Staff W was formed to address Franco's needs.

In exchange for gold, cash and raw materials from Spain, the Germans sent Franco an air force. On 31 July, a merchant steamer left Hamburg with 86 *Luftwaffe* pilots and support personnel and six Heinkel He 51 fighter aircraft. Over the next few months, Germany sent supplies, men and materiel to Spain by air and sea, building up the 'volunteer' force that came to be known as the *Legion Condor*.

■ **Examples of the planes used by German pilots fighting for the fascists during the Spanish Civil War. Although the fighters were obsolete with the introduction of the Bf 109, the bombers represented cutting-edge aviation technology in 1936.**

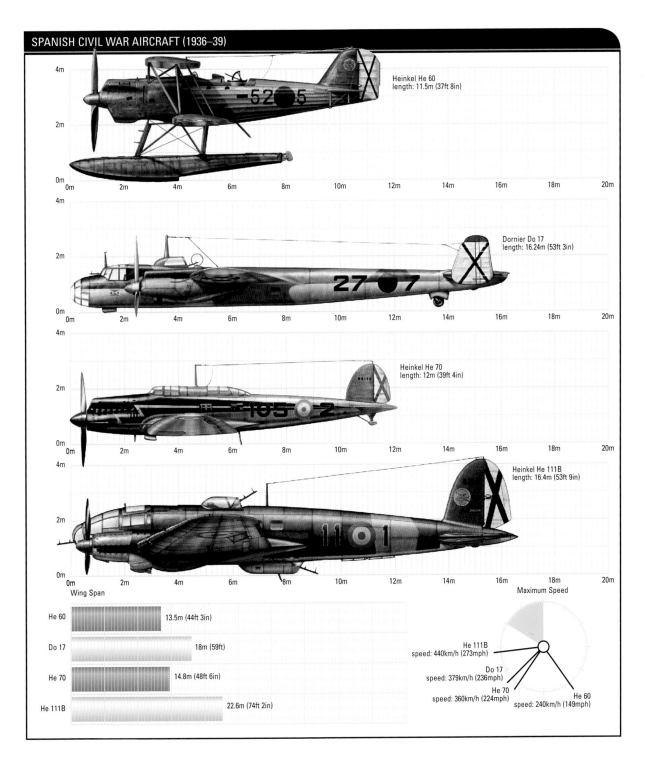

SPANISH CIVIL WAR AIRCRAFT (1936–39)

Heinkel He 60
length: 11.5m (37ft 8in)

Dornier Do 17
length: 16.24m (53ft 3in)

Heinkel He 70
length: 12m (39ft 4in)

Heinkel He 111B
length: 16.4m (53ft 9in)

Wing Span

Maximum Speed

He 60   13.5m (44ft 3in)

Do 17   18m (59ft)

He 70   14.8m (48ft 6in)

He 111B   22.6m (74ft 2in)

He 111B
speed: 440km/h (273mph)

Do 17
speed: 379km/h (236mph)

He 70
speed: 360km/h (224mph)

He 60
speed: 240km/h (149mph)

Legion Condor

The *Legion Condor* was commanded by General Hugo Sperrle, an aerial observer in World War I, and a dedicated Nazi. Sperrle's chief of staff was Wolfram von Richthofen, distant cousin of Baron Manfred von Richthofen – the Red Baron of World War I fame.

In three years, the *Luftwaffe* was able to make impressive advances in aerial combat and complementary doctrine. During the war, the Germans tested new airframes and capabilities, new roles and missions. And, given that it was facing a formidable enemy on the ground and in the air, the *Legion Condor* fared well. It was able to try and test new systems and ideas, and continued development of machines, men and missions as the *Luftwaffe* prepared for Hitler's gambles. By the end of the Spanish

■ The *Legion Condor*'s order of battle. The 'volunteer' pilots of the *Legion Condor* were sent to Spain to fight for the fascist Francisco Franco in his bid to overthrow the government in the Spanish Civil War of 1936–39. The Germans provided Franco's air assets during the conflict.

Civil War, the *Legion Condor* had made three significant contributions to Franco's successful campaign. First, the German airmen had solidified ideas about aerial combat and how to defeat an enemy in the air. These lessons were carried into the war that followed. Second, the Germans took important lessons away on the practice of bombing. They came to some interesting conclusions, and often counter to others' perspectives. Finally, the Spanish Civil War provided a diplomatic front for Germany; while it was going on, Hitler was allowed to concentrate on other issues.

Combat tactics

Aerial combat evolved during the Spanish Civil War. The Germans in the *Legion Condor* went to the fight with preconceived notions about how to fight in the air, based on lessons from World War I. What they realized very quickly was that a number of things had changed, and their doctrine had to evolve. In World War I, pilots like the infamous Red Baron had often taken to the skies alone to look for enemies. By the Spanish Civil War, the Germans realized that they had to

fight as teams. During the war, building on late World War I ideas, they developed the *Schwarm* tactic (in English known as the Finger Four), which was two pairs of fighters – one lead and one wingman – mutually supporting each other. The formation became standard in German fighter doctrine developed during the Spanish Civil War.

One of the main reasons for this development was the evolution of aircraft technology after World War I. As planes flew faster and armaments became more powerful, there was less time to react, and even good pilots needed lookouts and assistance in aerial combat.

A second reason was that the Soviets (and, to a lesser extent, the French) sent aircraft and pilots to the Republican side to counter the *Legion Condor*. The Germans faced organized, experienced pilots in comparable equipment, and had to evolve tactics. The *Schwarm* was an evolution of aerial doctrine into the modern era.

Fighter war

At the same time as Franco was begging for aircraft for his Nationalist

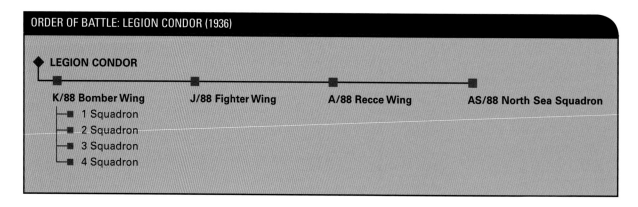

ORDER OF BATTLE: LEGION CONDOR (1936)

LEGION CONDOR

K/88 Bomber Wing | J/88 Fighter Wing | A/88 Recce Wing | AS/88 North Sea Squadron

- 1 Squadron
- 2 Squadron
- 3 Squadron
- 4 Squadron

AIRCRAFT STRENGTH: LEGION CONDOR (1936)

Ju 52	30
He 51	27
He 45	6
He 70	12
He 60	1
He 49	9

forces, the Republicans were also shopping for an air force. One source was the Soviet Union, which sent (after payment in gold) 500 Polikarpov I-16 fighter aircraft to the war. The I-16 was called the Mosca (Fly) by the Republicans, and these aircraft formed the backbone of the Republican air effort, immediately outclassing the *Legion Condor* machines.

The response was twofold. The Germans hastened the production of the newest fighter designs, and revolutionized tactics as mentioned above. The introduction of the Messerschmitt Bf 109 levelled the playing field in the air, and began the lasting legacy of that great aircraft. In time the Germans developed aerial tactics that proved effective, the *Schwarm* and ambush concepts, in which fighters would fly high cover over more vulnerable aircraft, then attack when the enemy was sighted.

By the end of the war, the *Legion Condor* could be proud of its incredibly successful record. In three years of war, the Germans had lost only 96 aircraft – 56 of those in accidents, and most of the accidents related to winter weather. Thus, only 40 combat losses were incurred. The exchange was 277 Republican aircraft shot down in air-to-air combat, and another 58 shot down by anti-aircraft fire (guns supplied and manned by

Germans). The fighter campaign was very successful by every metric.

Bombing raids

The *Legion Condor* also attempted bombing. In numerous raids against the Republican forces, German bombers rained death from above. In February 1937, new German bombers were sent to supplement the ageing aircraft in *Kampfgruppe* (Bomber Wing) 88. Thirty brand new Heinkel He 111B-1s and a follow-on 15 Dornier Do 17s made it to Spain to help the Nationalist cause and provide strategic bombing capability. Frequent bombing raids were carried out, with mixed results. When the aircraft bombed tactically (attacking men and machines on the ground in combat) or in an interdiction role (bombing supplies on their way to the front), the outcomes were superb. A number of sources recount the effectiveness of the German bombers to the immediate fight, and the destruction they delivered.

In one campaign, the results were more mixed. Against the Basques, the *Legion Condor* (and its Italian and Spanish support squadrons) was asked to provide air support for an offensive in the north. The bombers had four missions: to support the troops on the ground, to stop the flow of supplies to the front, to disrupt communications by bombing

■ **After sending a dozen transports, Hitler later asked for a volunteer organization to go to Spain to help the fascist cause. The *Legion Condor* took modern German equipment, pilots and ground crew to assist Franco in his civil war.**

headquarters near the front and, lastly, to destroy Basque villages with bombing. The ultimate goal was to defeat the anarchist forces in the north so that attention could be refocused against the Republican forces in the centre of Spain, around Madrid. The bombers set to work in March 1937.

The initial results were encouraging. *Legion Condor* aircraft were able to bomb forces in direct conflict with Nationalist troops – in other words, tactical bombing. Then they turned their attention to the rear areas, to hamper anarchist movement by bombing rail lines, roads and communications centres. This was also very successful, with continued attacks on Bilbao and Durango. The Basques were all but defeated – but refused to surrender. So the Germans loaded up their Ju 52s and bombed the cities. Durango was first and received a heavy bombing raid. For three days, the bombers dropped their lethal cargo, and destroyed a large section of the city. When it was over, 300 people were dead, and the city was a shambles. 'Strategic' bombing had worked inasmuch as it had destroyed buildings, but it was unsuccessful in making the Basques quit fighting – they did not.

Propaganda disaster
Two weeks later, German bombers attacked Guernica, destroying that city too. Militarily it was a huge success: the railyards were destroyed, buildings were burned and the city ceased to function. About 70 per cent of the city was destroyed and an estimated 300 were killed. But the Basques still did not surrender, and the international outcry was enormous. The Germans were roundly criticized for bombing civilians and destroying cities. Additionally, the bombing of Guernica encouraged Pablo Picasso to paint his interpretation of the horrors of bombing in order to bring international attention to the war. He painted *Guernica* during the war and it went on display at the 1937 World's

Fair in Paris. Today, the painting can be seen at the Reina Sofía National Museum of Art in Madrid.

From the bombing of the cities, the Germans took two important lessons. First, the international community did not condone aerial bombing, even in wartime. Second, it was not strategically decisive: it did not make the enemy surrender. For both of these reasons, the Germans refocused their efforts on changes in doctrine and procurement. First and foremost, they transitioned to a tactical and operational air force – a supporting force for the ground war. Second, they concentrated procurement on short- and medium-range bombers, with particular emphasis on dive-bombers. This change in doctrine would help the German war effort in the short run but plague them in the long term. But the lessons were learned: strategic bombing was not nearly as effective as once hoped, and long-range bomber technology was elusive.

Finally, and perhaps most importantly, the embryonic *Luftwaffe's* efforts in Spain provided a screen for Hitler's diplomatic manoeuvres. While not a big enough contribution to win the war outright, the *Legion Condor* did allow Hitler further gambles while international attention was focused on the civil war. The *Luftwaffe* became a tool of diplomacy and a symbol of strength as Hitler continued his plan of German rearmament and expansion.

As the Spanish Civil War drew to a close, Hitler continued to gamble in Europe and was successful in his aggressive diplomacy. By April 1939, Franco had won the Spanish Civil War, in part due to the contributions of the Germans and Italians, and expanded fascist influence in Europe. Although Franco subsequently declared neutrality when the wider European war broke out in September, he was friendly towards his erstwhile sponsor and Germany benefited from the arrangement.

Organization, 1938–39

When the Luftwaffe *was created in 1935, Hitler needed an organizational structure. Following the template of the army* (Heer) *and the* Oberkommando des Heeres *(OKH), or Army High Command, the new* Luftwaffe *High Command was known as* Oberkommando der Luftwaffe *(OKL).*

Even though the OKL fell under the German Armed Forces High Command (*Oberkommando der Wehrmacht*, or OKW), the personal ties between Göring (*Reichsminister* for Aviation and *Luftwaffe* C-in-C) and

Hitler gave the *Luftwaffe* a close connection to the *Führer*.

Competing commands
This greatly annoyed the chief of the OKW, *General der Artillerie* (General

of Artillery) Wihelm Keitel, who was also effectively Minister for War. To further convolute the issue, the OKW, although technically the high command, was later separated into the OKW and the *Oberbefehlshaber*

West (OBW), or Army Command West, initially under *Generalfeldmarschall* (Field Marshal) Gerd von Rundstedt. OBW was in charge of Western operations; meanwhile, the Army High Command (OKH) became the de facto command organization for the Eastern Front.

In short, Hitler enjoyed playing the commands off against one another other in order to maintain constant control over the course of the war, which in the end was extremely detrimental to the German war effort. The final organization under the OKW umbrella was the high command of the German Navy, the *Oberkommando der Marine* (OKM).

Luftwaffe structure

At the head of the *Luftwaffe* was Göring (a *Generalfeldmarschall* from February 1938), who controlled all *Luftwaffe* air assets in Germany as well as a few 'air'-designated ground units (which will be discussed below). The next layer down consisted, by 1939, of four *Luftflotten*, or air fleets, each of which had a geographic responsibility. *Luftflotte* 1 was in northeast Germany facing Poland; *Luftflotte* 2 was in northwest Germany facing the Low Countries and the Channel/North Sea; *Luftflotte* 3 was in southwest Germany, facing France; and *Luftflotte* 4 was in southeast Germany with jurisdiction over Austria and Czechoslovakia.

The commanders for each of the *Luftflotten* were: *General der Flieger* Albert Kesselring, based in Berlin (*Luftflotte* 1); *General der Flieger* Hellmuth Felmy, headquartered in Braunschweig (*Luftflotte* 2); *General der Flieger* Hugo Sperrle, based in

Munich (*Luftflotte* 3); and *General der Flieger* Alexander Löhr, based in Vienna (*Luftflotte* 4).

Each *Luftflotte* had control over its airfields and aircraft, including maintenance, procurement and air defence. The main components were the air assets but included engineers, communications, air defence and maintenance workers and security personnel. The *Luftflotten* had operational control over their territories and planning staffs for air campaigns originating in their sectors. The *Luftflotten* did coordinate for large operations,

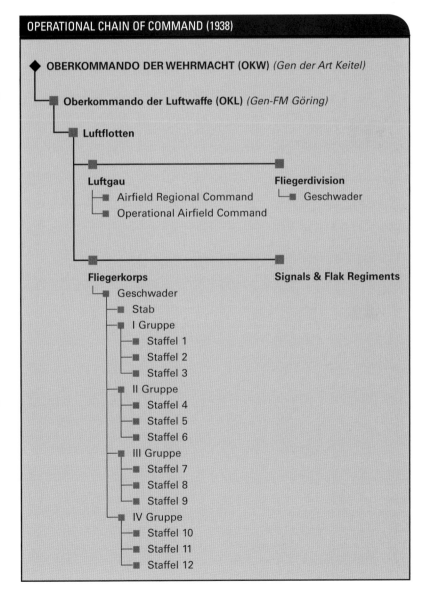

OPERATIONAL CHAIN OF COMMAND (1938)

◆ **OBERKOMMANDO DER WEHRMACHT (OKW)** *(Gen der Art Keitel)*

■ **Oberkommando der Luftwaffe (OKL)** *(Gen-FM Göring)*

■ **Luftflotten**

Luftgau
  ■ Airfield Regional Command
  ■ Operational Airfield Command

Fliegerdivision
  ■ Geschwader

Fliegerkorps
  ■ Geschwader
    ■ Stab
    ■ I Gruppe
      ■ Staffel 1
      ■ Staffel 2
      ■ Staffel 3
    ■ II Gruppe
      ■ Staffel 4
      ■ Staffel 5
      ■ Staffel 6
    ■ III Gruppe
      ■ Staffel 7
      ■ Staffel 8
      ■ Staffel 9
    ■ IV Gruppe
      ■ Staffel 10
      ■ Staffel 11
      ■ Staffel 12

Signals & Flak Regiments

but often their activities were divided according to the specific geographic regions.

Further *Luftflotten* were added as the war progressed. *Luftflotte* 5 was formed after the Norway campaign began. It was based in Oslo after April 1940 and was initially headed by *Generaloberst* (Colonel-General) Erhard Milch. *Luftflotte* 6 was formed well into the eastern war (temporally and geographically) when it was organized in May 1943 in Smolensk under the command of *Generaloberst* Robert Ritter von Greim.

Luftflotte Reich was the last such formation to be established. It was formed late in the war, specifically for the defence of the Reich in the final Allied aerial assaults. Created in Berlin in February 1944, it was commanded by *Generaloberst* Hans-Jürgen Stumpff.

Luftflotten structure

Luftflotten were subdivided into *Fliegerkorps* (flying corps), further dividing the areas of responsibility. *Fliegerkorps* could carry out independent operations, but were usually subordinate to its parent *Luftflotte*. Parallel organization for administrative duties came from the *Luftgaue* (air districts). While the *Fliegerkorps* were responsible for air operations, the *Luftgaue* focused on administration, supply and routine airfield maintenance.

Subdivision within the *Fliegerkorps* allowed for more efficient employment of air resources, by combining operations and commands. Typically, a *Fliegerkorps* oversaw 300–700 aircraft of all kinds, including combat aircraft as well as

LUFTFLOTTEN OPERATIONAL AREAS (1939)

■ Just prior to the German invasion of Poland, the *Luftwaffe* was organized into four *Luftflotten* (air fleets), each commanded by a *General der Flieger* (the equivalent of an RAF air marshal or a lieutenant-general in the USAAF). Each *Luftflotte* contained a complete mix of fighters, ground-attack aircraft, bombers and reconnaissance and transport aircraft, and its operations covered a designated area of territory.

The map here shows the territories covered by *Luftflotten* 1–4, prior to the great expansion in operational zones brought about by the conquest of Poland and Western Europe. *Luftflotte* 1 and *Luftflotte* 2 controlled northeast and northwest Germany respectively, while *Luftflotte* 3 and *Luftflotte* 4 took on the southwest and southeast areas of the country. *Luftflotte* 4 also had jurisdiction over Austria and Czechoslovakia.

liaison machines and transports. The *Fliegerkorps* was usually headed by a general officer and included an organization and planning staff. There were three to four *Fliegerkorps* in each *Luftflotte*.

Fliegerkorps structure

The *Fliegerkorps* were further divided into *Geschwader*. A *Geschwader* was a tactical unit roughly equivalent to an American air wing or a Royal Air Force group, and contained 100–120 aircraft. Each *Geschwader* was designated according to its mission – fighter, bomber, transport, or an equivalent tactical designation.

A *Geschwader* was usually commanded by an *Oberst* (colonel) but in extreme cases could be commanded by an *Oberstleutnant* (lieutenant-colonel) or a *Major* (major). Each *Geschwader* had a *Stab* (staff section), as well as communications officers, an adjutant for the commander, an air operations officer, a personnel officer and intelligence, navigation, and signals personnel. There were three to five *Geschwader* in each *Fliegerkorps*.

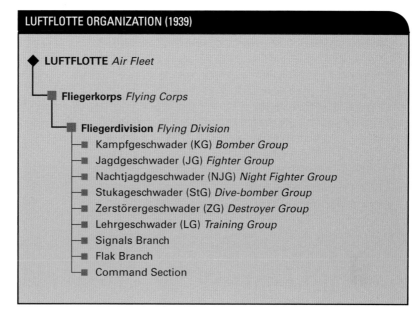

LUFTFLOTTE ORGANIZATION (1939)

◆ **LUFTFLOTTE** *Air Fleet*

■ **Fliegerkorps** *Flying Corps*

■ **Fliegerdivision** *Flying Division*
- ■ Kampfgeschwader (KG) *Bomber Group*
- ■ Jagdgeschwader (JG) *Fighter Group*
- ■ Nachtjagdgeschwader (NJG) *Night Fighter Group*
- ■ Stukageschwader (StG) *Dive-bomber Group*
- ■ Zerstörergeschwader (ZG) *Destroyer Group*
- ■ Lehrgeschwader (LG) *Training Group*
- ■ Signals Branch
- ■ Flak Branch
- ■ Command Section

■The operational *Luftwaffe* was organized into *Luftflotten* (sing. *Luftflotte*) – air fleets. Initially, there were four. During the war, the sectors were expanded, and eventually three more were added: 5, 6 – and *Luftflotte Reich*, specifically for the defence of the homeland towards the end of the war. Each *Luftflotte* ontained several *Fliegerkorps* (flying corps). Each *Fliegerkorps* was made up of a number of *Geschwader* – the equivalent of an air wing in the USAAF or a group in the Royal Air Force. In addition to aircraft and crews, each *Luftflotte* had a signals branch, a Flak (anti-aircraft) branch and a command organization – the *Luftgau*, or air district, which was responsible for airfield operations and supply.

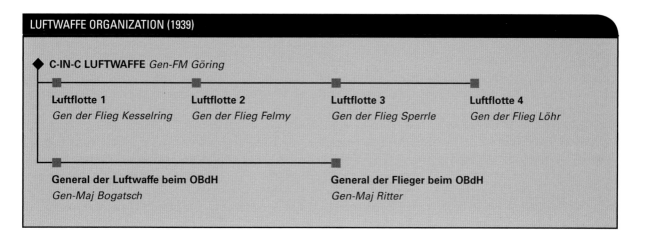

LUFTWAFFE ORGANIZATION (1939)

◆ **C-IN-C LUFTWAFFE** *Gen-FM Göring*

Luftflotte 1	Luftflotte 2	Luftflotte 3	Luftflotte 4
Gen der Flieg Kesselring	*Gen der Flieg Felmy*	*Gen der Flieg Sperrle*	*Gen der Flieg Löhr*

General der Luftwaffe beim OBdH
Gen-Maj Bogatsch

General der Flieger beim OBdH
Gen-Maj Ritter

The bulk of each *Geschwader*, though, was made up of the combat *Gruppen* (roughly equivalent to an American air group or an RAF wing). The typical fighter *Geschwader* (*Jagdgeschwader*, or JG) was made up of three *Gruppen* and a *Stab*, with four aircraft in the *Stab* plus 36–48 planes in each *Gruppe*. A *Gruppe* was commanded by a *Major* or a *Hauptmann* (captain) and usually had a home airfield but could share with another *Gruppe*. Each *Staffel* (squadron), of which a *Gruppe* had three or four, contained 12 aircraft (increased to 16 later in the war) – that is, three flights (*Schwärme*) of four aircraft each. Each *Schwarm* had a pair of *Rotten* (sections), each comprising a lead and a wingman.

Staffel and *Schwarm*

Jagdgeschwader 26 (JG 26) during the Battle of Britain provides a good illustration of the organization of the *Luftwaffe* in 1940. From 22 August, JG 26 was commanded by Adolf Galland, initially as a *Major*, and was assigned to an airfield in Pas-de-Calais, from where it flew Bf 109s against the RAF.

At this point, JG 26 contained three *Gruppen*, each with three *Staffeln* of 12 aircraft plus a four-plane *Gruppenstab* unit; in other words, each *Gruppe* had 40 planes. A five-plane *Geschwaderstab* unit led by Galland himself made up the inventory. JG 26's emblem was an 'S' in a shield, and the unit was named 'Schlageter' for Albert Leo Schlageter, a German World War I

veteran executed by the French in 1923 for sabotage. The unit also painted the noses of its aircraft a distinct yellow for identification and psychological purposes. JG 26 was was one of five fighter groups (along with JG 3, 51, 52, 54) assigned to *Jagdfliegerführer* 2 (Fighter Command 2) of *Luftflotte* 2.

Ground support units

In addition to flying units, each *Luftflotte* had command over land-based *Luftwaffe* units, among them the ground units that supported each airfield. While aircrew were the most visible component of the *Luftwaffe*, there were masses of men and women on the ground as well. These included the mechanics and

GESCHWADER ALLOCATION

LEVEL ONE

Luftflotte 1	Luftflotte 2	Luftflotte 3	Luftflotte 4
Geschwader 1–25	Geschwader 26–50	Geschwader 51–75	Geschwader 76–100

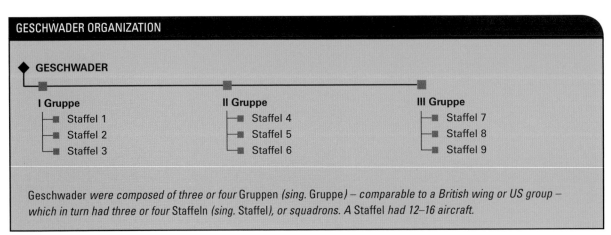

GESCHWADER ORGANIZATION

GESCHWADER

I Gruppe	II Gruppe	III Gruppe
Staffel 1	Staffel 4	Staffel 7
Staffel 2	Staffel 5	Staffel 8
Staffel 3	Staffel 6	Staffel 9

Geschwader *were composed of three or four* Gruppen *(sing.* Gruppe*) – comparable to a British wing or US group – which in turn had three or four* Staffeln *(sing.* Staffel*), or squadrons. A* Staffel *had 12–16 aircraft.*

DER SCHWARM

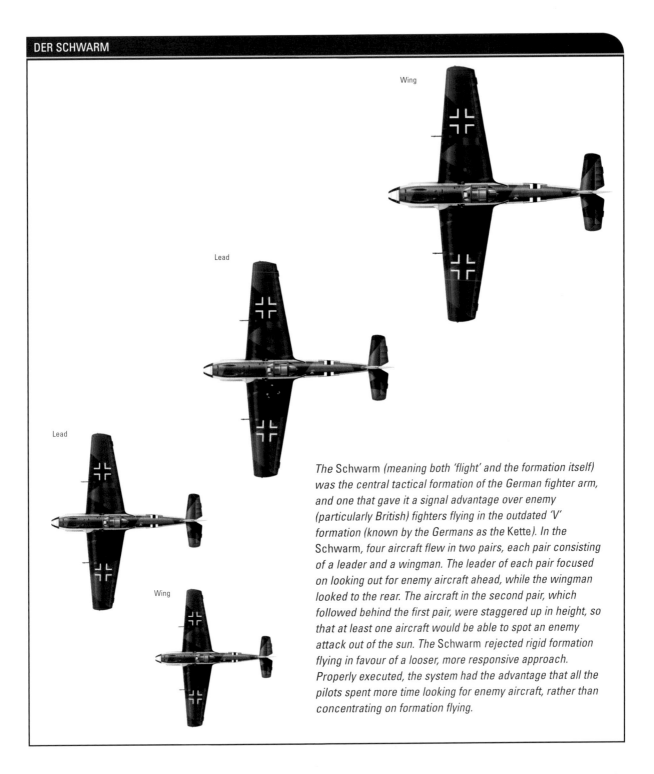

Wing

Lead

Lead

Wing

The Schwarm (meaning both 'flight' and the formation itself) was the central tactical formation of the German fighter arm, and one that gave it a signal advantage over enemy (particularly British) fighters flying in the outdated 'V' formation (known by the Germans as the Kette). In the Schwarm, four aircraft flew in two pairs, each pair consisting of a leader and a wingman. The leader of each pair focused on looking out for enemy aircraft ahead, while the wingman looked to the rear. The aircraft in the second pair, which followed behind the first pair, were staggered up in height, so that at least one aircraft would be able to spot an enemy attack out of the sun. The Schwarm rejected rigid formation flying in favour of a looser, more responsive approach. Properly executed, the system had the advantage that all the pilots spent more time looking for enemy aircraft, rather than concentrating on formation flying.

maintenance personnel for aircraft operations, engineers and workers for airbase construction and operations. Security personnel and staff personnel rounded out airbase staff, providing necessary support.

Each *Luftwaffe* command included communications and intelligence people, as well as planners and even medical staffs. Additionally, the *Luftwaffe* was in charge of ground-based air defence and thus also required anti-aircraft personnel. Finally, German paratroopers not only dropped from *Luftwaffe* aircraft but were indeed part of the *Luftwaffe*. They gained infamy in several campaigns, specifically in Norway, Belgium and later Crete.

Interestingly, an entire division that was related to the *Luftwaffe* but not commanded by it was the *Panzerdivision Hermann Göring*, which participated in a number of battles and gained notoriety in North Africa and on the Eastern Front. It had been originally designed and incorporated by Göring, but as a ground unit was under OKH control. Later renamed *Fallschirm-Panzerdivision Hermann Göring*, the unit was still fighting on the Eastern Front when the war ended.

Aircrew Readiness

An essential component of the air war was the provision of the pilots necessary for combat operations. Initially the Germans were well positioned to train and supply pilots for their fighters and bombers.

However, in this one area, the Germans eventually fell behind with an outdated model for pilot training. In 1935, when the *Luftwaffe* was announced to the world, the Germans had access to a small number of experienced pilots inside the country. There were a few pilots who had served in World War I, but these men were quickly reaching an age at which they were no longer fit for duty. But even under the constraints of the Treaty of Versailles, which forbade combat pilots, an aviation culture had been promoted in Germany and a number of interested men had joined sport-flying and gliding clubs. Thus when Hitler declared it 'legal' once again, there was a small cadre of experienced pilots available. Two *Lehrdivisionen* (training divisions) were set up to instruct new pilots in operations and tactics, consisting of 12 active units. Four within *Lehrgeschwader* (LG) 1 were for He 111 training; two within LG 2 were specifically for Do 17 training; four units instructed fighter pilots (three Bf 109 and one 110); and one was for dive-bomber pilots flying Ju 87s. The final unit was for basic instruction on the Henschel Hs 126, whose pilots went on to transport and liaison aircraft.

Training

Luftwaffe training before and in the first year of the war was similar to that in other pilot-training organizations around the world. Pilots received initial aircraft training in a variety of training types, mastering the art of flying at the most basic level. Initial instruction was around 80 hours of flight time – about six to eight weeks of instruction. Then, when they were deemed ready for combat types, the pilots were promoted to their type-specific training, usually fighters or bombers. An additional six to eight weeks followed in *Lehrdivision* 1 or 2, on the necessary skills for combat pilots. Theoretically, this prepared the pilots for more intensive operations in high-technology machines, preparing them for actual combat operations. Once these courses were completed, the pilots were shipped off to operational units, where training continued under the guidance of the unit commander and other experienced pilots.

The German system was adequate for the start of the war. More than 2300 pilots were ready to fill the ranks of 302 *Staffeln* in September 1939. But the German training system was not adequately organized for a long war of attrition; the system was deficient before anyone realized. When compared with the Allied training programmes, which could draw from a greater combined population base, the Germans simply lacked the manpower for air, sea and land warfare over an extended conflict. The Germans had to rely on their best pilots for the entire war, and did not have a coherent replacement system.

Endurance test

Whereas Allied pilots flew a specific number of missions and then were rotated out to become instructors, German pilots like Adolf Galland flew throughout the war, from start to finish, from the first missions of the war (in addition to his flight time in the Spanish Civil War) up to the very final days of the Reich in 1945. German pilots flew until they could not fly any more – because they were injured or killed.

Thus the experts got better (and German pilots had the most impressive combat victory tallies), but young pilots received less and less training throughout the war. Finally this was constrained by lack of aircraft to train in and not enough fuel for adequate training.

By the end of the war, German pilots came in only two flavours – the very experienced and the undertrained: replacements of any other kind were simply unavailable. The Allies, on the other hand, had a steady stream of highly trained pilots who not only survived but could count on an 'end' to their war if they made it to a certain number of missions. In a short war, the German system could have worked; in a long war of attrition, it was doomed to fail.

AIRCREW READINESS (AUGUST 1938)

In August 1938, the Luftwaffe *had a total of 3714 authorized crews on its books. As is so often the case with military data, the figures need unpacking somewhat. Training output lagged behind operational requirements, so only 1432 crews were fully operational, whereas 1145 had a partially operational status. Nevertheless, in terms of fully operational crews, it was the all-important fighter and medium-bomber forces that were best supported.*

Strategic Reconnaissance 84 Operational/228 Authorized

Tactical Reconnaissance 183 Operational/297 Authorized

Fighter 537 Operational/938 Authorized

Bomber 378 Operational/1409 Authorized

Dive-bomber 80 Operational/300 Authorized

Ground-attack 89 Operational/195 Authorized

Transport 10 Operational/117 Authorized

Coastal and Navy 71 Operational/230 Authorized

CHAPTER 2

Luftwaffe Production

By 1939, the Germans had built up impressive aircraft production capabilities. With the massive rearmament of the 1930s, the aviation industry was reborn. Historically, in World War I, the Germans had produced some of the finest military aircraft in the world, culminating in the all-metal monoplane (Junkers D.1 and CL.1), the high-speed fighter (the Albatross D.VII) and massive strategic bombers like the Gotha R-planes.

The planes were so advanced and potentially threatening that the Allies at the end of the war declared that the Germans were restricted in the types of aero engine they could develop and prohibited from building further military aircraft under the conditions of the Treaty of Versailles. German industry languished for a few years, and could have collapsed altogether.

This rather crowded scene shows He 115 seaplanes (foreground) and He 111 bombers (background) on the production line.

A War Economy

In the 1930s, the global economy was a shambles. The Germans were being forced to pay reparations for World War I based on the requirements of the Treaty of Versailles. The money, paid to the French and British, was returned to the Americans, for the repayment of wartime loans.

After Hitler was elected, he pulled out of the League of Nations (1933), and continued to defy the Treaty of Versailles. He stopped paying reparations – 132 billion Reichsmarks in gold had already been paid, further weakening the German economy – and by 1935 began open rearmament. The new German economy was based on the National Socialist model of economics – strength in Germany for the strength of Germany. One way to accomplish that was by enormous government spending programmes to stabilize the economy; Hitler concentrated government spending on infrastructure and military hardware. The German economy stabilized and then improved based on these strict government measures and increased spending. Hitler realized that there could be repercussions from violating the Treaty of Versailles but was confident that no one would defy him because their economies were also in a bad way. The British, French and Americans stood by idly as German economic might was reborn under the National Socialists.

Industrial might

By 1938, the German economy had made a full recovery. Industry based on high technology, hard science and new processes led the world. The Germans were recognized for their excellent tools and machines, and were feared for their newly built military power. And with a strong economy, the Germans were able to sell abroad to acquire resources in short supply in Germany. They turned to Sweden for steel and iron, to the Soviets for oil and grain and to France for bauxite, an essential ingredient for aluminum.

But Hitler knew that if he was going to expand the Third Reich, he would have to secure access to raw materials and additional industry, as well as farmland to feed an increasing population. Germany was not self-sufficient, and Hitler did not want to have to pay for resources.

In 1936, Hitler ordered Göring to initiate a Four-Year Plan to acquire vast amounts of resources for the Reich. Göring set to work gathering stockpiles of raw materials at unprecedented levels for the security of the Reich. He focused primarily on raw materials from countries that could potentially become enemies if the Germans sought war, buying up quantities of metals, petroleum and timber for expected military production. At the same time Fritz Todt was put in charge of infrastructure programmes aimed at constructing buildings, roads, canals and rail lines. Most of the transportation network had a dual purpose: in peace it facilitated transportation for German industry and civilians; during wartime it would act as a conduit for faster mobilization and logistics.

When the war started, the Germans commanded an impressive economy as well as vast quantities of raw materials. The Americans and Soviets both had great potential but were still reeling from the global depression. This caused Hitler to overestimate his own economy, and consequently underestimate others. The Germans went to war with a rapidly expanding industrial base, while the British, French and nearly everyone else struggled to revitalize theirs.

Captured potential

In the first two years of the European war (1939–40), Hitler captured vast quantities of resources and industry, forcing them into the German sphere and retooling them for military production. France's impressive industrial base was immediately put to work to produce German military goods. Thus even though the Germans were expending resources and material in the war, their growing industrial base produced more, and German military production increased.

One shortfall the Germans faced was in oil and petroleum products. This lack of oil was compensated for in two ways: first by German industrial techniques in synthetic fuels, and second by conquest. The German spring offensive in 1942 towards the Caucasus oilfields was designed to capture these resources for German use. Up to 1944, the Germans were able to produce enough synthetic fuel and received

GERMAN MILITARY EXPENDITURE IN RM MILLIONS (1933–39)

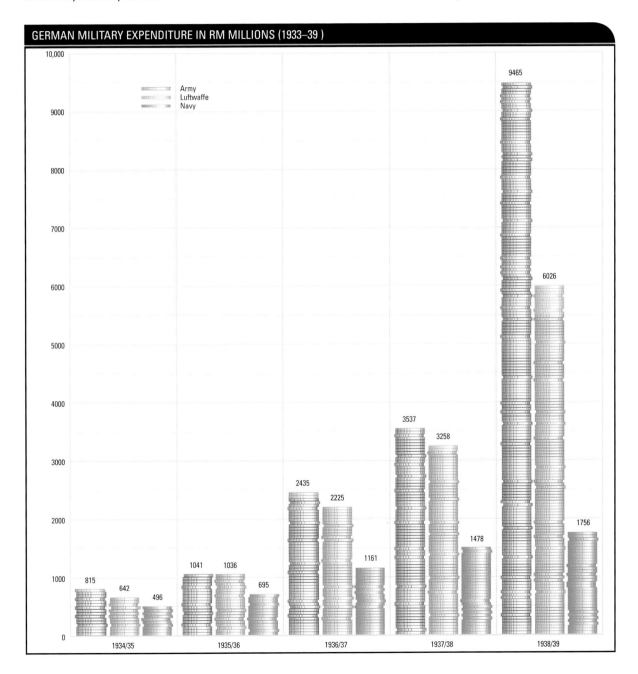

Army
Luftwaffe
Navy

enough fuel from Axis partners to maintain a fairly steady flow. But after the loss of Romania, the situation grew increasingly dire. By

the end of the war, Germany relied entirely on synthetic fuels produced at home and a declining supply of reserves. The main target for Allied

bombers was the German oil industry; the Americans hoped to strangle the German military by cutting off the necessary fuel.

WAR EXPENDITURE COMPARED, AS PERCENTAGE OF NATIONAL INCOME (1939–45)

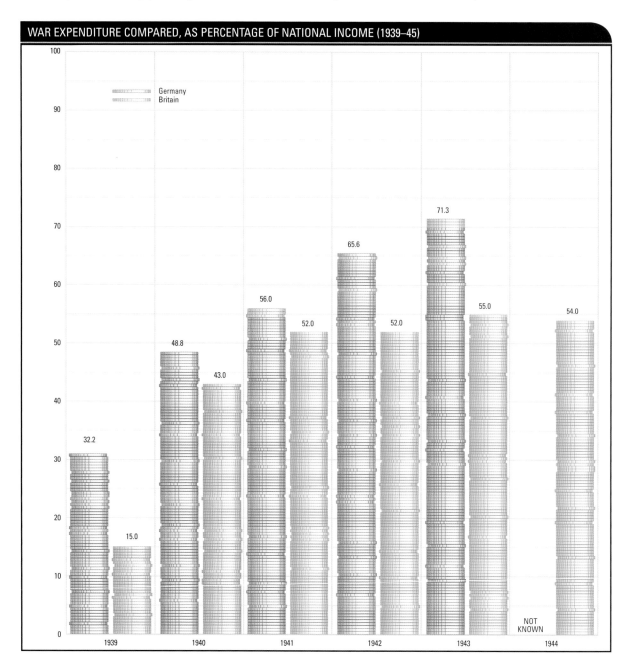

Germany
Britain

As the war progressed, the Germans were able to increase industrial production and their overall economic viability. Through 1943, output of materials for the German armed forces increased, producing some of the best weapons of the war. By 1944, however, the Germans faced increasing amounts of Allied hardware, and were forced to reinvent industrial processes and step up output. Albert Speer was named Minister of Armaments and moved to increase German production still further. His initiatives instituted new production schedules, fewer government restrictions and prioritized industry's efforts. Into 1944, German wartime production reached its highest levels of the war, and the Germans had more equipment than before. One illustration is indicative: German aircraft production reached its highest levels in 1944, increasing to over 40,000 units that year (up 160 per cent on 1943). At the same time, German gross domestic product (GDP) continued to rise, reaching $437 billion before the ultimate collapse in 1945.

The fall

However, when the collapse came, it was precipitous. Facing the combined economies and industry of the resurgent USSR and United States, the Germans were simply overwhelmed. Even at the height of their industrial production, the Germans were fighting the combined weight of two impressive and revitalized industrial nations; while Germany was producing the 40,000 aircraft cited above in 1944, American and Soviet industry combined to

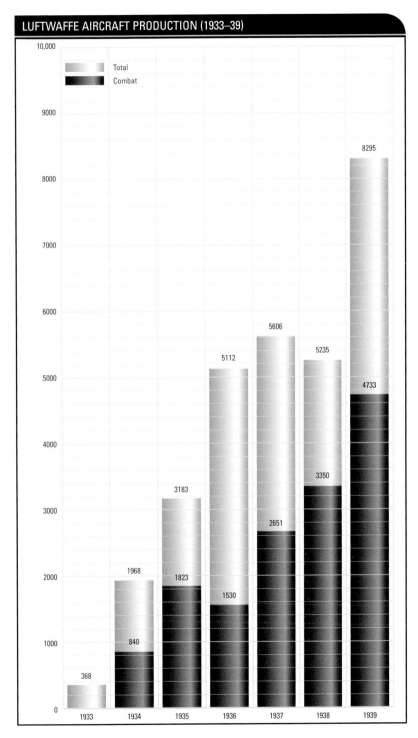

LUFTWAFFE AIRCRAFT PRODUCTION (1933–39)

produce 136,000 aircraft. By the end of the war, the Allies had produced almost 600,000 aircraft, whereas the Germans had built 120,000. And bear in mind that these figures are for aircraft only. The Germans were out-produced across the board, including tanks, aircraft, ships, machine guns, trucks and artillery pieces. The Germans may have had the best equipment (and they did), but in the end it did not matter; they were

GERMAN EXPENDITURE ON SELECTED ARMAMENTS IN RM MILLIONS (1939–41)

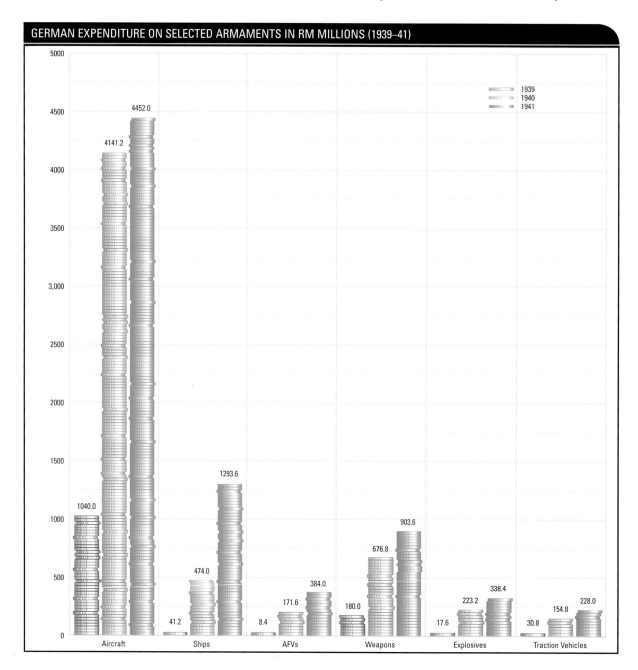

overwhelmed by Allied production and economic capabilities.

With Allied bomber attacks on German industry and oil, the invasion and liberation of France and the Soviets surrounding Berlin, the German economy and industry collapsed. Germany was out of materials, manufacturing was destroyed or disrupted and the entire oil industry was a shambles. As well, the transportation system collapsed, food and (heating) fuel were in short supply and the entire system fell in on itself. Germany's economy and industry ceased to exist under the combined weight of the Allied offensives and the cumulative effects of five years of war. The German defeat was complete; by 1945, Germany existed in name alone.

Manufacturers and Production, 1935–39

The Germans capitalized on the restrictions of the Treaty of Versailles by rethinking engine and aircraft engineering, and leapfrogged a number of inter-war mistakes made in Britain, France and the United States.

Instead of getting mired in evolutionary incremental changes, the German aviation industry, when finally allowed to rebuild, developed revolutionary designs and processes that had set the industry standard by 1935. And by learning from Allied mistakes, German industry was able to produce cutting-edge designs by the end of the 1930s. The earlier Versailles restrictions actually helped German aviation pioneers jump-start their industry when the time came.

Added to this were lucrative government contracts in 1935 that provided necessary funds for the development of high-technology aircraft. Hitler's government provided enormous sums of money for rearmament, the lion's share going to the *Luftwaffe*. The German aviation industry had the time, money and expertise to rebuild the *Luftwaffe* from the ground up, focusing on the latest technologies, and quickly surpassed all their rivals. By the start of the war, the Germans fielded some of the best military aircraft in the world, purpose-designed for the specific roles requested by the military and qualitatively better than anyone else's. Across the board, with the exception of a heavy bomber (which, incidentally, no one else had until later in the war), German aircraft were superior.

Maximum output

The *Luftwaffe*'s qualitative dominance was matched by quantitative superiority as well. The Germans began rearmament in 1935, well before any other nation, and their industry was working at high capacity when the European war began in 1939. However, this was a two-edged sword. The Germans were in a position to field the best and most numerous air force for a short war, but a long war of high-intensity attrition could potentially doom German industry. It was thus in Germany's best interests to win decisive campaigns quickly.

Furthermore, if a very powerful industrial nation became involved (for example, the United States), German quality could be overwhelmed by numerical quantity. Hitler was determined to wage a short, decisive war to make sure that German initial numerical and qualitative superiority would not be surpassed.

One final matter needs mention. By 1939, German industry was in full swing and was producing close to required levels for the German military. That said, it was the consensus among the armed forces and industry that more production was needed to fight a general European war, and both the industrialists and military leaders tried to convince Hitler to delay war until 1941. Their opinion was that the German armed forces would be best suited for war at that point, with qualitative and quantitative superiority over any foe.

However, Hitler demurred. In his opinion – in reality, the only opinion that mattered – such a delay would give Germany's enemies time to ramp up production as well. Hitler thought that it was best to strike immediately. German equipment was better at that point – and would only get better – and an immediate strike would equate to continued German supremacy even in a high-intensity war. Hitler won the argument; the German military prepared to carry out his orders.

New engine designs

The German aviation industry was at the cutting edge of design and manufacture by 1939. The Germans boasted some of the finest aircraft and engine manufacturers of the era – world leaders in their respective technologies.

INITIAL LARGE ORDER FOR AIRCRAFT (30 SEPTEMBER 1935)	
Aircraft	*Type*
150 bombers	Do 11
222 bombers	Do 13, later Do 23
450 auxiliary bombers	Ju 52
19 fighters	Ar 64
85 fighters	Ar 65
141 fighters	He 51
14 naval fighters	He 51W
12 naval fighters	He 38
320 long-range recce	He 45
270 short-range recce	He 46
51 dive-bombers	He 50
81 naval recce	He 60
21 long-range flying boats	Do 16 Wal
21 multi-purpose naval a/c	He 59
9 bombers	Do 17
9 bombers	He 111
3 bombers	Ju 86
72 recce aircraft	He 70
4 flying boats	Do 18
Total ordered	1954 aircraft

In engines, German manufacturing was impressive, and a number of aviation engine companies were hard at work providing ample supplies of engines for the German air force. The Daimler-Benz company, known worldwide for their internal combustion petrol engines, produced excellent powerplants for the *Luftwaffe*, including the DB 601 (later upgraded to the 605).

The DB 601 was an inverted V, liquid-cooled, 12-cylinder aviation engine that incorporated fuel injection and a single-stage supercharger for better performance at high altitude. By 1939 the DB 601, weighing 590kg (1320lb), produced over 900Kw (1200hp), impressive by industry standards.

Series production of the DB 601 had begun in 1935, and over 19,000 units were delivered to the *Luftwaffe* before the 601 was upgraded to the 605 in 1942. In addition, Junkers Motorenwerke (Jumo) and Bayerische Motoren Werke (BMW) also produced aircraft engines for the *Luftwaffe*, such as the Jumo 211 inverted V-12 that powered the Ju 87 and Ju 88.

Other high-performance engines were of another type: the radial. Air-cooled radial engines came from Siemens-Schuckert (later designated Bramo), as well as from BMW. Specifically, the pre-war BMW 801 was a twin-row, air-cooled, 14-cylinder radial aero engine, supercharged for high-altitude performance and initially producing 1050kW (1400hp) from a weight of 1000kg (2200lb). In general, radial engines were hampered by the large frontal area, which increased drag,

and were not seen as ideal engines for fighters. But continued improvements to the BMW design made it a more attractive proposition, and the 801 eventually powered the Focke-Wulf Fw 190 fighter.

The benefit of the radial was that it had fewer moving parts – it did not require delicate liquid-cooling plumbing – and was more resilient and reliable. But German radials took time to develop, whereas in 1939 German in-line aviation engines were cutting-edge. Other firms supplying the *Luftwaffe* with engines included Argus Motoren and Heinkel's in-house engine department.

Messerschmitt airframes

The airframe industry was equally diverse, providing a varied menu of aircraft for the *Luftwaffe* at very high production rates. Willi Messerschmitt's Bayerische Flugzeugwerke (Messerschmitt A.G. after 1938) set the tempo with high production of the Bf 109 as well as a number of additional airframes. By the start of hostilities, Messerschmitt had produced 1076 Bf 109s (from 1935 to September 1939), including prototypes and early production models that did not see combat.

When the war began in September 1939, Messerschmitt produced about 150 109s a month, with an average of 120 delivered to and accepted by the *Luftwaffe*. The official figures are 449 produced and accepted between September 1939 and the end of that year. After the start of the war, as recognition of the necessity for replacements emerged, Messerschmitt increased production as he expanded operations. By the last full year of the war, over 1000 109s were produced every month, for a war's total of over 30,000 examples. Thus even at the beginning of the war, with new technology and demands, Messerschmitt was producing significant quantities of fighters for the *Luftwaffe*.

In addition to this airframe, Messerschmitt's factory also produced the twin-engine Bf 110 heavy fighter for the *Luftwaffe*, not in the same numbers as the 109 but in significant quantities. Almost 400 Bf 110s were available for combat in 1939, with Messerschmitt producing around 75 per month. Although initially successful, the 110 was no competition for advanced British fighters like the Spitfire, and by 1940 was relegated to other roles. Of the 6000 units completed during the war, most were used on the Eastern Front or converted to night-fighters.

In the meantime, Messerschmitt had an active experimental design organization in full swing. Messerschmitt designers were working before the war to come up

with improvements to all of the existing Messerschmitt aircraft, as well as some radical solutions for aerial warfare. The improved version of the 109 – the Me 209 – was in the design phase. Replacements for the 110 were envisioned in the Me 210 and 410, neither of which were very successful. Messerschmitt also designed a heavy bomber in the Me 264, a reconnaissance/liaison aircraft in the Me 161 and its successor the Me 162, and also embarked on radical designs with his rocket plane, the Me 163 Komet, and the world's first operational jet fighter, the Me 262. Messerschmitt was the primary producer of *Luftwaffe* fighters and set the pace for the entire German aircraft manufacturing industry.

Focke-Wulf and Heinkel
A few other companies tried to compete with Messerschmitt in fighter development. Focke-Wulf, which produced the Fw 200 Condor naval reconnaissance and potential bomber aircraft, was one of these.

Led by its designer Kurt Tank, Focke-Wulf eventually challenged Messerschmitt's monopoly with the excellent Fw 190, but few others threatened the firm's position. Companies like Heinkel, Dornier and Junkers focused on bombers, producing such aircraft as the He 111, Do 17 and Junkers Ju 87 and 88.

Each had exemplary production centres, producing (initially) sufficient quantities for the *Luftwaffe*, as well as important in-house experimental programmes. Ernst Heinkel, who ran his own aircraft manufacturing company, wanted to break Messerschmitt's monopoly and constantly harassed the *Luftwaffe* high command to let him add to the *Luftwaffe* inventory. His He 112 was an early competitor but was rejected by the *Luftwaffe*, and he followed up

■ **The table below shows the strength authorized by the Reich Aviation Ministry (*Reichsluftministerium*; RLM) in 1938. Note the carrier squadrons; Germany laid down its first carrier in 1936, but it was never completed.**

RLM AUTHORIZED AIRCRAFT (1938)

Bomber groups (KG)	58
Destroyer groups (ZG)	16
Dive-bomber groups (StG)	8
Short-range recce groups (NaG)	10
Long-range recce groups (FaG) for army liaison	10
Long-range recce groups (FaG) for Air HQ	13
Ground-attack groups (SchG)	1
Ship/Carrier squadrons (Bord- und Trägerflugzeugstaffeln)	36
Transport groups (TG)	4
Fighter groups (JG)	16

with a night-fighter, the He 219, which was deployed later in the war. Heinkel also developed experimental aircraft such as the rocket-powered He 176 and jet-powered He 178, both of which flew in prototype in 1939. Heinkel even proposed a twin-engine jet fighter to compete with the Me 262, his He 280, which was developed entirely in-house and used his own HeS 8 engines.

However, the *Luftwaffe* regarded Heinkel as a producer of bombers in order to maintain a steady stream of available aircraft. Dornier, meanwhile, followed the Do 17 with an improved Do 17Z, enhancing the *Luftwaffe*'s ability to conduct deep, high-speed bombing raids. Junkers was a jack-of-all-trades, producing the Ju 87 Stuka for dive-bombing, the Ju 86 and 88 medium bombers, which doubled as reconnaissance aircraft, and the ubiquitous Ju 52 transport and liaison aircraft. More than 4800 of the latter were eventually built, providing an important transport capability for the *Luftwaffe*.

Other manufacturers

Additional aircraft manufacturers included Arado, Henschel and Bachem, plus late-war experimental aircraft from Horton. In all, the German aircraft manufacturing industry was well poised in 1939 to produce the needed aircraft for the *Luftwaffe*, building on excellent inter-war development and designs. When the war started, and attrition became an important consideration, all were able to increase production to supply necessary aircraft for the fight.

Aircraft Production, 1939–45

German aircraft production was impressive both before and during the war, with a total of almost 120,000 aircraft of all types produced between 1938 and 1945. Early in the war production included all types of aircraft – fighters, bombers, dive-bombers, transports and trainers – but later on the focus changed to fighters for the defence of the Reich.

The Germans began the war with more aircraft than any one other of their early opponents. German production began in earnest in 1935, when Hitler disobeyed the Treaty of Versailles and ordered the reconstitution of the German air force. At that time, there was an emphasis on trainers and transports, in an effort to prepare the *Luftwaffe* for operations. Immediately thereafter, the foremost aircraft manufacturers were contracted to produce the newest and most modern fighters and bombers for the air service. Messerschmitt, Junkers, Heinkel and Dornier led the field and produced impressive numbers of these types, as well as transports, for

the nascent air force. By 1939, the *Luftwaffe* had incorporated a number of new designs that outclassed all of their early opponents qualitatively as well as quantitatively.

By the end of 1940, Germany was producing more than 10,000 aircraft per annum. Some industrialists (specifically shipbuilders but aircraft and tank manufacturers as well) warned Hitler that their production figures would not be ready for sustained combat operations until 1941, but Hitler refused to delay the outbreak of hostilities; he believed that any additional time would give Germany's enemies the opportunity to also build and renovate their forces to stand against Germany. His

decision for war in 1939 was based on the idea that the Germans were at that point ahead, and could maintain the lead through what he hoped would be quick, decisive victories. Initially he was correct.

There were few substantial revisions to production schedules and demands in the first year of the war. Each company was given quotas to fill, and each complained about the lack of materials and workers, but in the end, based on a 40-hour working week, German aircraft manufacturers continued to produce, and increase production of, the latest designs.

The German high command was shocked by the high loss rates in the opening phases of the war and requested higher output. Fortunately, for the *Luftwaffe*, the early campaigns, though costly, were short, and losses were made up. Early in the war, the *Luftwaffe* lost less than 10 per cent of total strength to combat, and industry was able to replace the aircraft.

Losses versus production

In 1940, a heavy year of fighting in Norway and France, as well as being the year of the Battle of Britain, German losses were again high, but production increased to fill gaps. In 1940, the Germans lost nearly 4000 aircraft but produced some 10,800.

Although the losses were high, the successes of the 1940 campaigns, with the exception of the 'draw' in the Battle of Britain, led the Germans to believe that they were acceptable. The higher losses should have warned the Germans that higher rates of attrition could be expected from competent industrialized foes, especially if they were locked into battles of attrition. However, the Germans continued to plan for further conquests, basing their production, training and operational figures on optimistic assessments of German capabilities and overestimation of enemy weakness.

The year 1941 emerged as a watershed for the *Luftwaffe* and for Germany as a whole. That summer, Hitler opened an aggressive attack on the Soviet Union, and by December the United States was also involved in the war. German production capabilities, able to survive during the conquest of Poland and France, and barely able to withstand a very costly campaign against the British, were no match for either the Soviets or the Americans, let alone both.

Regardless, Hitler opened Operation *Barbarossa*, the attack on the Soviet Union, in June 1941. In his

LUFTWAFFE AIRCRAFT STRENGTH (1940–41)

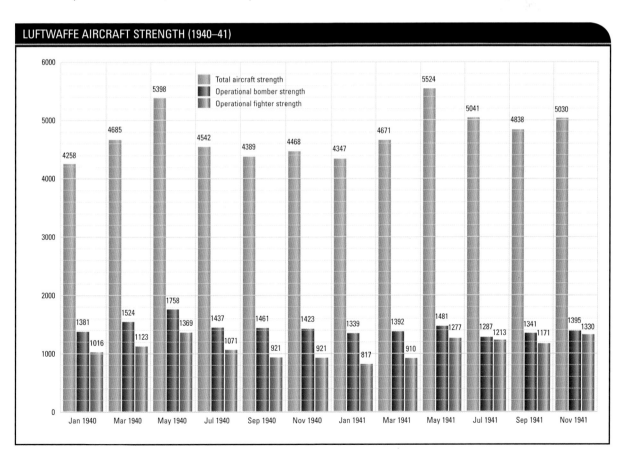

estimation, German forces would roll over the Soviets in a matter of weeks, destroying them, before having to deal with any other contingencies. Had he proven correct, the *Luftwaffe* might have been able to survive the attrition it faced in the USSR. In the opening months of the campaign, it looked as if Hitler would prove to be correct.

However, by the time winter hit, the Soviets had not surrendered and then the Americans joined in the war. The *Luftwaffe* became embroiled in a costly war of attrition with the Soviets, and would soon face the combined material and industrial weight of the Allies.

Struggling to keep up

In 1941, the Germans lost over 3000 aircraft (and a further 2000 in non-combat-related circumstances) but were able to replace them with the production of almost 12,000 new machines, including the brand new Fw 190. German total strength stood at 4300 aircraft at the start of the year but was no higher than 5100 aircraft available for combat at its end.

The following year was a time of battles for the *Luftwaffe*, and then in 1943 the tide began to turn. That year, the *Luftwaffe* was bolstered by new types of fighters, including the newest version of the Bf 109 (the G-6). In 1943 the first jet aircraft designed for combat were tested, and showed immediate promise. The *Luftwaffe* also sloughed off unworkable designs that plagued production schedules and refocused on the production of realistic combat-ready models.

Yet even though the German aircraft industry produced 25,500 airframes, and many new versions and models, 1943 was destructive on the *Luftwaffe*. It was locked into an increasingly devastating war of attrition against the Soviets, and

LUFTWAFFE BOMBER AIRCRAFT STRENGTH (1939–45)

Type	1939	1940	1941	1942	1943	1944	1945	Total
Arado Ar 234	–	–	–	–	150	64	–	214
Dornier Do 17	215	260	–	–	–	–	–	475
Dornier Do 217	1	20	277	564	504	–	–	1366
Heinkel He 111	452	756	950	1337	1405	756	–	5656
Heinkel He 177	–	–	–	166	415	565	–	1146
Junkers Ju 88	69	1816	2146	2270	2160	661	–	9122
Junkers Ju 188	–	–	–	–	165	301	–	466
Junkers Ju 388	–	–	–	–	–	4	–	4

LUFTWAFFE FIGHTER AIRCRAFT STRENGTH (1939–45)

Type	1939	1940	1941	1942	1943	1944	1945	Total
Dornier Do 17	9	–	–	–	–	–	–	9
Dornier Do 217	–	–	–	–	157	207	–	364
Dornier Do 335	–	–	–	–	–	7	4	11
Focke-Wulf Fw 190	–	–	228	1850	2171	7488	1630	13,367
Focke-Wulf Ta 152	–	–	–	–	–	34	?	~150
Focke-Wulf Ta 154	–	–	–	–	–	8	–	8
Heinkel He 162	–	–	–	–	–	–	116	116
Heinkel He 219	–	–	–	–	11	195	62	268
Junkers Ju 88	–	62	66	257	706	2513	355	3959
Messerschmitt Bf 109	449	1667	2764	2657	6013	12,807	2798	29,155
Messerschmitt Bf 110	156	1006	594	501	641	128	–	3026
Messerschmitt Me 163	–	–	–	–	–	327	37	364
Messerschmitt Me 210	–	–	92	93	89	74	–	348
Messerschmitt Me 262	–	–	–	–	–	564	730	1294
Messerschmitt Me 410	–	–	–	–	271	629	–	900

LUFTWAFFE GROUND-ATTACK AIRCRAFT STRENGTH (1939–45)

Type	1939	1940	1941	1942	1943	1944	1945	Total
Focke-Wulf Fw 190	–	–	–	68	1183	4279	1104	6634
Henschel Hs 129	–	–	7	221	411	302	–	941
Junkers Ju 87	134	603	500	960	1672	1012	–	4881
Junkers Ju 88	–	–	–	–	–	3	–	3

began to feel the weight of Allied aerial might around the periphery.

War on many fronts

In North Africa, and later Sicily and Italy, and in counter-bomber operations in northern Europe, *Luftwaffe* losses mounted. The German air force lost 7400 aircraft in combat and another 6000 in non-combat accidents in 1943, including more than 1100 transport aircraft lost in the failure to resupply Stalingrad at the start of the year. With the disappearance of transports from the inventory, the *Luftwaffe* lost an important facet of its logistics chain, which was never recovered. Compounding the problem for the *Luftwaffe* was the increasing pressure from the Combined Bomber Offensive, the joint American and British bombing campaign.

By late spring 1943, the British (by night) and the Americans (by day) began a systematic bombing campaign against Germany and the occupied territories, intending to destroy German industry and cities, and force a surrender. The Germans responded by sending up fighter interceptors day and night to stem the Allied campaign. While costly for both sides, the combination of the three major theatres of combat steadily wore at *Luftwaffe* operational status and replacement programmes. Sources show that German losses continued to increase throughout the year. Added to the requirement for replacement aircraft was the need for more pilots and spare parts, as well as a demand on the German transportation network to deliver the parts and, especially, fuel.

Thus, although there were more aircraft produced, operational numbers increased only slightly. In January 1943, the *Luftwaffe* could commit 5400 aircraft to combat; by the end of the year, this number had risen to only 6500.

Decline

By 1944, the situation was increasingly dire. Although the German aircraft industry had been reorganized, and production rates increased further, the *Luftwaffe* was losing more heavily. By the middle of

LUFTWAFFE TRANSPORT AIRCRAFT STRENGTH (1939–45)

Type	1939	1940	1941	1942	1943	1944	1945	Total
Gotha Go 244	–	–	–	43	–	–	–	43
Junkers Ju 52	145	388	507	503	887	379	–	2809
Junkers Ju 252	–	–	–	15	–	–	–	15
Junkers Ju 352	–	–	–	–	1	49	–	50
Messerschmitt Me 323	–	–	–	27	140	34	–	201

LUFTWAFFE RECONNAISSANCE AIRCRAFT STRENGTH (1939–45)

Type	1939	1940	1941	1942	1943	1944	1945	Total
Dornier Do 17	16	–	–	–	–	–	–	16
Dornier Do 215	3	92	6	–	–	–	–	101
Focke-Wulf Fw 189	6	38	250	327	208	17	–	846
Focke-Wulf Fw 200	1	36	58	84	76	8	–	263
Henschel Hs 126	137	368	5	–	–	–	–	510
Junkers Ju 88	–	330	568	567	394	52	–	1911
Junkers Ju 188	–	–	–	–	105	432	33	570
Junkers Ju 290	–	–	–	–	23	18	–	41
Junkers Ju 388	–	–	–	–	–	87	12	99
Messerschmitt Bf 109	–	–	26	8	141	979	171	1325
Messerschmitt Bf 110	–	75	190	79	150	–	–	494
Messerschmitt Me 210	–	–	2	2	–	–	–	4
Messerschmitt Me 410	–	–	–	–	20	93	–	113

LUFTWAFFE MARITIME AIRCRAFT STRENGTH (1939–45)

Type	1939	1940	1941	1942	1943	1944	1945	Total
Arado Ar 196	22	104	94	107	104	–	–	431
Blohm & Voss Bv 138	39	82	85	70	–	–	–	276
Blohm & Voss Bv 222	–	–	–	–	4	–	–	4
Dornier Do 18	22	49	–	–	–	–	–	71
Dornier Do 24	–	1	7	46	81	–	–	135
Heinkel He 115	52	76	–	–	141	–	–	269

the year, the *Luftwaffe* had lost more than could be replaced, not necessarily because of the airframes available, but because of a shortage of pilots. Young *Luftwaffe* pilots were thrown into combat with a mere 20 hours' training, and that number continued to decrease as the war dragged on. There were almost 40,000 aircraft produced in 1944, but many sat empty on airfields or at manufacturers waiting for pilots to fly them; and the *Luftwaffe* continued to haemorrhage. Losses on the Eastern Front were atrocious, and there were fewer planes and pilots because of both attrition and the decision to pull more squadrons back to Germany to fight the Allies. The Soviet Union rolled on, achieving complete air superiority by the middle of the year.

In June the Allies landed in France, achieving local air superiority over Normandy. While the Allies flew more than 14,000 sorties on 6 June, the *Luftwaffe* defenders in *Luftflotte* 3 flew only 100. This single day was indicative of the declining strength of the *Luftwaffe* by summer 1944. Throughout the rest of the year, the Germans fought bravely against overwhelming odds. On two fronts, they faced enormous industrial output from the Soviets and Americans, whose industries were invulnerable to German offensives. The Allies were able to destroy German might both on the ground

■ A pair of Focke-Wulf Fw 190s patrol somewhere on the Eastern Front. The Fw 190 was considered the most advanced fighter of its type in the world when it first appeared in the summer of 1941.

and in the air, increasing the attrition of the *Luftwaffe*.

American historians recount the importance of the North American P-51D Mustang's contribution to the fight. Once it had been fitted with long-range drop tanks, the Mustang could escort bombers to Berlin and back. The Mustang was qualitatively better than every German aircraft (except the Messerschmitt Me 262 jet) and broke the back of the *Luftwaffe*, whose pilots and planes were decreasingly effective.

Last gasp

In 1944, the *Luftwaffe* launched its final offensive of the war in support of the December Ardennes Offensive. A coordinated air and ground attack, the operation was designed to strike the Americans and British to knock them out of the war. In the end, it backfired; it cost the Germans heavily and did not achieve its ends. On 1 January 1945, the *Luftwaffe* initiated Operation *Bodenplatte*, a last-ditch effort to destroy the Allied air forces and recover ground. It too was an abysmal failure; the *Luftwaffe* was crushed.

In 1944, the *Luftwaffe* lost 10,000 aircraft up to Operation *Overlord* in June, and another 14,000 aircraft in the last six months of the year. By the end of the year, the *Luftwaffe* had no more than 6000 aircraft of all types available for combat, and only 1600 of these were single-engine fighters. Having been divided between two fronts, and then having thrown away resources in the Ardennes, the *Luftwaffe* had virtually no aircraft to contest Allied air superiority at the start of 1945.

In the last five months of the war, the Germans produced a meagre 7500 aircraft of all types as industry collapsed. The *Luftwaffe* ceased operations in May but had been defeated prior to that. On both fronts, Allied air forces roamed the skies and attacked with impunity.

The Allies destroyed the *Luftwaffe* with a combination of attritional warfare, two-front attacks and the destruction of the transportation infrastructure in Germany. By the end of the war, there were aircraft available, but no more *Luftwaffe* pilots and no fuel for the planes. The demise of the *Luftwaffe* was complete.

AIRCRAFT PRODUCTION: MAJOR POWERS COMPARED (1938–45)

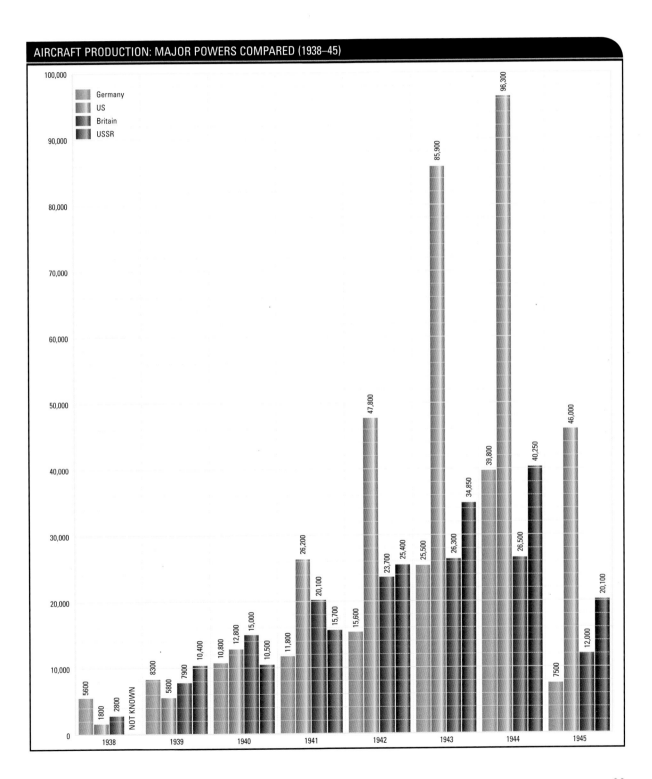

Legend:
- Germany
- US
- Britain
- USSR

1938: Germany 5600, US 1800, Britain 2800, USSR NOT KNOWN

1939: Germany 8300, US 5800, Britain 7900, USSR 10,400

1940: Germany 10,800, US 12,800, Britain 15,000, USSR 10,500

1941: Germany 11,800, US 26,200, Britain 20,100, USSR 15,700

1942: Germany 15,600, US 47,800, Britain 23,700, USSR 25,400

1943: Germany 25,500, US 85,900, Britain 26,300, USSR 34,850

1944: Germany 39,800, US 96,300, Britain 26,500, USSR 40,250

1945: Germany 7500, US 46,000, Britain 12,000, USSR 20,100

CHAPTER 3

Invasion of Poland to the Fall of France

In the early hours of 1 September 1939, the German Army, supported by the Luftwaffe, rolled into Poland, opening the initial phases of the invasion. Years of training and development, as well as a dry run in Spain, had built up to this campaign. Employing all of its abilities and the latest and best aerial weapons, the Luftwaffe quickly emerged as an able and deadly force of military might.

Hitler was determined to expand the German Empire – the Third Reich. His ultimate goal was Lebensraum (literally 'living space') in the East, but he did not want to become embroiled in a two-front war, remembering first-hand the quagmire of World War I. The Nazi–Soviet Non-Aggression Pact was signed days before the German invasion of Poland, guaranteeing that the Germans and Soviets would not have to fight each other, for now. Hitler had successfully persuaded Stalin that in exchange for half of Poland, the Soviets would not have to fight Germany in a struggle for which they were unprepared.

A Junkers Ju 87 goes into its trademark dive in ground-attack operations, somewhere over Poland, September 1939.

Invasion of Poland, September 1939

On the morning of 1 September 1939, German tanks rolled across the Polish border and Luftwaffe *planes flew attack missions into Poland. Two weeks later, the Soviets attacked Poland from the other side; Poland was doomed.*

The *Luftwaffe* began the campaign with an assortment of aircraft: strategic bombers, air-superiority fighters and dive-bombers. The collection totalled 4000 aircraft: 1200 fighters – Messerschmitt Bf 109s and 110s; 1200 medium bombers – Heinkel He 111s and Dornier Do 17s; about 400 Junkers Ju 87 dive-bombers; and around 1200 transport, reconnaissance, liaison and obsolete types, the last-mentioned of which were being phased out but were still useful against the outclassed Polish air effort.

Lightning war
The new German battle doctrine of *Blitzkrieg* was put to the test. Instead of sending massive numbers of men into the attack across a wide front,

which had been the tactic of World War I, the Germans reconceived warfare, incorporating the latest technology. Air units coordinated by radio combined with fast-moving mechanized ground units (armoured and motorized) to penetrate deep into enemy territory, avoiding pockets of resistance and cutting off front-line troops from supply and command. This 'lightning war', defined by surprise, manoeuvre and coordination, worked best against an acquiescent adversary, and came to define the German way of war in subsequent years. Also known as Combined Arms Warfare, these methods aimed at attacking enemy weak points with overwhelming force and exploiting gains quickly. The combined attacks on Poland,

with Panzers (tanks) spearheading the attack and supported from the air, were incredibly successful against the Polish forces, who were simply unprepared for the German onslaught.

In the opening phases of the battle for Poland, German Panzer units supported by *Luftwaffe* bombers and dive-bombers drove deep behind Polish forces, cutting them off.

■ **Number of Luftwaffe squadrons prepared for operations September 1939. At this early stage of the war, the number of observation and bombing squadrons were higher than fighter squadrons; German twin-engine bombers were effective as the front line of attack in German blitzkrieg combined arms attacks.**

LUFTWAFFE SQUADRON STRENGTH (AUGUST 1939)

Reconnaissance squadrons 55
Staff units 13
Bomber squadrons 90
Dive-bomber squadrons 27
Fighter squadrons 40
Pursuit-interceptor squadrons 27
Ground-attack squadrons 3
Weather recce squadrons 1
Naval aviation squadrons 20

Further German infantry then moved in to clean up the rear areas, gathering prisoners. If the Germans encountered strongholds, the *Luftwaffe* targeted them with bombers. This method of warfare proved extremely successful.

Luftflotten 1 and 4 were the two main commands in the Polish campaign. Twenty *Kampfgeschwader* (bomber groups) of He 111 and Do 17 aircraft faced Poland, ready to bomb it into submission. There were also five *Stukageschwader* (Stuka groups), flying Ju 87s at the point of the *Blitzkrieg* spear. Polish forces facing them were primarily unmechanized ground troops. Without a viable air weapon, and with few anti-tank weapons, the Poles were outmatched in the sky

and on the ground. With the Germans attacking out of Germany, occupied Czechoslovakia and East Prussia, Poland faced a triple threat.

Airfields bombed

The *Luftwaffe*'s primary targets were Polish airfields. For the *Luftwaffe* to gain (and maintain) air supremacy, the Polish Air Force would have to be destroyed. Fighters covered the bombers as the Polish airfields were targeted. Many Polish planes were caught on the ground on the opening day, and as the conflagration opened, the Polish Air Force was destroyed. Its PZL aircraft were hopelessly outclassed by the German Bf 109 fighters, but a few were able to harass the German bombers. Unfortunately for the Poles, their

airfields were quickly destroyed, and the few fighters they had, were shot down. In the first few days of the war, the Polish Air Force ceased to exist. Over 800 aircraft (of which no more than 400 were modern types for combat operations) were either shot down or destroyed on the ground.

In ground combat, the *Blitzkrieg* tactics were also successful. The Poles had little defence against either the German dive-bombers or

LUFTWAFFE STRENGTH (SEPTEMBER 1939)	
Type	Total
Staffeln	302
Ready crews	2370
Operational combat aircraft	2564

LUFTWAFFE BOMBER, DIVE-BOMBER & GROUND-ATTACK AIRCRAFT STRENGTH (SEPTEMBER 1939)

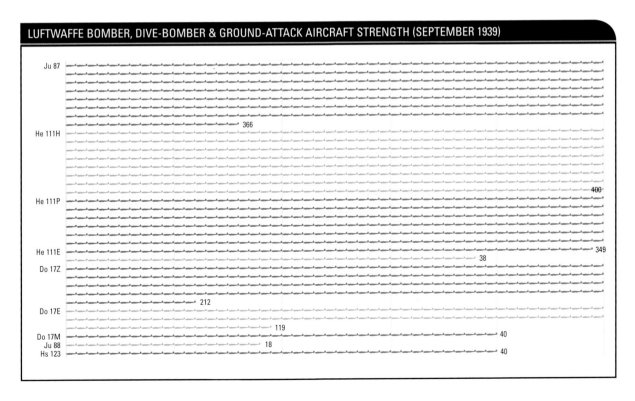

Ju 87

He 111H — 366

He 111P — 400

He 111E — 349

Do 17Z — 38

Do 17E — 212

Do 17M — 119

Ju 88 — 18 — 40

Hs 123 — 40

Panzers; the Polish Army was quickly overcome. Ju 87s spearheading the Panzers attacked ground targets with impunity. The dive-bombers crushed Polish resistance as the Panzers rolled on.

Bombers over Warsaw

Only the deep-strike bombers faced organized resistance. On the first morning of hostilities, He 111s of KG 27, subordinate to *Luftflotte* 2, were sent deep into Poland to bomb Warsaw, escorted by Bf 110s. The Poles were able to prepare for this raid and mustered around 50 PZLs to combat the German bombers. In this operation the Poles were somewhat successful, although Warsaw was bombed, and the PZLs of the Pursuit Brigade claimed six German aircraft destroyed. But the Germans

recovered quickly. That afternoon, in the second attack of the day, the bombers were escorted by Bf 109s as well as 110s, and the Poles lost seven valuable fighters. The Poles were up against the most advanced military in Europe and were outmatched across the board.

In subsequent days, the Germans continued both strategic bombing attacks, with heavy fighter escort, and combined arms attacks against the Polish Army in the field. The *Luftwaffe*'s learning curve was very steep, as it made significant and important corrections continually, from the tactical level upwards. The combined attacks became more precise and deadly; the bombing raids became more concentrated and successful. Ju 87s pinpointed Polish tanks, roads and bridges,

destroying Polish weapons and supply. Bf 110s attacked troop concentrations and supply lines. Bombers escorted by fighters bombed Polish cities into submission. The Polish Air Force was swept from the air, and by the second week of the war the *Luftwaffe* was able to fly without resistance, increasing its efficiency still further.

Soviet invasion

On 17 September, the Soviets invaded Poland from the east, sealing the country's fate. What was left of the Polish Air Force– about 25 per cent – fled to Romania in order to escape the carnage. The *Luftwaffe* focused its attention on Warsaw. With the successful combined arms campaigns, and crumbling resistance in the field, all

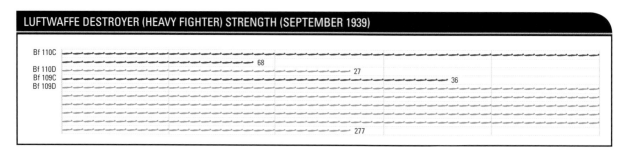

LUFTWAFFE DESTROYER (HEAVY FIGHTER) STRENGTH (SEPTEMBER 1939)

Bf 110C — 68
Bf 110D — 27
Bf 109C — 36
Bf 109D — 277

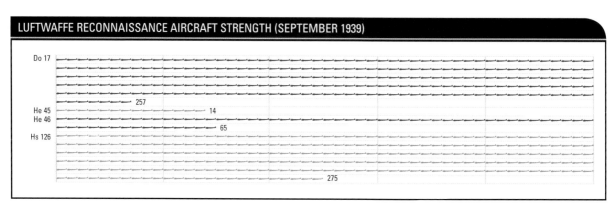

LUFTWAFFE RECONNAISSANCE AIRCRAFT STRENGTH (SEPTEMBER 1939)

Do 17 — 257
He 45 — 14
He 46 — 65
Hs 126 — 275

LUFTWAFFE DAY- & NIGHT-FIGHTER STRENGTH (SEPTEMBER 1939)

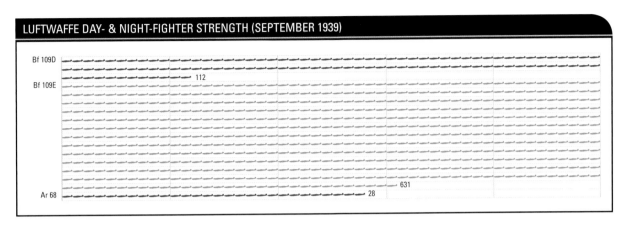

Bf 109D

Bf 109E — 112

— 631

Ar 68 — 28

LUFTWAFFE TRANSPORT AIRCRAFT, SEAPLANE & FLYING BOAT STRENGTH (SEPTEMBER 1939)

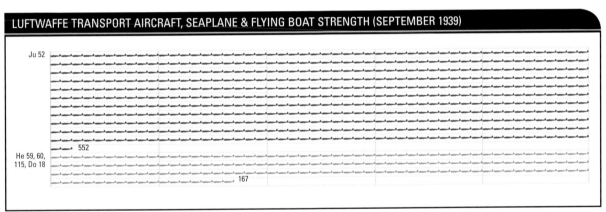

Ju 52

— 552

He 59, 60, 115, Do 18

— 167

that was left was for the Poles to surrender. On 25 September, the *Luftwaffe* began the final phases of the battle, bombing Warsaw into submission. Using He 111s, Do 17s plus Ju 52s operating in the bombing role, the *Luftwaffe* attacked the city with explosives and incendiaries. Three days later, Poland surrendered. Poland was divided between the

■ **Messerschmitt Bf 110s from** *Zerstörergeschwader* **(ZG) 26 fly over Poland. Bf 110s were initially used as fighter escort for He 111 bombers but later graduated to a ground-attack role.**

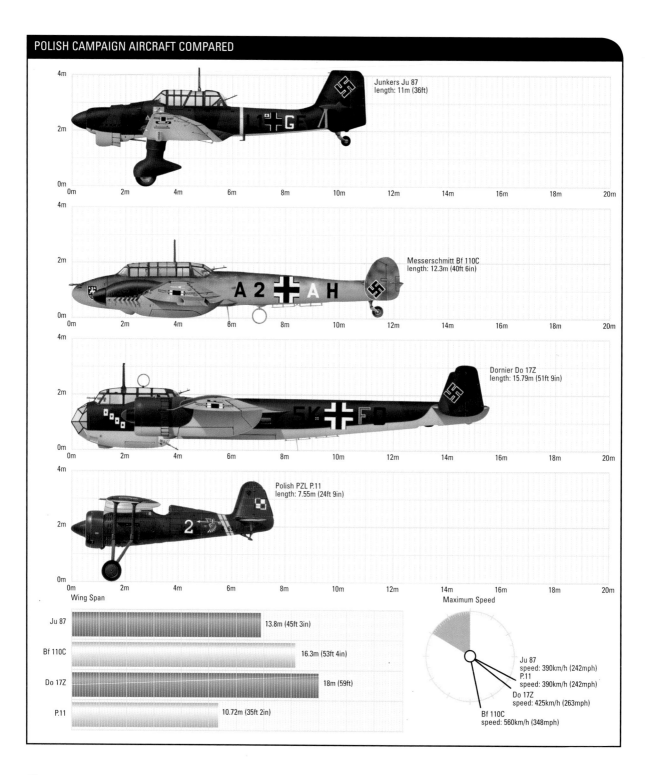

POLISH CAMPAIGN AIRCRAFT COMPARED

Junkers Ju 87
length: 11m (36ft)

Messerschmitt Bf 110C
length: 12.3m (40ft 6in)

Dornier Do 17Z
length: 15.79m (51ft 9in)

Polish PZL P.11
length: 7.55m (24ft 9in)

Wing Span

Ju 87 — 13.8m (45ft 3in)

Bf 110C — 16.3m (53ft 4in)

Do 17Z — 18m (59ft)

P.11 — 10.72m (35ft 2in)

Maximum Speed

Ju 87
speed: 390km/h (242mph)
P.11
speed: 390km/h (242mph)
Do 17Z
speed: 425km/h (263mph)
Bf 110C
speed: 560km/h (348mph)

LUFTFLOTTE 2 AIRCRAFT STRENGTH (SEPTEMBER 1939)

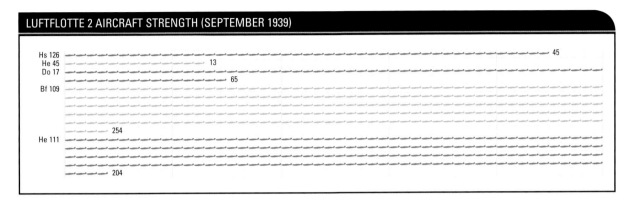

Hs 126 — 45
He 45 — 13
Do 17 — 65
Bf 109
He 111 — 254
204

■ *Luftflotte* 2 was the organizational command for the Polish campaign. Above are the numbers and types of aircraft ready for operations against the Poles in September 1939.

Soviets and Germans, the latter turning their attentions westwards while the former watched German intentions with a wary eye.

Combat record

The record of the *Luftwaffe* in the Polish campaign was instructive; many lessons emerged. Strategic bombing of Polish cities had been successful in terms of the destruction caused but had brought with it a cost. In addition, the high-intensity combat of *Blitzkrieg*, as well as air combat with the Polish Air Force, indicated the high attrition rate of modern warfare. Even flying against the Poles, with their inferior anti-aircraft weapons and obsolete aircraft, the Germans incurred high losses. Over the course of the four-week campaign, the Germans lost 281 aircraft of all types in combat while accounting for the destruction of 335 Polish planes. While they had been victorious, the Germans had learned valuable lessons about attrition, tactics and the need for increased production.

■ Poland lost 335 aircraft in the campaign – most of its air force. The Germans lost 281 aircraft shot down, and another 263 or 273 (depending on source) damaged, only 70 of which could be repaired.

POLISH AND GERMAN AIRCRAFT LOSSES COMPARED

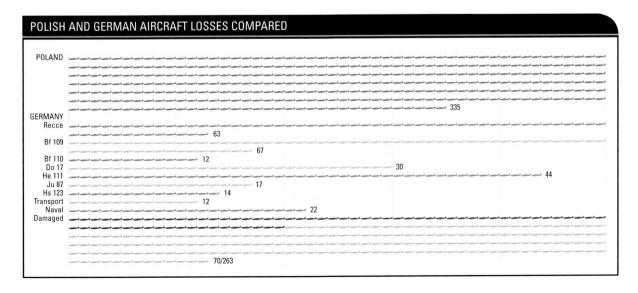

POLAND — 335
GERMANY
Recce — 63
Bf 109 — 67
Bf 110 — 12
Do 17 — 30
He 111 — 44
Ju 87 — 17
Hs 123 — 14
Transport — 12
Naval — 22
Damaged — 70/263

The 'Sitzkrieg', October 1939 – April 1940

Poland was defeated and dismantled. Poland's allies, Britain and France, had declared war on the third day of the Polish campaign (3 September 1939), and were organizing their mighty empires and industries for an eventual showdown with the Germans, but for now they sat back and waited.

The defensive mindset of both of these countries dictated that they would wait for German aggression rather than take the fight to the powerful German military machine. A period began that was dubbed, among other things, the Phoney War and the '*Sitzkrieg*', the latter label being a play on the German term *Blitzkrieg*, or 'lightning war'.

France in particular did not have any intention of striking at Germany. It was still reeling from the losses of World War I and had adopted a defensive stance, militarily, socially and politically. France, worried about future German aggression, had put money and effort into defensive border fortifications, in lieu of the offensive spirit that had characterized the previous war. The French government, as fractured as it was, had decided to concentrate on defensive measures above all, the ultimate example being the Maginot Line.

This series of defensive fortifications along the Franco-German border was intended to protect France from a future German attack, forcing the Germans to go on the offensive and destroy themselves in the process. Little expenditure was put into planes, tanks or offensive military capabilities; the French were content to make the Germans take

the offensive. That is not to say that the French lacked good equipment; quite the contrary. However, their defensive mindset hampered production of modern military equipment until it was too late.

Air defence

Likewise, the British were content to protect Britain, offer token assistance to the French on the Continent and keep the shipping lanes in the Atlantic open for supply. The British focused on defensive air technology, with continued development of a strategic air force, and the power of the Royal Navy at sea. The small, professional but ill-equipped British Expeditionary Force (BEF) was sent to France to assist the French armies in case of a German attack.

The Nazi–Soviet Non-Aggression Pact had stunned the British and French; they were convinced that Stalin would not bargain with Hitler. When he did, it removed the Soviets from the Allied camp. Without the second front to tie up German forces, the British and French were unwilling to attack the German military juggernaut in the West, and provided no help for the flailing Poles. With Poland defeated, and the Soviets complacent, the British and French sat on the defensive and awaited the eventual German attacks.

In the United States, the consensus was non-involvement. The Americans were against being drawn into a second European war just two decades after the first, and were more than willing to sit idly by and watch. That said, with the attack on Poland, the British and French placed lucrative orders with American arms manufacturers for materiel. Realizing that they were behind in equipment, and that their own industry did not have time to catch up, the British and French hoped to tap into American industrial capacity for military hardware. Orders were placed for aircraft, ships and every other kind of military equipment imaginable. US manufacturers were happy to accept the enormous cash infusion.

In one example, a marginal aircraft became an important commodity as France and Britain sought to boost their lack of quantity. Both countries placed orders with the Bell Aircraft factory – by this time in Buffalo, New York – for the P-39 Airacobra. While the Americans considered it to be of only marginal value in a future war, the Europeans saw the Airacobra as a stop-gap for the coming conflict. The British ordered 400; the French, 250. Bell began series production of the aircraft in autumn 1939.

Meanwhile, the Germans began a re-evaluation. It was unwise to begin offensive operations in the autumn or winter, and they were equally willing to sit and wait without Allied interference. Germany ramped up production to replace losses in the air and on the ground, and began planning for a series of spring offensives in the West.

One target was the German long-time enemy – France. Under the guise of *Fall Gelb* (Case Yellow), the Germans planned the invasion of France, keeping in mind the (nearly) impregnable Maginot Line. The opening phases of *Fall Gelb* were to take the Germans into the Netherlands and through Belgium into France. Meanwhile, other planning focused on Denmark and Norway (*Fall Weserübung* – Case Weser Exercise).

Fall Gelb

German operational doctrine did not alter significantly for *Fall Gelb*. The *Luftwaffe*, using the same aircraft and tactics as in Poland, were tasked with attacking enemy airfields, destroying enemy aircraft and gaining air superiority. Fighters and dive-bombers were to spearhead the Panzer units as they drove through Belgium and into France, using a different route from that followed by the Schlieffen Plan of World War I.

Germany focused on bolstering production numbers and increasing quantity for the *Luftwaffe*, and waited for spring. Emphasis was placed on replacing the planes that had been lost in Poland and increasing production for what would be a

■ **Aircrew load bombs beneath a Dornier Do 17Z, spring 1940.**

longer campaign against France. Between the fall of Poland and the operations of spring 1940, German industry did as ordered. New Bf 109s and 110s rolled off the production line in significant numbers, planes that were to turn the tide of the air war over France.

Luftflotten 1 and 2 began operational training with new aircraft, fresh off the assembly lines. The combat units prepared by going over tactics and training for the upcoming conflicts, which would be against a more formidable military than the Poles. The French and British were better prepared for the German onslaught – the aircraft of the RAF and France's *Armée de l'Air* were superior to and more numerous than those of the Polish Air Force. But before the battle for the Low

Countries and France, the Germans had to attend to other business.

By spring 1940, the *Sitzkrieg* was over, but it had given the Germans time to recover from the Polish campaign. New resources had been gathered for the upcoming onslaught: industry had provided the materials; fresh pilots had been trained in the *Lehrdivisionen*. By May, the *Luftwaffe* had grown substantially. It boasted 1100 bombers (He 111s and Do 17s) as well as over 400 Ju 87 dive-bombers. Fighter cover (for protection and ground attack) was provided by as many as 850 Bf 109s and another 350 Bf 110 heavy fighters. In addition, *Luftwaffe Fallschirmjäger* (paratroopers) played an important role in unfolding events. First came the attack on Denmark and Norway, Operation *Weserübung*.

Fall Weserübung: Denmark and Norway

The North Sea was a strategic causeway. In World War I, the Royal Navy had maintained control of the waterway, and had imposed a distant naval blockade on Germany, choking the country off from needed supplies, both military and civilian.

Hitler recognized the significance of losing control of this area. He was determined to secure it through the *Kriegsmarine* (German Navy) and deny the Royal Navy the opportunity to control this important waterway.

■ **The chart below enumerates the forces allocated to the aerial invasion and air support of Norway in the spring of 1940. The chart on the opposite page details *Luftwaffe* losses in the aerial campaign to all causes, including shot down (in the air and from the ground), crashed and other accidents. Note the high number of transport losses.**

To control the North Sea, Hitler needed to secure ports in Denmark and Norway, by force if necessary. Added to this, airbases in Norway would provide a strategic advantage to the *Luftwaffe* as well as another set of attack routes against Britain. *Fall Weserübung* was the codename of the operation to capture Denmark and Norway for German use.

However, the German Navy was not nearly as strong as the Royal Navy; the Germans needed to maximize their resources to secure these areas. Denmark could be defeated with land forces, but an air bridge was deemed necessary to

defeat Norway. A joint force attack was planned. In addition to having the strategic importance of geography, Norway produced iron, a strategic raw material that the Germans hoped to secure. On 9 April 1940, the plan was put into action.

Denmark

The campaign for Denmark was the shortest of the war. The German ambassador to Denmark, Cecil von Renthe-Fink, informed the Danish Foreign Minister that the Germans were moving to 'protect' the Danes from the French and British. German troops marched across the border

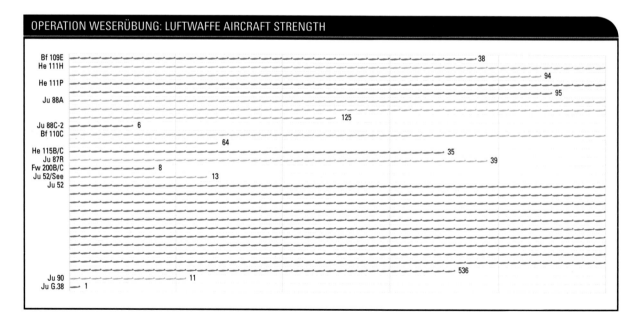

OPERATION WESERÜBUNG: LUFTWAFFE AIRCRAFT STRENGTH

Aircraft	Strength
Bf 109E	
He 111H	38
He 111P	94
Ju 88A	95
Ju 88C-2	6
Bf 110C	125
He 115B/C	64
Ju 87R	35
Fw 200B/C	8
Ju 52/See	39
Ju 52	13
	536
Ju 90	11
Ju G.38	1

and a force of 1000 waded ashore at Copenhagen to secure the port. An additional company of paratroopers (4./FJR 1) dropped at the airbase at Aalborg, overpowering the defences quickly. In exchange for domestic control over the population, King Christian X decided to capitulate to German demands almost immediately, surrendering that morning.

In the six-hour fight, the Germans employed the *Luftwaffe* in two phases – two units of bombers (one of He 111s; one, Do 17s) dropped leaflets on the Danish capital, Copenhagen, urging the population to surrender, while two units of fighters (Bf 110s) attacked the main Danish airfield at Værløse and destroyed 11 aircraft on the ground and severely damaged another 14. With little resistance, Denmark fell under German control.

Norway

The main focus of the campaign was Norway. On the same morning as the invasion of Denmark took place, a more formidable force attacked Norway. Employing joint warfare doctrine, elements of the German Navy, Army and *Luftwaffe* carried out a spectacular campaign against Norway in an effort to secure the territory, its raw materials and the strategic waterways of the North Sea and Baltic. The air component was assigned to X *Fliegerkorps*, and included elements of 19 *Luftwaffe* units, amounting to more than 1000 planes.

The majority of the aircraft were transport Ju 52s from nine units, which were employed to ferry troops to Norway to secure airfields and cities. Additional support came from three units of fighters (one of Bf 109s and two of Bf 110s), while bombing duties were performed by five bomber units. Maritime air support came from a unit of Fw 200s and another of Ju 52 seaplanes. An additional paratroop company combat-jumped onto the airfield at Sola Air Station to secure it.

The attack went off as planned. Bombers dropped their bombs on the cities, heralding the attack. Fighters escorted the bombers and fought the Norwegian Air Force quickly and efficiently. Ju 52 transports landed at the airfields in Oslo and Kjevik, securing the bases for further troops.

At sea, the *Kriegsmarine* was initially uncontested, but requests to the British were soon honoured, and the Royal Navy set sail to confront the Germans. As the ground offensive gained strength, the Norwegians were defeated. Although not as rapidly as Denmark, Norway was swiftly reduced. The royal family fled, and the *Luftwaffe* continued to bomb Norwegian cities. Eventually, even though there was continued fighting over the port city of Narvik (against British and French troops), Norway surrendered, on 10 June 1940.

Butcher's bill

The *Luftwaffe*'s record in Norway was a bit more mixed. While the *Luftwaffe* was very successful in its missions, losses mounted, especially in terms of transport aircraft. While losses of bombers and fighters were relatively light, many German transports were lost to crashes and accidents due to the pace of combat. It is estimated that the *Luftwaffe* lost 1300 aircrew in the battle for Norway, with 300 killed and another 450 missing. Although the losses were predominately from transports,

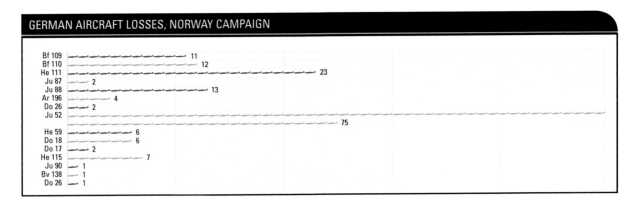

GERMAN AIRCRAFT LOSSES, NORWAY CAMPAIGN

Aircraft	Losses
Bf 109	11
Bf 110	12
He 111	23
Ju 87	2
Ju 88	13
Ar 196	4
Do 26	2
Ju 52	75
He 59	6
Do 18	6
Do 17	2
He 115	7
Ju 90	1
Bv 138	1
Do 26	1

SAYVILLE LIBRARY

they included fighter and bomber losses as well.

By 15 May, the air units in Norway had been redesignated *Luftflotte* 5, under the command of *Generaloberst* Erhard Milch, and their numbers were bolstered by the addition of further aircraft.

Aircraft losses

By the end of the campaign, the *Luftwaffe* had lost 166 aircraft to Norwegian aircraft, ground fire and accidents. The most unfortunate losses were the 75 Ju 52 transport aircraft – Ju 52s were already in short supply. In all, the *Luftwaffe* lost almost two dozen front-line fighters (11 Bf 109s and 12 Bf 110s), and

40 bombers (including 23 He 111s, a pair of Ju 87 dive-bombers and 13 of the new Ju 88s).

However, the heavy transport losses were the most important figures on the list as far as later *Luftwaffe* campaigns were concerned. By 1940, the Ju 52 was nearing obsolescence, but the *Luftwaffe* had no emerging replacement for the ageing platform. Once again, with a short-war mindset, the *Luftwaffe* (and, by extension, the German military as a whole) did not have cogent plans for transport or logistics. The Ju 52 was the best the *Luftwaffe* had, and it remained the backbone of the German aerial transport arm

throughout the war. Unfortunately for the Germans, this was not the last time that a lack of foresight concerning transportation and logistics would jeopardize operations.

Pushing ahead

However, even with mounting losses in the air war, the German high command pressed on with their plans. Although attrition was high, they thought that a short war would result in victory, even if they were in danger of running out of planes and pilots. As long as they had enough, it would have to do. Production continued, and planning continued for subsequent campaigns.

The Low Countries

In the context of World War II, the Low Countries means the Netherlands, Belgium and Luxembourg. Occupying the area formed by the deltas of the Rhine, Scheldt and Meuse rivers, these lowland regions bore the initial brunt of Hitler's campaign in the West.

Kings and nations had fought across this ground for centuries. Indeed, Belgium had traditionally been referred to as the 'Cockpit of Europe' because of the number of battles it had witnessed. The region's flat terrain, crossed by rivers, canals and strategically located bridges, is ideal for mobile warfare. At the beginning of World War I, the Germans implemented the Schlieffen Plan, marching four entire armies through the Low Countries, in an effort to outflank the Belgians, the British Expeditionary Force and the French,

who were situated in the area. By 1940, it was still the easiest path of advance into France.

Build-up

Luftflotte 2 began planning and equipping for the upcoming campaign. *General der Flieger* Albert Kesselring organized his forces – fighters, bombers and ground-attack planes – to support the land offensives of the army. Employing the successful *Blitzkrieg* tactics of combined operations, the Germans planned to attack through the Low

Countries and into France, taking advantage of the geography and at the same time avoiding the French defensive fortifications of the Maginot Line. The Germans were aware that the Belgians were likely to fight but were making inquiries into guaranteeing their neutrality. The Germans were also aware that there was a significant BEF contingent, complete with RAF aircraft, and the French were well equipped even if they were overrated. The German plan was a quick attack through the Low Countries into France, where

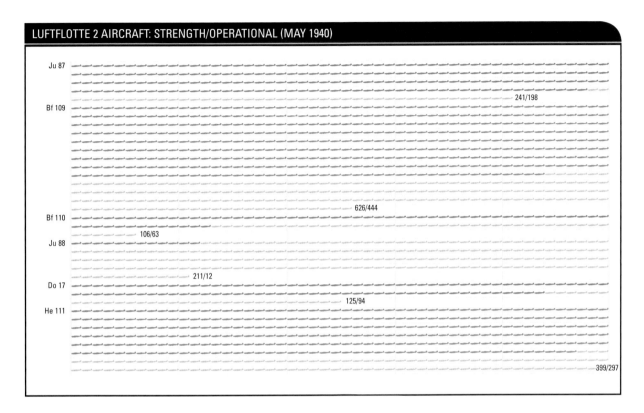

LUFTFLOTTE 2 AIRCRAFT: STRENGTH/OPERATIONAL (MAY 1940)

Ju 87

Bf 109 — 241/198

Bf 110 — 626/444

Ju 88 — 106/63

Do 17 — 211/12

He 111 — 125/94

399/297

■ *Luftflotte* 2 strength at the opening of the campaign for the Low Countries and France. Between the Polish campaign and the attack on France, the *Luftflotte* had rebuilt and rearmed with new planes supplied in increased numbers.

they would split the French forces, forcing capitulation.

The *Luftwaffe* was ready. Losses from the Polish campaign had been made up and an impressive force was arrayed for the upcoming battle. Known as *Fall Gelb* (Case Yellow), the attack into the Low Countries and on into France was planned out in great detail, maximizing German strengths and taking advantage of enemy weaknesses.

Air component
Organizing a force of more than 3000 planes was not an easy task. *Luftflotten* 2 and 3 commanded over 850 Bf 109s plus an additional 350 Bf 110s. Added to this were the 1100 bombers that would carry out attacks against strategic and operational targets and the 400 Ju 87s that would coordinate with the ground forces in tactical assault. Over 500 transport aircraft stood ready to ferry men and supplies as needed.

Aligned against the Germans were the most advanced aircraft they had yet faced, in the shape of British and French fighters. However, even these were outmatched by the *Luftwaffe*.

The British committed 680 aircraft, but most of these were completely

obsolescent Fairey Battles, with a few marginally effective Hawker Hurricanes. The French had some 1562 aircraft available, but theirs were also obsolescent compared with the contemporary German designs. The Belgian Air Force, of just under 200 aircraft in total, were completely overwhelmed by the approaching *Luftwaffe* onslaught.

Outdated equipment
First, the Belgians. They faced the Germans with outdated equipment, bought from a number of different countries. Their eclectic collection included Italian Fiats, home-built Renards and an interesting mix from British factories. Of all their planes, only the Hawker Hurricane Mk Is

were even close to competent against the latest *Luftwaffe* designs, and they only had 11 of them.

The British Expeditionary Force boasted some of the most modern aircraft, but all were poorly suited to repelling the Germans. British standing orders kept the newest, the Supermarine Spitfire Mk 1, at home for possible German attack on Britain. Therefore, in terms of modern aircraft, the BEF had only Mk I Hurricanes with which to defend French airspace, and no more than half of the air contingent were Hurricanes. The remaining BEF aircraft were Fairey Battles, completely overmatched by the *Luftwaffe*'s machines.

A dire situation prevailed in the French Air Force, the *Armée de l'Air*, which had postponed significant upgrades until it was too late. Also flying obsolescent aircraft against the Germans, the French had only a few handfuls of the latest aircraft, Dewoitine D.520s and Morane M.S.406s, to combat the Germans. All other designs – and, in fact, most of the French Air Force – were completely outmatched.

The campaign opened on 10 May 1940. The Germans did not attack the Maginot Line, concluding correctly that the French defences were stout at that point. Instead, the Panzer

spearhead roared through the Ardennes forest, catching the French forces off guard. Another German advance drove into Belgium through the Netherlands.

The Netherlands

Luftwaffe operations against the Netherlands included 250 bombers and 150 fighters against a mere 144 Dutch aircraft. As in Poland, the *Luftwaffe* destroyed over half of the Dutch planes on the ground, effectively defeating the Dutch Air Force in the first few hours of the campaign. A few of the remaining planes were shot down in combat, but in effect the *Luftwaffe* gained air superiority quickly. After the bombing of Rotterdam, the Dutch surrendered, five days into the campaign.

Belgium

In Belgium, the story was the same. The *Luftwaffe* gained air superiority rapidly by attacking airfields. Almost all of the Belgian Air Force, the *Aéronautique Militaire Belge*, was destroyed on the ground, again giving the *Luftwaffe* complete mastery of the skies. The strongest resistance was at the strategic Albert Canal crossing, protected by the fort at Eben-Emael, which covered the junction where the canal and the Meuse River joined.

■ **Opposite: Graphic representation of *Luftwaffe* and Allied aircraft types, spring 1940. Whereas half the British contingent were Hurricanes and compared favourably with *Luftwaffe* types, most of the French aircraft were outclassed.**

On the first day of the campaign, *Luftwaffe* gliders landed on the concrete and steel fort, and assault troops neutralized its guns. *Luftwaffe* paratroopers secured the river crossings, overwhelming the Belgian defenders and forcing their retreat. The British and French thought that the Eben-Emael assault was the main German attack, and refortified a more northerly position to counter the German advance.

Despite all efforts, the Belgians were completely outmanoeuvred and outmatched; even though they offered strong resistance, they were overwhelmed by the German onslaught. Belgium capitulated in 18 days.

■ **Operational aircraft strengths of the British, Belgian and French defenders at the beginning of the campaign for the Low Countries and France. Although the sheer numbers look reasonably healthy compared with the German air fleet, most of the Allied aircraft were out of date.**

ALLIED AIRCRAFT STRENGTH (MAY 1940)

BEF	
France	680
	1562
Belgium	192

LOW COUNTRIES CAMPAIGN AIRCRAFT COMPARED

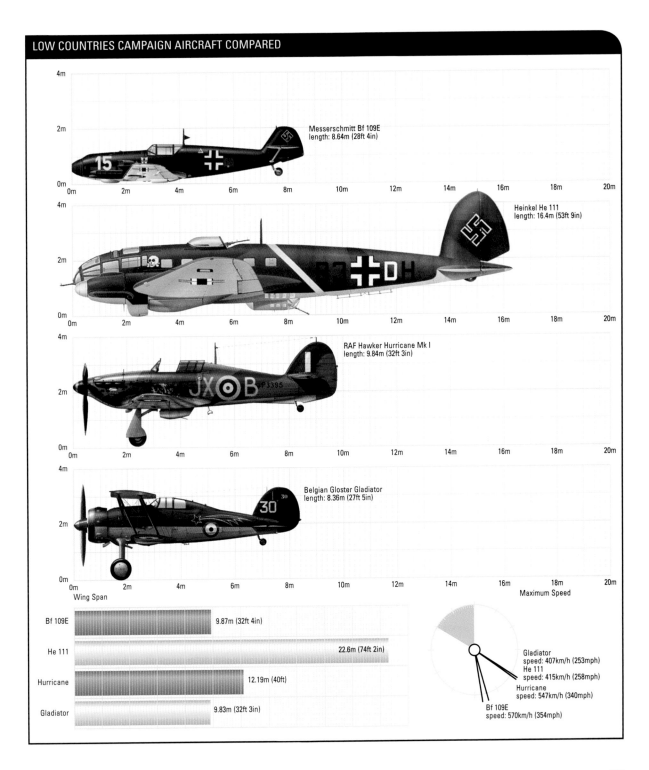

Messerschmitt Bf 109E
length: 8.64m (28ft 4in)

Heinkel He 111
length: 16.4m (53ft 9in)

RAF Hawker Hurricane Mk I
length: 9.84m (32ft 3in)

Belgian Gloster Gladiator
length: 8.36m (27ft 5in)

Wing Span

Bf 109E	9.87m (32ft 4in)
He 111	22.6m (74ft 2in)
Hurricane	12.19m (40ft)
Gladiator	9.83m (32ft 3in)

Maximum Speed

Gladiator
speed: 407km/h (253mph)
He 111
speed: 415km/h (258mph)
Hurricane
speed: 547km/h (340mph)
Bf 109E
speed: 570km/h (354mph)

France and the BEF

The German invasion of Western Europe in 1940 concentrated on the Netherlands, Belgium and Luxembourg in order to bypass France's Maginot Line fortifications. Three Army Groups took part: 'B' attacked in the north and 'A' further south, while 'C' acted as decoy, keeping the Maginot Line occupied.

While Germany's Army Group B under *Generaloberst* Fedor von Bock, fought through northern Belgium, Army Group A, led by *Generaloberst* Gerd von Rundstedt, powered through the 'impassable' Ardennes forest. Thinking that the Ardennes was too dense for the German Panzers, the French had only lightly defended this sector. However, Army Group A drove through and surprised

the French defenders. Led from the air by two *Stukageschwader*, the Panzer divisions drove deep into the heart of the French defences, cutting a line between the First and Second French Armies. The BEF was also to

the north of the dividing line, fighting with the French First Army.

As in previous campaigns, *Luftwaffe* bombers destroyed airfields and planes, this time French; *Luftwaffe* fighters took care of

■ **This chart shows *Luftflotte* 3's operational numbers in May 1940. In addition to those of *Luftflotte* 2, these aircraft flew combat operations against the French in May 1940. The *Luftwaffe* was willing to take high losses if the end result was a quick, decisive campaign.**

LUFTFLOTTE 3 AIRCRAFT: STRENGTH/OPERATIONAL (MAY 1940)

Aircraft	Strength/Operational
Ju 87	
Bf 109	80/67
Bf 110	601/425
Ju 88	174/127
Do 17	62/22
He 111	354/271
	447/302

French planes that were able to take off for attack. The dive-bombers led the Panzers in tactical attacks against French land targets.

Across the Meuse

The first formidable defence came at the river Meuse. Combining bomber and dive-bomber forces, the *Luftwaffe* led the way in crossing the Meuse, shattering the French defences at the *Schwerpunkt* (focal point) and avoiding heavy resistance. Once the Germans crossed the Meuse, the French retreat turned into a rout. By the morning of 14 May, the French forces, with little air cover, were a shambles.

The German attack was on a roll. *Luftwaffe* fighters and bombers continued to control the skies, and the Panzers rolled forward. By the morning of the 20th, the Germans had reached the Channel coast and had effectively cut off the French First Army and the BEF from the rest of the French armies.

The situation was dire. The new British Prime Minister, Winston Churchill, flew to Paris to confer with the French government and high command. He saw despair and defeatism and was convinced that the French were overwhelmed by the German attack. Although the French forces in the north were ordered to fight south to defeat the German advance, they could not, and were soon trapped, making their way to Dunkirk on the coast.

Trapped

By 24 May, the BEF and French First Army were trapped at Dunkirk, surrounded by German tanks and being harassed by the *Luftwaffe*. Over 350,000 Allied troops were trapped. Churchill realized the gravity of the situation and ordered the Royal Navy to begin a withdrawal plan. Hitler, in a controversial decision, ordered his Panzers to halt for three days, offering the Allies a bit of breathing room. This order was in part due to assurances from Göring that the *Luftwaffe* alone could destroy the trapped armies.

The *Luftwaffe* bombed and dropped leaflets urging the soldiers to surrender, but the British had other plans. In a spectacular retreat, the Royal Navy, assisted by a variety of French and British commercial ships and boats, evacuated the bulk of the trapped soldiers, saving about 330,000. Dunkirk was evacuated, the BEF was saved and about 100,000 French troops also left the Continent, forming the Free French under newly promoted Brigadier-General Charles de Gaulle. The *Luftwaffe* was not able to destroy the trapped forces because they had no plan to execute and the Royal Air Force stepped up aerial coverage of the retreat. Dunkirk was a retreat, but it was successful.

The Germans turned south. The new plan was named *Fall Rot* (Case Red), organized to drive on Paris and complete the conquest of France. The disorganized French put up little resistance, and German troops marched into the French capital on 16 June. By 22 June the campaign was over; France surrendered. Northern France was occupied; southern France was governed by a newly formed French regime with its seat at Vichy.

The campaign was difficult for the Germans but not without substantial rewards. The planes of *Luftflotten* 2 and 3 proved successful in the six-week battle, but at a cost. For the Germans, the invasion of Western Europe showed once again that the pace of modern warfare required substantial preparation and logistical support. During the course of the Battle for France, the French, Dutch and Belgian air forces were destroyed, but the *Luftwaffe* had suffered tremendous losses, which would have to be made up quickly. Fortunately for the Germans, industry was on track to make up the losses by summer 1940.

Losses

In the course of the battle, the *Luftwaffe* suffered 1400 losses of aircraft of all types, or about a third (36 per cent) of its front-line forces. The heaviest losses were among the Ju 87 Stuka dive-bombers, which were quickly nearing obsolescence in a modern air war environment. Nevertheless, the *Luftwaffe* controlled the skies over all of Europe, and was soon building and refurbishing bases on the northern coast of France for a new battle against Britain.

In addition to the facilities in newly conquered Norway (*Luftflotte* 5), the *Luftwaffe* had gained advanced bases in Western Europe for future combat. For the German high command, the conquest of northern France, in addition to Norway, meant that the German Navy was also in a position to surround and blockade Britain from the sea. The stage was set for the Battle of Britain.

CHAPTER 4

The Battle of Britain

By mid-summer 1940, the Germans stood triumphant on the continent of Europe. They had gained new allies to the south; Italy joined the Axis for a number of reasons on 10 June. The Italian leader, Benito Mussolini, was also a fascist, and the Italian regime had a lot in common with its German counterpart. Both were dedicatedly anti-communist, and the Italians were still angry at the British and French about the outcome of World War I.

The Italians were also expansionist; Mussolini wanted to re-create an Italian Empire in the Mediterranean basin, including territory in North Africa. Bulgaria would eventually join the Axis, and Romania was also close to joining the grouping. In the Pacific, Japan and Germany had reached an agreement to fight international communism; the Japanese had already begun expanding to create their Greater East Asia Co-Prosperity Sphere. With the Soviets quiet, and the United States still neutral, Hitler considered his options for the only belligerent left, Britain.

A British RAF recovery team examine the fuselage and cockpit of a shot-down Junkers Ju 88 bomber, July 1940.

Preparation

By the summer of 1940, Luftwaffe production was in full swing. Messerschmitt's Bf 109 plant was churning out 50 aircraft a day. Across the compound another assembly line was producing almost five Bf 110 heavy fighters a day as well; 150 of the aircraft were delivered per month that summer.

Bomber factories were also replacing losses from previous campaigns. He 111s, Do 17s and Ju 87s and 52s were coming off the assembly lines in significant numbers.

The newest airframe for *Luftwaffe* use, the Junkers Ju 88 fast medium bomber, was still having substantial teething problems but was almost ready for use. Controversy surrounded this aircraft; it had been envisioned as a fast medium bomber, but significant changes were requested that put production behind schedule. Because it could only deliver a small bomb load, the *Luftwaffe* leadership demanded that the Ju 88 must have dive-bombing capabilities. This led to significant redesign and modification, some historians claiming that over 15,000 modifications were incorporated into production models. These changes obviously hampered series production. Although available in small numbers for the attack on France, the Battle of Britain became the showcase for the Ju 88.

Good economics

Financially, the Germans were in good shape. Although campaigning was costly, the successes, especially the defeat of France, meant that the Germans had access to more raw materials, industrial capacity and money than before. There was little concern for the costs of the war as the Germans took over French industry. These newly acquired assets began production for the German war machine almost immediately. Even though the French industries focused on small arms and peripheral military hardware, raw materials from France and Scandinavia (both bought and appropriated) provided more than enough resources for German military manufacturing.

In fact, there was money and materials left over in the major aircraft manufacturing companies for independent research and development (R&D) and design for new prototypes and models. Each of the major manufacturers (and a few that will appear later in the story) was able to increase wartime production as well as continue substantial R&D programmes for future development, while at the same time paying high wages and turning a profit. This was a heady time in Germany; there was little concern for financial matters.

The campaigns to this point, while costly, had been short and decisive. *Luftwaffe* strength by summer 1940 had increased; losses were replaced. German aircraft manufacturing made up the numbers, even though the losses had been higher than planned.

Likewise, pilot strength was up. German pilots who had been captured were returned; pilot training was running at full speed. That said, however, the Germans were still not adequately prepared for a long campaign of attrition and counted on short, decisive, successful battles to avoid deficiencies in both production and training. The Germans who paid attention knew that a long campaign against an industrialized enemy would be disastrous for Germany, just as World War I had been. However, few offered the opinion. The German war machine had to this point been successful; it was counter-productive to morale and prospects to suggest that subsequent campaigns would not be equally short and decisive. In summary, few were concerned.

Hitler eyed Britain with great suspicion. Some historians argue that Hitler would have been content

■ **Opposite: Four of the main types of *Luftwaffe* aircraft to participate in the Battle of the Britian (from top) – the Bf 109 fighter, He 111 bomber, Ju 87 dive-bomber and Ju 88 bomber. The *Luftwaffe*'s bombers were very small compared with the strategic bombers later employed by the Allies, but this suited their main intention: to destroy the RAF on the ground and in the air.**

BATTLE OF BRITAIN LUFTWAFFE AIRCRAFT COMPARED

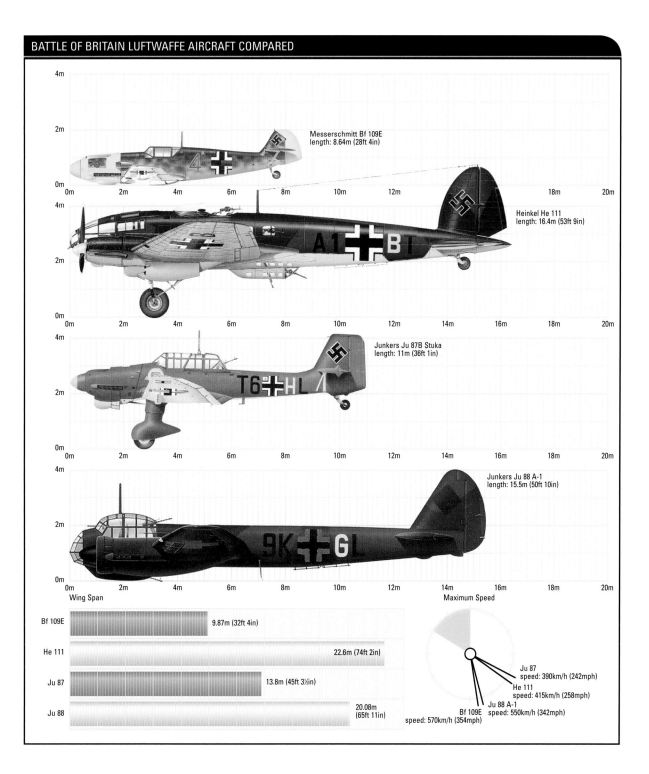

Messerschmitt Bf 109E
length: 8.64m (28ft 4in)

Heinkel He 111
length: 16.4m (53ft 9in)

Junkers Ju 87B Stuka
length: 11m (36ft 1in)

Junkers Ju 88 A-1
length: 15.5m (50ft 10in)

Wing Span

Bf 109E — 9.87m (32ft 4in)

He 111 — 22.6m (74ft 2in)

Ju 87 — 13.8m (45ft 3½in)

Ju 88 — 20.08m (65ft 11in)

Maximum Speed

Ju 87
speed: 390km/h (242mph)

He 111
speed: 415km/h (258mph)

Ju 88 A-1
speed: 550km/h (342mph)

Bf 109E
speed: 570km/h (354mph)

to let Britain become neutral; others suggest that Britain was a danger to German grand strategy. In the end, Hitler was willing to force Britain to capitulate, using overwhelming military might, but he did not have an equally coherent diplomatic plan. Britain, and Prime Minister Churchill, did not want to be conquered and prepared the population for the ultimate threat. The British organized to fight Hitler's Germany.

ALBERT KESSELRING

■ **Kesselring in full dress uniform, February 1943.**

Albert Kesselring, an infantry officer in World War I, became the chief of staff of the Luftwaffe *in 1936. He led* Luftflotte *1 during the Polish campaign, and was promoted to the head of* Luftflotte *2 for the war in the West. He continued the war as an excellent air commander facing the toughest opponents: the Soviets in 1941, the Allies in the Mediterranean theatre in 1942 and the Allies in Western Europe in 1944. He ended the war as the commander-in-chief of the* Luftwaffe *for Southern Europe. Post-war, as an American prisoner, he helped to write the official history of the* Luftwaffe. *He was released from captivity in 1952.*

BIRTH:	30 November 1885
DEATH:	16 July 1960
PLACE OF BIRTH:	Marktsteft, Kingdom of Bavaria, German Empire
FATHER:	Adolf Kesselring
MOTHER:	Rosina Kesselring
PERSONAL RELATIONSHIPS:	Luise Anna Pauline (Liny) Keyssler (married 1910)

MILITARY SERVICE:

1904: Officer Cadet, 2nd Bavarian Foot Artillery Regiment
1905–6: Military Academy, promoted to Lieutenant
1909–10: School of Artillery and Engineering (Munich)
1915: transferred to 1st Bavarian Foot Artillery
19 May 1916: promoted to Captain
1916: transferred to 3rd Bavarian Foot Artillery
1916: Iron Cross 2nd and 1st class
1917: posted to General Staff, sent to Eastern Front as a staff officer
1918: returned to Western Front as a staff officer with the II and later III Bavarian Corps
1933: discharged; appointed head of Department of Administration of the Reich Commissariat for Aviation with rank and pay of Colonel
1934: promoted to *Generalmajor*
1936: promoted to *Generalleutnant*
1936: appointed Chief of Staff of the *Luftwaffe*
1 October 1938: promoted to *General der Flieger*, and commander of *Luftflotte* 1
12 January 1940: became commander of *Luftflotte* 2
November 1941: appointed Commander-in-Chief South, transferred to Italy
19 July 1944: awarded Knight's Cross with Oak Leaves with Crossed Swords and Diamonds by Hitler
10 March 1945: appointed *Oberbefehlshaber West* (OB West)
6 May 1945: surrendered to American forces and taken into captivity

Britain had two enormous advantages over the defeated Polish and French. First and foremost, the Channel offered a natural barrier from the Continent; and second the Royal Navy was the force to defend it. The last successful invasion of England had come in 1066, when the Normans had crossed the Channel. In the interim, the French, Spanish and others had either attempted or planned for the occasion; none had been successful.

Hitler would have to be very creative for a successful invasion of Britain. After the fall of France, Hitler ordered planning for Operation *Seelöwe* (Sealion). It was to be a blueprint for the invasion of England across the Channel, using a combined air, sea and land force to compel British capitulation. The plan was outlined in three steps: achieve air superiority over the Royal Air Force, defeat the Royal Navy – at least in the Channel – and then transport the invasion force across. And the plan had to be put into action before the weather turned in late autumn. The German high command set to work.

British response

By August 1940, the British were in dire straits. All of their allies had been defeated by the Germans; they could only count on the United States for supplies. And these supplies were under constant attack from German U-boats.

The British knew that an attack was forthcoming, most likely sooner rather than later. But while concerned, they had a few advantages that would help them against the impending storm. As

mentioned above, the Channel and the Royal Navy provided a defensive geographical and military barrier against the Germans. While good on land, the Germans (with the exception of the Norway campaign) had not crossed water, and it was reasonable to expect that it was not a speciality. The Royal Navy concentrated on patrols in the Channel, mining the waters and preparing coastal defences against potential German attack from the sea.

On land, Britain began preparing defensive fortifications in coastal areas, as well as in the cities, to hamper German advances in the case of an invasion. The Home Guard was called up and army troops were distributed throughout southern England. Civilians were issued gas masks in case the Germans resorted to chemical attacks reminiscent of World War I. Prime Minister Churchill motivated the population with a number of rousing speeches and public appearances. One of the most gifted speakers of the twentieth century, Churchill was a light in a dark time. Stockpiles were laid, shelters were prepared, the population was galvanized in preparation for the upcoming crisis.

In the air, the RAF was ready. Fortuitous decisions and innovations in the inter-war period had unwittingly prepared the RAF for the approaching onslaught. Although its fate was not assured, the British air arm held significant advantages by summer 1940. One of the most important was radar. It had been developed in the mid-1930s, and the RAF had perceived the importance of 'radio direction and ranging' to 'see' aircraft and ships

approaching from a distance – specifically enemy planes coming from the Continent – and also for naval gun-laying. By 1940, the British had a series of radar stations along the English coast, positioned to spot approaching German aircraft.

Although very primitive, radar was an effective early warning system for the RAF. It was combined with improved communications and centralized control at RAF Fighter Command. Located just south of London, Fighter Command HQ received radar reports, landline (phone) and radio signals, and charted enemy activity on a giant map table. From HQ, specific squadrons could be mobilized to battle the *Luftwaffe*, rather than mounting constant aerial patrols, which caused wear and tear on men and machines. A coordinated centralized Fighter Command with improved communications technology was key to the defence of Britain.

New fighters

The final piece of the puzzle concerned the RAF aircraft themselves. The British could 'see' the Germans and could prepare a defensive stance but needed a weapon to defeat the German aerial armada. Fortunately, this was also available by summer 1940 in the shape of the Supermarine Spitfire. The Air Ministry had placed an order for 310 airframes in 1936 but was reluctant to order more; the focus at the time was on bombers. When the crisis came in 1939 with the declaration of war on Germany, the Air Ministry reviewed priorities and upped the original orders.

By the summer of 1940, British high-performance fighters came in two types: the Spitfire and the Hawker Hurricane. The Hurricane was heavier and slower but better armed; the Spitfire was faster and newer, but fewer were available.

First in service in 1937, the Hurricane was ready in numbers in spring 1940, the main fighter for RAF squadrons. Fighting was intense in the Battle for France, and when the RAF was recalled to Britain there were only about 500 Hurricanes available. That said, about 75 were

being produced each week on average, bolstering Fighter Command forces. Hurricanes made up about 65 per cent of Fighter Command; Spitfires much of the balance.

Still, there were not many to go round. On Day One of the Battle of Britain, there were 250 Spitfires ready, but their production rate was a significant 25 per week on average. These production numbers can be attributed to one person – Lord Beaverbrook, Minister of Aircraft Production. Born in Canada as Max Aitken, he decided in spring 1940 to

streamline British aircraft production, leading to significant changes in output and repair during the Battle of Britain.

■ **The two main RAF fighters during the Battle of Britain were the Hawker Hurricane Mk I and the Supermarine Spitfire Mk I. The Hurricane was stout but outclassed by the German Bf 109 and concentrated its efforts on German bombers. The Spitfire was comparable to the main German fighters. During the battle, the RAF had more Hurricanes than Spitfires in a consistent ratio of 65:35.**

RAF AIRCRAFT COMPARED, BATTLE OF BRITAIN

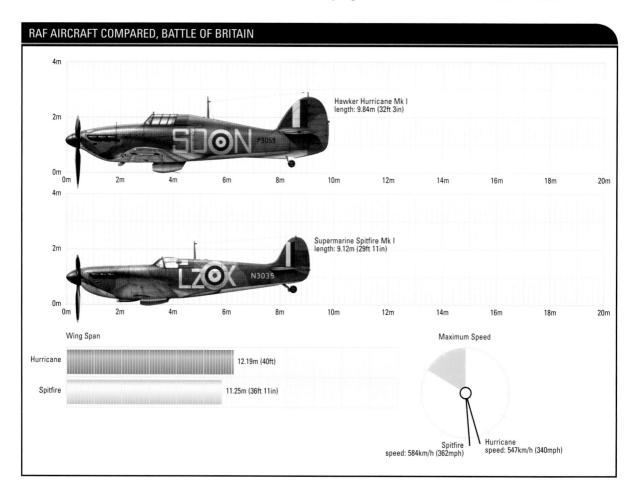

Hawker Hurricane Mk I
length: 9.84m (32ft 3in)

Supermarine Spitfire Mk I
length: 9.12m (29ft 11in)

Wing Span

Hurricane — 12.19m (40ft)

Spitfire — 11.25m (36ft 11in)

Maximum Speed

Spitfire speed: 584km/h (362mph)

Hurricane speed: 547km/h (340mph)

RAF pilot training was also a significant factor. The RAF had an adequate system to train pilots but also benefited from the far-reaching empire; numerous pilots came from Canada, New Zealand, South Africa and Australia. As well, Polish and Czech pilots, who had escaped from their defeated countries, continued to fight with the British against the Germans. The Free French offered some pilots, and there were a handful of American volunteers. Pilots made up one element of which there was not a significant Allied shortage.

Home advantage

One final consideration was that the British were playing with 'home field' advantage. If a German pilot was shot down but lived, he became prisoner. If a British pilot was shot down over England and lived, he often climbed into a new aircraft later that day to fight again. There were numerous accounts of RAF pilots continuing the fight in new planes, provided that they were well enough to fly.

Over the Channel was another story. On average, German sea

rescue was better than British, but it depended on weather and proximity to either side. The Germans more often used seaplanes to recover downed pilots, whereas the British relied on Royal Navy ships. Thus the Germans could be faster, but the RN could loiter.

RAF organization

By the opening stages of the Battle of Britain, the combined variables of RAF Fighter Command gave the advantage to the British, but they would still have to fight for it. Fighter Command was organized into groups, numbered 10, 11, 12, and 13. 10 Group was responsible for southwestern England and south Wales. Commanded by Air Vice Marshal Sir Quintin Brand, it was one of the quieter sectors and the staging area for squadrons of Gloster Gladiators and Boulton Paul Defiants, obsolete by 1940 and used for coastal patrol.

11 Group shouldered a heavier load of the fighting, defending London and southeast England. It was commanded by Air Vice Marshal Keith Park, a New Zealander.

Because of its location, 11 Group was the busiest sector during the battle and thus flew almost exclusively Hurricanes and Spitfires.

Under the command of Air Vice Marshal Trafford Leigh-Mallory at his HQ in Notttinghamshire, 12 Group covered the Midlands, East Anglia and the rest of Wales. 13 Group, meanwhile, served northern England and Scotland and also supported the overworked 11 Group. 13 Group was based at Newcastle-upon-Tyne and led by Air Vice Marshal Richard Saul. It had a larger contingent of long-range aircraft (in addition to its Spitfires and Hurricanes) for North Sea patrols and defence against German bombers from Norway. (Incidentally, from 1940 to 1943, 14 Group was formed in northern Scotland to fly sea patrols against German U-boats in the Atlantic.)

All of the groups were controlled from Fighter Command HQ at Bentley Priory, where the central command structure outlined above was located. Air Chief Marshal Sir Hugh Dowding commanded Fighter Command during the Battle of Britain.

Luftwaffe Dispositions

The Germans were confident, but rightfully so. They had completed a significant treaty with the Soviets, securing their Eastern Front. The Poles were defeated in a matter of weeks, and the war machine rolled on. Their long-time foe, the French, had been defeated in a few months of intensive campaigning.

Germany had won every campaign to date and acquired vast resources in the process. Added to this, further

countries were joining the Axis camp and continued to have successes in every theatre of battle. It was a heady

time for the Axis as Hitler prepared to fight the British. They were the lone enemy by summer 1940, and though

Hitler may have preferred to have them as non-belligerent neutrals, he prepared an offensive plan nonetheless. The planned invasion was codenamed *Seelöwe* (Sealion).

For an invasion of Britain, the *Luftwaffe* first needed to achieve air superiority over the most modern and coordinated air force it had faced to date. The RAF stood directly in the way, but once it was out of the way the Royal Navy could be defeated in the Channel and the invasion could commence. Hitler requested the aerial campaign from Göring, who passed orders down to the commander of *Luftflotte 2*, *Generalfeldmarschall* Albert Kesselring. 'Smiling' Albert Kesselring was up to the task and set to preparing his *Luftflotte* for the upcoming battle.

Quick outcome

With aircraft production in full swing, the *Luftwaffe* could count on replacements of aircraft for the planned short campaign. Hitler needed a quick decision against the RAF if the navy and army were to coordinate a successful invasion before the weather turned in the autumn. Kesselring knew that he would take heavy losses, but if Britain could be knocked out of the war, the *Luftwaffe* would have succeeded no matter the amount of damage. He set to planning a quick, decisive air campaign to defeat the RAF.

In this battle, the *Luftwaffe* was the main thrust. There would be no army to race across the plains to occupy airfields and commandeer aircraft factories, it was all up to the air component of the German *Blitzkrieg*. The *Luftwaffe* alone would have to

destroy the RAF in order to win the Battle of Britain. With that in mind, Kesselring organized his plan.

Luftflotten 2 and 3

Luftflotte 2 had vast resources at its disposal. Dive-bombers – Ju 87 Stukas – would begin the fight by attacking ships in the Channel, destroying Royal Navy assets where they appeared. Then *Luftwaffe* bombers, escorted by fighters, would destroy the RAF at its bases and in the factories. *Luftflotte 2* bases were relocated to the northern

BF 109 UNITS				
Unit	Base	Type	Strength	Operational
Stab/JG2	Beaumont-le-Roger	Bf 109E	4	3
I./JG2	Beaumont-le-Roger	Bf 109E	32	27
II./JG2	Beaumont-le-Roger	Bf 109E	33	24
III./JG2	Le Havre	Bf 109E	29	20
Stab/JG3	Wiere-au-Bois	Bf 109E	2	2
I./JG3	Grandvilliers	Bf 109E	30	24
II./JG3	Samer	Bf 109E	34	30
III./JG3	Desvres-le-Touquet	Bf 109E	34	25
Stab/JG26	Audembert	Bf 109E	4	2
I./JG26	Audembert	Bf 109E	34	24
II./JG26	Marquise-Ost	Bf 109E	35	29
III./JG26	Caffiers	Bf 109E	39	33
Stab/JG27	Cherbourg-Ouest	Bf 109E	5	5
I./JG27	Lumetôt	Bf 109E	39	39
II./JG27	Crépon	Bf 109E	39	27
III./JG27	Arques	Bf 109E	39	32
Stab/JG51	Wissant	Bf 109E	4	2
I./JG51	Pihen-bei-Calais	Bf 109E	29	23
II./JG51	Marquise-Ouest	Bf 109E	25	25
III./JG51	St Omer-Clairmarais	Bf 109E	39	39
Stab/JG52	Coquelles	Bf 109E	2	1
I./JG52	Coquelles	Bf 109E	45	36
II./JG52	Peuplingues	Bf 109E	35	23
III./JG52	Zerbst	Bf 109E	31	16
Stab/JG53	Cherbourg	Bf 109E	4	4
I./JG53	Rennes	Bf 109E	39	37
II./JG53	Dinan	Bf 109E	30	26
III./JG53	Brest	Bf 109E	39	21
Stab/JG54	Campagne-les-Guines	Bf 109E	4	3
I./JG54	Guines-en-Calais	Bf 109E	34	24
II./JG54	Hermelingen	Bf 109E	38	36
III./JG54	Guines-en-Calais	Bf 109E	36	39
Stab/JG77	Stavanger/Trondheim	Bf 109E	–	–
I./JG77	Stavanger/Trondheim	Bf 109E	42	40
II./JG77	Stavanger/Trondheim	Bf 109E	39	35
II.(S)/LG2	Böblingen	Bf 109E-7	38	36

coast of Belgium and France to get closer to the eventual theatre of combat. The 4000 aircraft were arranged in multiple squadrons, poised for the attack. Of this 4000, about 900 Bf 109s were operational in five *Jagdgeschwader* (JG 3, 26, 51, 52, and 54). Another two groups of Bf 110 heavy fighters – *Zerstörergeschwader* (ZG) 26 and 76 – were also ready with about 200 aircraft.

Fighters from *Luftflotte* 3 were also available, and were committed to the fight later, including *Jagdgeschwader* 2, 27 and 53 along with heavy fighters from *Zerstörergeschwader* 2. The remainder of the *Luftwaffe* strength was represented by bombers, the He 111 being the most numerous type. The bombers would fly from bases in northern France, Belgium and distant

Norway. The majority were from *Luftflotte* 2 (HQ in Brussels), but others came from *Luftflotten* 3 (HQ in Paris) and 5 (HQ at Stavanger, Norway). The bombers from *Luftflotte* 5 flew long-distance attacks against central and northern England and Scotland, without fighter escort. German aircraft production received highest priority.

Although the *Luftwaffe* was to experience heavy losses, the predicted damage was going to be made up through increased production and concurrent pilot training. Losses were high, but production kept pace; the German numbers remained steady throughout the campaign. With men and materiel in place on its new airfields in France and Belgium, the *Luftwaffe* was poised for the attack on Britain. With fighter bases right on the Channel coast, the limited range of its aircraft was maximized. The bombers flew from inland bases, allowing them to form up over France for concentrated attacks in formation. Supplies of bombs and munitions were husbanded for the campaign as the *Luftwaffe* prepared single-handedly to bring the British to their knees.

■ **Fighters in the early years were designed for manoeuvrability rather than firepower. This diagram shows the weight of fire from a three-second burst of the Spitfire Mk I and Bf 109E. As the war progressed, fighters mounted ever more powerful armaments, and by 1944, interceptors such as the Fw 190A could bring to bear 16.8kg (37lb) of firepower.**

LUFTWAFFE STRENGTH DEPLOYED AGAINST BRITAIN (AUGUST 1940)			
Unit Type	Total Units	Nominal	Operational
Kampfgruppen	42	1482	1008
Stukagruppen	9	365	286
Sclachtgruppen	1	39	31
Jagdgruppen	26	96	853
Zerstörergruppen	9	244	189
Nachtjagdgruppen	3	91	59
Seefliegerstaffeln	14	240	125

THREE-SECOND BURST: WEIGHT OF FIRE COMPARED (1940)

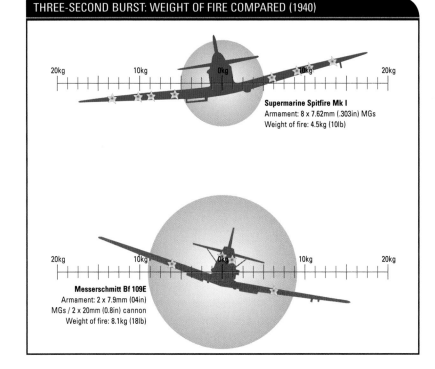

Supermarine Spitfire Mk I
Armament: 8 x 7.62mm (.303in) MGs
Weight of fire: 4.5kg (10lb)

Messerschmitt Bf 109E
Armament: 2 x 7.9mm (04in) MGs / 2 x 20mm (0.8in) cannon
Weight of fire: 8.1kg (18lb)

BATTLE OF BRITAIN (JULY–OCTOBER 1940)

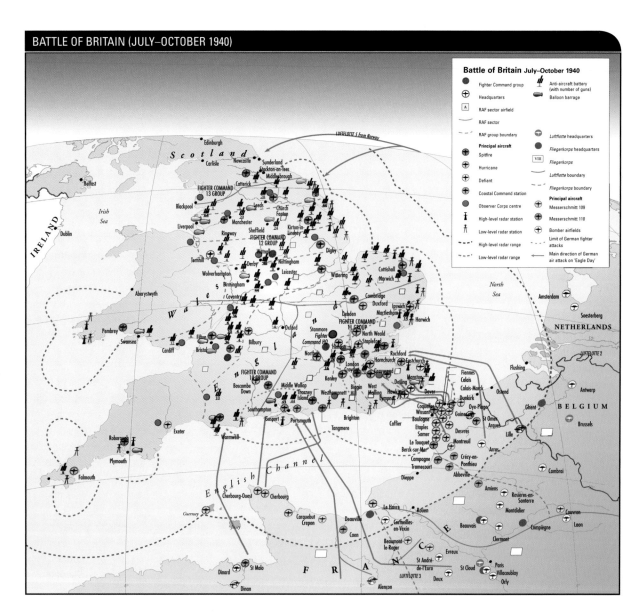

■ This map of the Battle of Britain campaign illustrates some of the challenges faced by the *Luftwaffe* in executing an air war against the UK mainland. The critical importance of southeastern England as the primary battleground is illustrated by the massive concentration of German airbases on the opposite coast, this thick cluster of units straddling the dividing line between *Luftflotten* 2 and 3. Yet even flying in from these distances meant that the loiter/combat time of the German fighters was restricted compared with that of their adversaries based in southeast England, and should bombers be bound for more distant targets they might need to make do without single-seat fighter escort. This situation pales into insignificance when compared with the lot of *Luftflotte* 5, whose planes were flying in from bases in Scandinavia, the distance precluding single-seat fighter escort altogether and demanding the use of Bf 110s.

The Battle of Britain

While the Battle for France was still raging in June 1940, the Luftwaffe *used a small portion of its force to reconnoitre airfields and give crews experience of flying over the British Isles. When the Battle of Britain finally began, it was divided into four phases.*

Phase I: *Kanalkampf*

In the first phase of the battle, *Luftwaffe* Ju 87 Stuka dive-bombers attacked shipping in the Channel. Running from 10 July to 12 August, this early phase of the campaign was intended to disrupt shipping and clear the Channel of the Royal Navy's presence. What it actually did was amplify the shortcomings of the Ju 87 in modern warfare. The Stukas were easy prey for the RAF fighters, due to slow speed and poor defensive armament. In a few weeks, the *Luftwaffe* lost 59 destroyed and 33 damaged, a full 20 per cent of the Stuka force, prompting the decision to limit the Ju 87's use over Britain. On the other side of the water, the British saw equal obsolescence in the Boulton Paul Defiant; it too was withdrawn from the fight after being savaged by *Luftwaffe* fighters.

Phases II and III: *Adlerangriff*

The first actual attacks on RAF airfields in Britain started on *Adlertag* (Eagle Day), 13 August 1940. The attacks began with bombing raids on RAF airfields and radar sites, in an effort to not only destroy the early warning system but also wipe out the defenders, similar to previous campaigns. Over the first 24 hours, which included a night attack against the Spitfire factory, the *Luftwaffe* flew 1485 sorties against the RAF's 727 and lost 46 aircraft to the RAF's 14; attrition warfare had begun. That first day began an intensive period of aerial combat over Britain. During the first week of *Adlerangriff* (Eagle Attack), the tactic was to neutralize the RAF to gain air superiority and the period saw concentrated operations against coastal radar installations, *Luftwaffe* fighters escorting bombers into the attack.

The sixth day of operations, 18 August, saw both sides take their heaviest casualties of the campaign as the *Luftwaffe* mounted 750 sorties against radar installations and airfields. The RAF's 11 Group made up the defence, flying every operational aircraft against the Germans. This day marked the last of the Ju 87 attacks against British targets as an elevated number of Stukas fell to British fighters. Over 30 per cent of the now vulnerable planes did not return. Aircraft from *Luftflotten* 2 and 3 concentrated on the Poling radar station and the air station at Croydon. *Luftflotte* 5 mounted 170 sorties from Norway but lost 75 aircraft to RAF fighters from 12 and 13 Groups. However, the RAF also lost 34 in the north. In the south, the Germans lost 61 aircraft to the RAF defenders, who also lost heavily, with 30 Hurricanes and seven Spitfires shot down.

By the end of the week, Göring had called off the persecution of the radar installations, and ordered his planes to shift focus to RAF Fighter Command specifically. The *Luftwaffe* concentrated on attacking RAF airfields, with a few bombing raids on aircraft manufacturing factories. The new plan was inherently attritional;

BATTLE OF BRITAIN AIRCRAFT LOSSES: PHASE I (10 JULY – 12 AUGUST 1940)

RAF

127

Luftwaffe

261

the *Luftwaffe* wanted to destroy the RAF on the ground, but if it chose to fight in the air, the Bf 109s would shoot its aircraft down.

Over the next two weeks of fighting, air supremacy was contested. The *Luftwaffe* increased operational tempo, averaging 1000 sorties per day, while the RAF fought to deny them, nearing 850 sorties per day. Both sides lost heavily; the Germans had the initial advantage of more aircraft, but the British could replace more quickly. Lord Beaverbrook, the Minister of Aircraft Production, had instituted an additional replacement plan using civilians, who cannibalized damaged planes to produce operational aircraft.

End of the beginning

By the end of the third phase of the Battle of Britain, which ran from 24 August to 6 September, both sides had suffered huge losses, but the RAF was closer to defeat. In this crucial phase of the battle, *Luftflotte* 2 focused its aggression on 11 Group, mounting attacks on 53 airfields as it

concentrated on destroying the RAF. In an interesting example of poor German intelligence-gathering, Göring was convinced at this point that the RAF was all but destroyed. He believed he had achieved air superiority over Britain, and conveyed this message to Hitler. Göring thought incorrectly that he had destroyed more than 50 per cent of RAF strength, at the cost of only 10 per cent of his own forces lost. He was convinced that the RAF had lost about 800 aircraft and was down to fewer than 100 fighters and pilots.

True figures

The accurate figures are much more interesting. Fighter Command had suffered badly, losing 444 planes over the period, including 410 Spitfires and Hurricanes. However, with factories running at full steam, and replacement pilots in training or recruited from the Commonwealth, RAF strength was not substantially degraded. RAF Fighter Command, by 6 September, held steady at 738 aircraft (Spitfires and Hurricanes,

with increasing numbers of Spitfires) ready for operations, and an additional 256 planes in reserve, as ordered by Beaverbrook.

The Germans, for their part, had also lost in significant numbers – more than 440 fighters plus an additional 440 bombers (with significant losses of Ju 87s, which were now out of the fight). The Germans, too, were replacing aircraft, holding steady at around 1400 operational fighters and an equal number of bombers. Göring, though, thought that while the *Luftwaffe* was replacing their aircraft, the RAF was not and was close to breaking. He did not believe that the British could make up their losses.

Luftwaffe aces

During the battle, a number of *Luftwaffe* pilots achieved significant success. Flying fighter sweeps, their new tactics were revolutionary and effective. The fighter *Schwarm* was a new idea. The tactic had four fighters flying together, with a lead and his wingman backed up by a second *Rotte* (section) comprising another

---

BATTLE OF BRITAIN AIRCRAFT LOSSES: PHASES II & III (13 AUGUST – 6 SEPTEMBER 1940)

RAF

Luftwaffe — 385

629

---

lead and wingman. The four planes were mutually supportive. Using this formation, the *Luftwaffe Schwarm* maximized the effectiveness of the lead pilot, usually the best and highest-ranking officer.

One example clarifies. At the start of the Battle of Britain, Adolf Galland was the *Gruppenkommandeur* of III *Gruppe* of *Jagdgeschwader* 26 (III./JG 26). Galland had gained notoriety during the Spanish Civil War, where flying for the *Legion Condor* he shot down 12 Republican aircraft. In August 1940, as group commander, he flew lead in his *Schwarm* and took part in frequent combat operations against Royal Air Force pilots during the Battle of Britain. To the credit of his wingmen, Galland was not shot down during the campaign. By mid-September, by which time he was *Geschwaderkommodore* of JG 26, he had achieved 40 victories and was awarded the Oak Leaves to his Knight's Cross. By the end of the year he had an additional 18 victories, bringing his total to 58.

Galland's machine during the Battle of Britain was the Messerschmitt Bf 109 E-4. The Bf 109 was better in all respects than the British Hawker Hurricanes it fought, and equal to the Supermarine Spitfire, depending on comparisons. The Bf 109's armament was better, with two 7.92mm (0.31in) MG 17 machine guns and one 20mm (0.79in) Oerlikon MG FF aerial cannon. The Spitfire Mk 1, which flew in the Battle of Britain, had eight 7.7mm (0.303) machine guns, so the edge went to the German planes armed with aerial cannon. Although the engines were similar – both liquid-cooled supercharged V-12s (German:

Daimler-Benz 601A; British: Rolls-Royce Merlin III) at about 825kW (1100hp) each – the German engine was fuel-injected while the Rolls-Royce was carburetted. The edge went to the 109 once again; it could dive better. The Spitfire was better in a turning battle, and both were equal in climb and speed.

Meanwhile, the Bf 109 outclassed the Hurricane across the board. In the campaign, the stouter Hurricanes concentrated on shooting down the German bombers (and avoiding being shot down themselves), while the Spitfires fought the German fighters.

Galland was equally successful against both types. Over the course of the campaign (according to his log book from 24 August to the end of the year), he shot down 22 Spitfires, 22 Hurricanes and a single Boulton Paul Defiant. Among the pilots he shot down during the Battle of Britain were a number of aces. Allied pilots who fell to Galland included Pilot Officer Johnny Allen (7⅓ confirmed victories), Sub-Lieutenant Francis Dawson-Paul (7¼), New Zealand Flight

Lieutenant Al Deere (17⅓) and Count Manfred Czernin (17), who was born in Germany to an Austrian aristocrat and an English mother and flew for 17 Squadron RAF. The count bailed out, later to become an agent for the Special Operations Executive (SOE).

Galland's attitude to the Spitfire was one of respect. Indeed, when asked at one point by Göring what it would take to win the battle, Galland replied, 'Give me a squadron of Spitfires!' This did not impress Göring; the pilot and his boss maintained a constant feud throughout the war.

In all, there were 40 *Luftwaffe* fighter pilots who chalked up at least 10 victories during the campaign. Thirty had 10 to 20 kills; the top 10 had between 23 and 45 each. Helmut Wick (42 victories) of *Jagdgeschwader* 2 is given credit as the highest-scoring German pilot for the recognized dates of the campaign (10 July–31 October); he was killed on 28 November 1940, when his plane was shot down over the Channel. On that very day, he had become the highest-scoring ace of the war.

TOP 12 LUFTWAFFE ACES IN THE BATTLE OF BRITAIN		
Pilot	*Unit*	*Kills*
Oberleutnant Helmut Wick	I/JG 2	42
Major Adolf 'Dolfo' Galland	III/JG 26, Stab JG 26	35
Hauptmann Walter Ösau	III/JG 51	34
Major Werner 'Vati' Mölders	Stab JG 51	28
Oberleutnant Hermann-Friedrich Joppien	I/JG 51	26
Oberleutnant Herbert Ihlefeld	I/LG 2	24
Hauptmann Gerhard Schöpfel	III/JG 26	23
Hauptmann Hans-Karl Mayer	I/JG 53	22
Oberfeldwebel Siegfried 'Wurm' Schnell	II/JG 2	18
Hauptmann Horst 'Jakob' Tietzen	II/JG 51	18
Oberleutnant Hans 'Assi' Hahn	III/JG 2	17
Leutnant Erich Schmidt	III/JG 53	17

The Blitz

By 7 September, the British still had not surrendered. They had been subjected to destructive attacks but still held their own in the air. Göring was convinced that the RAF was close to annihilation; Hitler wanted results. He ordered the Luftwaffe *to bomb London.*

Phase IV: the Bombing of London, 7–18 September

On both sides, the war had escalated. Harking back to Giulio Douhet's prediction that bombing a civilian population would result in the surrender of a country, both the British and the Germans considered the idea. The Germans had already tried it, even as early as the Spanish Civil War, but the results had been mixed. But by September 1940, Hitler was ready to escalate the war against Britain. Warsaw had been bombed, to get the Polish to surrender. But the Polish surrender had been more directly linked to the destruction of the Polish Army by both German and Soviet forces. France surrendered before a coordinated *Luftwaffe* bombing campaign began. But with Britain, Hitler was convinced that bombing was the logical progression of the campaign. It was the way to get London to capitulate.

Retaliatory bombing

Once the strategic 'gloves' were off, both sides practised bombing. The British had mounted small bombing raids at German ports, ostensibly to bomb dockyards and ships but also causing 'collateral damage' – a military euphemism for civilian casualties. But RAF Bomber Command was not (yet) specifically targeting civilians; that came later. That said, Bomber Command launched a punitive raid on Berlin on the night of 24/25 August, prompting historians ever since to suggest that the British began the practice of 'terror bombing civilians'. However, the Germans were already bombing in south England, and inflicting collateral damage, no matter what the intent. With the moral barrier broken, bombing London was an understandable strategic choice.

East London docks

On 7 September, 350 bombers from *Luftflotte* 2 attacked the east London docks in three waves in the middle of the day. Over 600 fighters provided escort, but the Bf 109 had a short range and could not loiter for more than 10 minutes over London (to say nothing of targets further north), and was ill equipped to protect the bombers. This provided an opportunity to the RAF fighters, who simply had to wait for the *Luftwaffe* escort to turn back before they attacked the bombers. On this day, the three waves of *Luftwaffe* bombers were attacked by fighters of 11 Group, which sent up six squadrons to combat the first wave, eight against the second and whatever could be mustered for the final wave later in the afternoon. All of the operational fighters in 11 Group flew and fought that day to repel the *Luftwaffe*. The high-altitude raid (as opposed to earlier low-level bombing against RAF airfields) was a bit trickier for the radar to estimate, and Fighter Command planes had a more difficult time reaching altitude at short notice. This would be overcome with new tactics; the evolution of aerial warfare continued.

The London 'Blitz', as it came to be known, continued by day for another 11 days. During this time, the *Luftwaffe* lost heavily; on the worst

■ **Opposite: This map of the bombing campaign against Britain between September 1940 and May 1941 shows that, between the three *Luftflotten,* there was no corner of the United Kingdom that the *Luftwaffe* could not reach. During the attacks on coastal cities in February–May 1941, for example, even Belfast in Northern Ireland was struck, as well as several other ports down the eastern Irish coastline. Targets in the north of England, such as Liverpool, Hull and Sheffield, were the responsibility of *Luftflotte* 2, while *Luftflotte* 5 could take on targets as far north as Glasgow, in addition to its maritime role of interdicting North Sea naval traffic.**

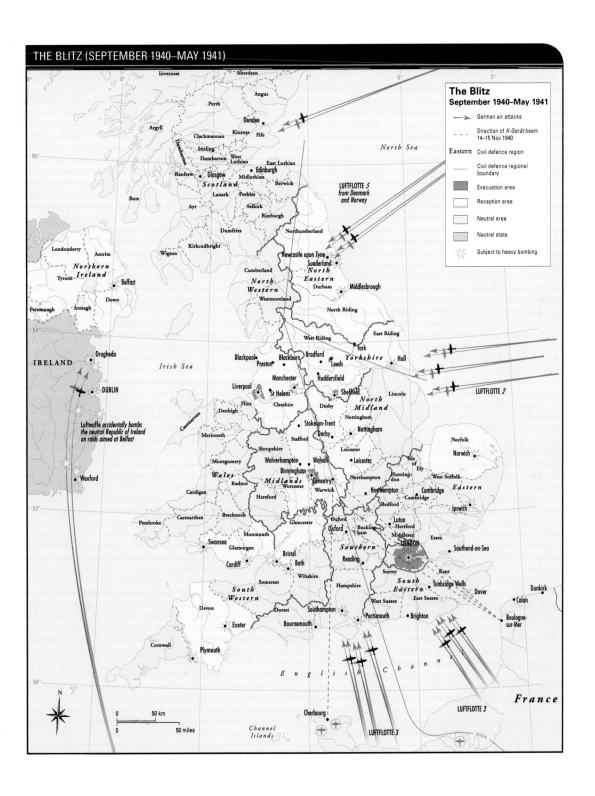

THE BLITZ (SEPTEMBER 1940–MAY 1941)

The Blitz
September 1940–May 1941

→ German air attacks

- - - Direction of *X-Gerät* beam
14–15 Nov 1940

Eastern Civil defence region

Civil defence regional
boundary

Evacuation area

Reception area

Neutral area

Neutral state

✳ Subject to heavy bombing

North Sea

LUFTFLOTTE 5
from Denmark
and Norway

Inverness

Aberdeen

Perth

Angus

Dundee

Argyll

Clackmannan

Kinross

Fife

Stirling

West
Lothian

Dumbarton

East Lothian

Renfrew

Glasgow

Edinburgh

Midlothian

Berwick

Scotland

Bute

Lanark

Peebles

Ayr

Selkirk

Roxburgh

Dumfries

Northumberland

Kirkcudbright

Wigton

Newcastle upon Tyne

Sunderland

*North
Eastern*

Cumberland

Durham

Middlesbrough

*North
Western*

Westmoreland

North Riding

Londonderry

Antrim

*Northern
Ireland*

Tyrone

Belfast

East Riding

Down

West Riding

York

Fermanagh

Armagh

Yorkshire

Hull

Irish Sea

Blackpool

Blackburn

Bradford

Preston

Leeds

IRELAND

Drogheda

Liverpool

Manchester

Huddersfield

St Helens

Sheffield

Lincoln

*North
Midland*

DUBLIN

Cheshire

Flint

Derby

*Luftwaffe accidentally bombs
the neutral Republic of Ireland
on raids aimed at Belfast*

Denbigh

Stoke-on-Trent

Nottingham

Caernarvon

Derby

Nottingham

Merioneth

Stafford

Leicester

Norfolk

Shropshire

Norwich

Wexford

Montgomery

Wolverhampton

Walsall

Eastern

Birmingham

Leicester

Isle
of
Ely

West Suffolk

Wales

Radnor

Midlands

Coventry

Northampton

Hunting-
don

Cardigan

Worcester

Warwick

Cambridge

Ipswich

Hereford

Northampton

Bedford

Brecknock

Pembroke

Carmarthen

Oxford

Bucking-
ham

Luton

Hertford

Gloucester

Oxford

Middlesex

Essex

Swansea

Southern

LONDON

Southend-on-Sea

Glamorgan

Bristol

Reading

Surrey

Kent

Cardiff

Bath

*South
Eastern*

Tunbridge Wells

Dover

Somerset

Wiltshire

Hampshire

Dunkirk

*South
Western*

Dorset

Southampton

West Sussex

East Sussex

Brighton

Calais

Devon

Bournemouth

Portsmouth

Boulogne-
sur-Mer

Exeter

Cornwall

Plymouth

E n g l i s h   C h a n n e l

France

N

0 — 50 km

0 — 50 miles

Cherbourg

LUFTFLOTTE 2

LUFTFLOTTE 3

*Channel
Islands*

XXXX

day, as much as 25 per cent of its bombing force. On the 15th, the most active day for both sides, the *Luftwaffe* sent 200 bombers (in three waves) escorted by more than 300 fighters, to face 300 RAF fighters, both Spitfires and Hurricanes. Although the RAF claimed 185 enemy shot down, the figure was actually 34 bombers and 26 fighters, for a loss of 26 RAF fighters. The high claims led to this day later becoming known as 'Battle of Britain Day' – the RAF had seemingly turned the tide. Three days later – the 18th – the *Luftwaffe* mounted a 70-bomber raid, losing 19 planes while the RAF lost 12.

An unintended consequence of the city bombings was that the RAF gained a valuable pause. Close to breaking point after the targeted raids on airfields, the RAF had time to recover when the *Luftwaffe* switched to city bombing. Indeed, the RAF

recovered quickly and was able to put up an increasingly more effective defence as time went on. With losses exceeding sustainable limits, the *Luftwaffe* entered the last phase of the Battle of Britain.

Phase IV(b): Night Blitz, 19 September – spring 1941

After the dreadful losses of daylight bombing, the *Luftwaffe* switched to night bombing of London and other cities. The benefit was that the RAF fighters would have a harder time finding the bombers and would thus be less able to shoot them down, thereby leading to fewer losses.

The drawback came in two forms: the *Luftwaffe* could not use fighter escorts for protection and they would have a tougher time finding targets. However, London was a big city, and using a combination of radio direction finding and celestial navigation, the

Luftwaffe bombers pressed the attack. For 53 nights, the *Luftwaffe* bombed London. The attacks petered out by November because of bad weather, then diminished to a trickle as the *Luftwaffe* prepared for other operations.

During the course of the raids, the *Luftwaffe* dropped 16,250 tonnes (16,000 tons) of bombs on London in September, and another 13,200 tonnes (13,000 tons) until the cessation of raids in mid-November. These bomb loads were split fairly evenly between high-explosive and incendiary munitions. While massively destructive to London (and other cities), the raids were not, contrary to Douhet's prediction, enough to force a British surrender. Britain held fast; Hitler eventually cancelled Operation *Seelöwe* and turned his attention to planning for the invasion of the Soviet Union.

During the Blitz, over 60 per cent of London was damaged or destroyed. The death toll was over 43,000 killed and another two million left homeless. Over the entire campaign, the RAF lost 915 aircraft but was able to make up losses and even to increase its operational numbers. The *Luftwaffe* lost 1733 aircraft but also

AIRCRAFT LOSSES IN THE LONDON 'BLITZ'

Date	Force	Aircraft Type	Strength	Losses
15 Sep 1940	Luftflotte 2	bomber	200	34
	Luftflotte 2	fighter	300	26
	RAF	fighter	–	26
18 Sep 1940	Luftflotte 2	bomber	70	19
	RAF	fighter	–	12

BATTLE OF BRITAIN AIRCRAFT LOSSES: PHASE IV (7–18 SEPTEMBER 1940)

RAF

Luftwaffe 238

411

LUFTFLOTTE 2 AIRCRAFT: STRENGTH/OPERATIONAL (15 SEPTEMBER 1940)

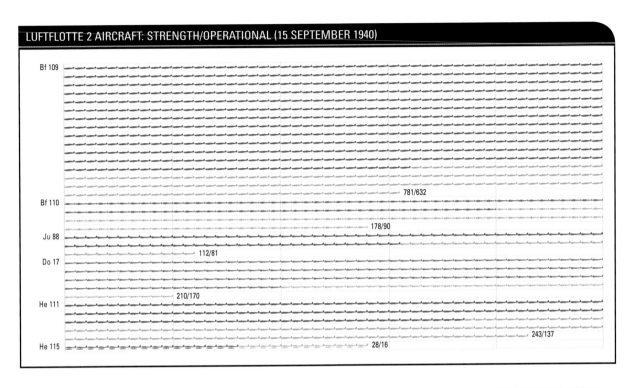

Bf 109   781/632

Bf 110   178/90

Ju 88   112/81

Do 17   210/170

He 111   243/137

He 115   28/16

LUFTFLOTTE 3 AIRCRAFT: STRENGTH/OPERATIONAL (15 SEPTEMBER 1940)

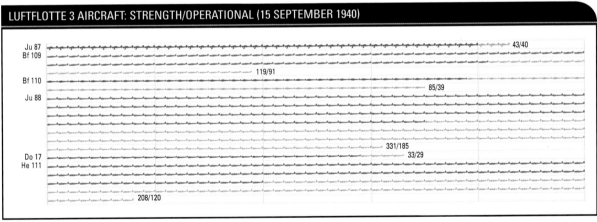

Ju 87   43/40

Bf 109

Bf 110   119/91

Ju 88   85/39

Do 17   331/185

He 111   33/29

208/120

LUFTFLOTTE 5 AIRCRAFT: STRENGTH/OPERATIONAL (15 SEPTEMBER 1940)

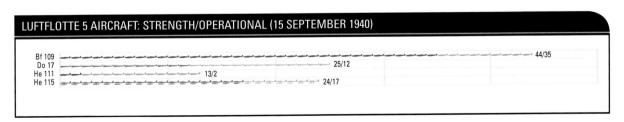

Bf 109   44/35

Do 17   25/12

He 111   13/2

He 115   24/17

made up losses with increased production. In the end, it was a stalemate, and the victory went to the 'home team'. The *Luftwaffe* did not subdue the RAF; the invasion of Britain never materialized. Although the RAF was not yet prepared to attack Germany in a similar fashion, the defence of Britain was complete, the British remained in the war and the Germans had been handed their first defeat. Materially the campaign was costly but not decisive. Psychologically it was a victory for the Allies; it proved that the Germans could be defeated in modern industrial warfare.

The British survived, and prepared to fight the Germans for the Atlantic and in other theatres. The Germans turned their attention away from Britain and towards the East for the conquest of the Soviet Union.

New technologies

The Battle of Britain introduced new technologies to the history of warfare. Aircraft were relatively new but had been used in World War I. In 1940, though, electronics played an increasingly important role in warfare. On the British side of the electronics war, it was signals intelligence and code-breaking. On the German side, it included range and direction finding (RDF), an early term for radar, in the form of navigation and bombing aids.

In countering the *Luftwaffe*, the British worked tirelessly on signals intelligence. With the realization that the Germans relied heavily on radio traffic, the British instituted an impressive signals intelligence section early in the war, located at Bletchley Park and known as 'Station X'. The Germans had a very sophisticated electro-mechanical cipher machine, Enigma, which they used to encode and decode radio signals that conveyed orders to the troops. The Germans believed the Enigma cipher to be unbreakable.

The programme for decoding Enigma messages in Britain was called Ultra. The British had acquired an Enigma machine from Polish refugees and built others by reverse engineering; during the war they also constructed a machine, called Colossus, one of the first digital electric 'computers', to break the code. Its ability to compute algorithms quickly and efficiently allowed the British to successfully decode nearly all German radio traffic – with only a few 'blackout' periods – as the war dragged on. During the Battle of Britain, the Government Code and Cypher School

(GCCS or GC&CS) worked around the clock to break German signals traffic to warn of attacks and discern German movements.

Ultra was extremely secret and the British went to great lengths to keep the Germans from knowing that their codes had been broken. After the war, one British author suggested that Winston Churchill knew of the German bombing raid aimed at Coventry ahead of time but allowed the city to be bombed to protect the Ultra secret. The contention was later shown to be inaccurate; Ultra members later said that although they knew of a major raid, there were no indications that Coventry was the target. Ultra was an important advantage for the British and it played a substantial role later in the war in the battles for North Africa and the Mediterranean.

Direction finding

In Germany, another interesting electronics technology was in

TONNAGE OF BOMBS DROPPED BY LUFTWAFFE: BATTLE OF BRITAIN	
Month	*tonnes/tons*
September 1940	16,250/16,000
October 1940	13,200/13,000

BATTLE OF BRITAIN AIRCRAFT LOSSES: PHASE IV(b) (19 SEPTEMBER – SPRING 1941)

RAF

Luftwaffe — 152

— 297

■ **An He 111 bomber flies over London's East End docks area, autumn 1940.**

development. With the onset of the night-bombing campaign, *Luftwaffe* pilots were having trouble finding their targets in Britain. The British had taken a decidedly non-technological route and ordered cities to be 'blacked out' at night. Without landmarks, *Luftwaffe* bombers easily became lost. The German response was the *Knickebein* (Crooked Leg) system of radio beam direction finding. Based on the Lorenz system for blind landing, which directed aircraft to their airfields, the *Knickebein* system was directed at Britain. Two radio transmitters were set up to broadcast signals that crossed at the intended target. The aircraft, using a special radio receiver, would fly along one beam until it 'heard' the second signal, at which point it would drop its bombs.

The 'Battle of the Beams', as it was known, was a back-and-forth struggle to jam and un-jam the signals for accurate targeting. The German radio stations at Kleve (in western Germany) and Stolberg (northern Germany) struggled to broadcast stronger signals as the British worked to block, jam or 'bend' them. As the British grew more adept at jamming *Knickebein*, the Germans introduced their newest technology: *X-Gerät*.

The new system was more complex, with greater redundancy. It used multiple higher frequency signals, and the British had a tougher time with the new system until a

receiver was captured when an He 111 with the new equipment was shot down. The system used a main signal and radio signals crossing the main line at intervals. The bombers released based on the direction they were flying and timing patterns. The British countered by disguising signals and adding beams to confuse the German pilots.

The next German invention was *Y-Gerät*, an improvement on the earlier system. The Germans made the mistake of releasing the unofficial name for the system: Wotan, the name of a one-eyed god. The British correctly surmised that the new development was a one-beam system. The pilot, flying along the single beam, navigated by sending an echo back to the radio station, which computed the distance to the target. The British masked the signal with a shifted-phase radio beam, confusing

the Germans from the start. *Y-Gerät* was considered defective and abandoned after only a few attempts.

The Battle of Britain ushered in a new era of warfare for the destructive capabilities of aircraft as well as the constant interaction to defeat aerial assault. The German efforts in the campaign failed for a number of reasons, specifically a lack of a heavy bomber force, incoherent strategy and technological failures. To the Allies' credit, most of the German failures became lessons learned when the Allied strategic bombing campaigns began in earnest in 1943.

TOTAL AIRCRAFT LOSSES: BATTLE OF BRITAIN	
	Losses
RAF	915
Luftwaffe	1733

CHAPTER 5

The Mediterranean & North Africa

The Mediterranean theatre (North Africa, Sicily and Italy) and the Balkans have a curious status in terms of the overall strategic drama of World War II. As the war developed, Hitler's Germany would be crushed between the hammer of the Soviet advance from the east and the anvil of the Western Allies' onslaught from the west. By contrast, little was strategically decided in the Mediterranean theatre, apart from the fates of individual armies.

By 1945, the Allied attempt to push through to mainland Europe from the 'soft underbelly' of Italy, itself a stepping stone following victory in North Africa, had not been altogether successful, and was expending huge volumes of soldiers' blood for slow territorial gain. The war ended with both sides still locked into the rugged Italian landscape.

Float-equipped Ju 52/3m transport aircraft were used extensively in the Mediterranean theatre. This photograph was taken over the Aegean

Introduction

Italy was Germany's Axis partner in the south, and wanted to expand its influence in the Mediterranean. Benito Mussolini, the Italian leader, was also an early fascist, and gravitated towards the German camp for two reasons, political and diplomatic.

Their politics were similar, and the Italians were still angry with the Allies for the outcomes of World War I. The Italians entered the war on 10 June 1940, and immediately began their thrust east – into the Balkans – and south across North Africa.

However, the Italian Air Force was not as dominant as the *Luftwaffe*. Although one of the earliest air power theorists was Italian (Giulio Douhet), the Italian aircraft industry was not able to produce the amount or quality of machines that were needed. Further, historians have suggested that the Italian contribution to the Spanish Civil War – on the fascist side – was actually the height of Italian military power. As the Italians moved into the Balkans, Greece and North Africa, they needed increasing German assistance in their expansionist goals. German help was given, but this help in turn took away from other German efforts.

Reliance on Germany

At the height of the Italian expansion, the Italian Air Force increasingly relied on German equipment. Although the Italians had a nascent aircraft manufacturing industry, their machines were temperamental and delicate. As operations progressed, the Italians first relied on German aircraft engines (like the Daimler-Benz 601; first purchased, later license-built), and later German *Luftwaffe* coordination for air power.

The Balkans and Greece

Italy invaded Albania in the spring of 1939. Although the Italians faced strong resistance, the country fell quickly. When the Italians began operations elsewhere in the Balkans, things went badly for the invaders from the beginning.

The Yugoslavs were tougher opponents and the terrain hindered the Italian campaign. Mussolini asked Hitler for help, and the Germans sent ground troops as well as *Luftwaffe* assets to help the Italians. Angry that the Yugoslavs did not immediately join the Axis camp, Hitler ordered Operation *Strafgericht* (Punishment). Belgrade was bombed for four days (6–10 April 1941). The campaign consisted of over 500 sorties; the *Luftwaffe* dropped an estimated 221 tonnes (218 tons) of bombs. More than 2500 civilians were killed (some estimates are as high as 15,000), with the destruction of 'thousands' of buildings, including the royal palace and the National Library of Serbia. The centre of Yugoslavia fell to Axis forces as they turned their attention south to Greece.

Planes of the RAF as well as British Commonwealth forces, providing a stronger defence against the Axis advance, bolstered Greek forces. *Luftwaffe* Stuka dive-bombers were employed to greater effect in this campaign; there was little enemy aerial resistance to the vulnerable plane. As in previous *Blitzkrieg* campaigns, the *Luftwaffe* attacked Greek airfields first, destroying Allied air power and creating air supremacy. With the skies cleared, the *Luftwaffe* set to, attacking ground targets in advance of the land operations. The British were quickly driven from the Greek peninsula, and

BALKAN INVASION – LUFTWAFFE AIRCRAFT: STRENGTH/OPERATIONAL (5 APRIL 1941)

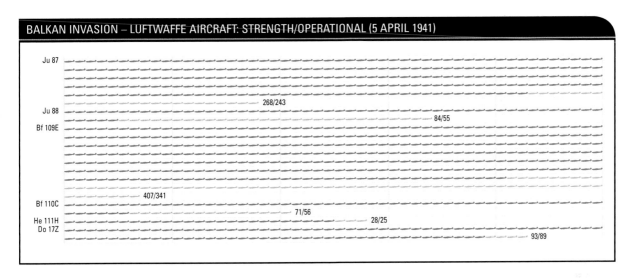

Ju 87

Ju 88   268/243

Bf 109E   84/55

Bf 110C   407/341

He 111H   71/56

Do 17Z   28/25   93/89

Greece fell on 30 April 1941. The *Luftwaffe* had shown once again the operational art of combined tactics, leaving devastation in its wake.

Battle for Crete

The last Allied stronghold in the region was the island of Crete, where British troops and RAF planes were camped ready to repel an Axis attack. As in the campaign against Britain, the *Luftwaffe* faced extreme difficulty in attempting to defeat an opponent through air power alone. However, the Germans added an extra element to their plan against Crete. To provide a ground component to the fight, the *Luftwaffe* landed paratroopers (*Fallschirmjäger*) in a combined attack.

The island of Crete became an Allied fortress. Over 50,000 Allied troops (mostly British and Commonwealth) had been ferried from Greece to the island by the Royal Navy, garrisoning the island against German attack. Crete was considered a strategic location

because of its position in the Mediterranean and for its excellent harbours. The British wanted to keep it; the Germans realized that they needed to take it.

The German campaign against Crete, Operation *Merkur* (Mercury), began in the early hours of 20 May 1941. More than 500 *Luftwaffe* transports (mostly Ju 52s) flew in 10,000 paratroopers for an aerial invasion of the island; another 750 troops would land in gliders. The paratroopers were from *7.Fliegerdivision* (7th Airborne Division), and coordinated by XI *Fliegerkorps*. Their task was to drop onto the three predesignated zones of the island and secure airfields, at which time they would be relieved by the 5th Mountain Division. German intelligence estimated that there were 5000 Allied troops plus an additional 10,000 Greeks, but these estimates were incorrect. In reality, the Germans were to face a combined force of approximately 40,000 on Crete.

The morning began poorly for the *Luftwaffe*. Although they quickly achieved air superiority over the island, the transports (and gliders) fared badly. The paratroopers were dropped off-target, and suffered heavy casualties in landing. The defences were stronger than anticipated; the German paratroopers lost 50–75 per cent of their initial invasion force to strong opposition. In one example, the 3rd Battalion of the 1st Assault Regiment lost 400 killed out of 600 against New Zealand defenders on the first day.

In addition to the airborne landings, the *Luftwaffe* also used fighters to sweep the skies, and bombers to bomb Cretan cities. Heraklion was bombed, causing massive damage. However, at the end of the first day, none of the German objectives had been met, resistance was still strong and losses were high.

Over the next four days, the British and Germans continued to reinforce the island; the British by sea and the Germans by air. The struggle for Crete

INVASION OF CRETE (20–31 MAY 1941)

Khania

Rethymnon

Heraklion

Sphakia

Allied evacuation routes

■ The map here clearly shows the principal German operational targets running along the northern coastline of Crete. What the map cannot reveal is the difficult, spiky nature of the terrain along this section of coast. A rocky, undulating landscape here made airborne landings treacherous at best – many German paratroopers became the victims of landing injuries, and German gliders were often wrenched apart by jagged surfaces. Nevertheless, over 11 days of fighting, the Germans managed to turn the situation their way. The Allied forces on Crete began evacuation on 29 May, those troops who did not get away surrendering to the Germans on 1 June.

was very costly for both sides. The British lost several ships to aerial attacks, while the *Luftwaffe* lost many transport aircraft in the operation. But the tide had turned. By 27 May, the British ordered a retreat to Egypt. Over the next few nights, more than 16,000 Allied and Greek troops were spirited off to Egypt in another strategic withdrawal. On 1 June, the remaining garrison of 500 Commonwealth troops surrendered to the Germans. The battle for Crete was over.

In the aftermath of Crete, a number of important military lessons were taken into consideration. First and foremost, *Luftwaffe* paratroopers had taken heavy losses. Hitler decided that the losses were too high, and refused to allow any airborne invasions for the rest of the war. Furthermore, *Luftwaffe* transport aircraft were savaged in the attack. Of the more than 370 *Luftwaffe* planes damaged or destroyed, the vast majority of losses were of invaluable transport aircraft, already in high demand. In the end, the campaign was a victory for the *Luftwaffe*, but it was also incredibly taxing. The *Luftwaffe* lost more than 4000 personnel killed; almost all the dead were paratroopers. On the Allied side, the British lost 3500 killed, and a further 7500 Cretan civilians were killed during or after the attack. Both sides were forced to reconsider military strategy in the aftermath of the Crete campaign.

Into Africa

The Italians continued their campaigns into North Africa, and a back-and-forth war began between the British forces in Egypt and the Italians in Libya. The Italians fared poorly, and quickly sought reinforcements from Hitler.

The Germans sent Erwin Rommel, the tank commander made famous in the campaigns against France, and the *Afrikakorps*, initially made up of the 5th Light Division. With the

Afrikakorps came *Luftwaffe* planes from *Luftflotte* 2, including portions of 22 air units. These included the fighter units JG 53 and 27, ZG 26 and 76, and bombers from KG 4, 26 and

30. Three *Gruppen* of Stukas, totalling a hundred or so dive-bombers, also arrived. In all, the *Afrikakorps* had around 450 aircraft by the time Rommel landed. These assets were

X FLIEGERKORPS (12 JANUARY 1941)		
Type	Strength	Operational
Ju 87B-1	164	109
Ju 88	123	72
Bf 109E-7	53	46
Bf 110D-3	55	40
He 111H-3	48	21
Ju 52/3m	77	60

under overall command of X *Fliegerkorps*, with a subordinate command, *Fliegerführer Afrika*, in North Africa itself. The aircraft flew fighter and bomber missions against Allied targets on land as well as against shipping in the Mediterranean. A large portion of the air fleet comprised transport aircraft, stretching the availability of Ju 52s across two continents.

Desert *Blitzkrieg*
The *Luftwaffe* provided air cover for the long-distance campaigns across the North African deserts. As in previous campaigns, the fighters and attack aircraft flew ahead of the rolling tanks, providing aerial coverage for Rommel's armour. Bombers were targeted at what few cities were within range but played a minor role in the campaigns. The *Luftwaffe* also provided much-needed aerial observation for Rommel's forces, contributing intelligence on Allied positions and strengths. The major constraint to the *Afrikakorps* was in supply; a mere 100 transports were available for the constant material requirements of the entire army. Most of the supplies had to be flown in – including aviation fuel and water – since the Germans

did not control the sea lines of communication (SLOCs) across the Mediterranean. The roadblock was the British garrison at Malta, and their access to compromised Enigma messages. The British on Malta, even with the few resources available to them, became very proficient at sinking German surface traffic resupplying North Africa, and were a nuisance in the air as well. Thus, Rommel's forces relied heavily on the transport aircraft of *Luftflotte* 2 for resupply, while at the same time the German transports were in short supply to other theatres.

This led directly to fuel shortages for the *Luftwaffe* aircraft supporting Rommel. At the beginning of 1941, Rommel's planes were restricted to only 100 sorties a day, when more

were necessary for both air support of ground operations and air cover for transport ships. The British were also able to tap into greater production at a time when the Germans were losing the attritional battles in the Mediterranean. Although effective against the RAF in Egypt, the *Luftwaffe* was hindered by other German interests, in particular the attack on the Soviet Union, as well as by a lack of fuel and parts. The Allies grew stronger while the *Luftwaffe* languished in the desert.

Another major concern for the *Luftwaffe* (which continues to plague air forces fighting in a desert environment) was the sand. The high-performance aircraft engines suffered from extended operations in the sand of North Africa, and a field

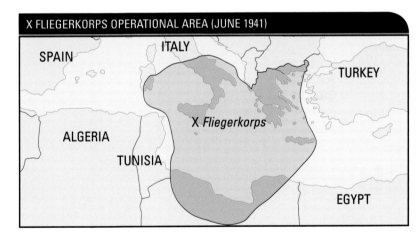

X FLIEGERKORPS OPERATIONAL AREA (JUNE 1941)

■ X *Fliegerkorps*, under *General der Flieger* Hans Geisler, commanding general of the formation since October 1939, was moved down from Norway and Denmark by the beginning of January 1941, being first based in Sicily. From its island headquarters, and from later bases on the North African mainland itself, its operational radius covered all of southern Italy and Sicily, the Balkans and coastal North Africa. X *Fliegerkorps*' jurisdiction also incorporated the area of sea between these territories, and the formation therefore was well placed to interdict Allied naval traffic fuelling the war effort in North Africa and Malta.

modification was necessary for the new theatre. Bf 109s brought to North Africa were fitted with sand filters on the engine intake. The new designation for these aircraft was the Bf 109F-2/Trop. The dust collector was adequate against the environment but reduced engine performance by as much as 10 per cent on take-off. Once the aircraft was off the ground, however, the filter could be opened.

The *Luftwaffe* fighters were initially effective against the RAF's Hurricane Mk IIs, but with the arrival of more RAF fighters plus additional American-built aircraft, the *Luftwaffe* in North Africa could not compete.

With losses due to enemy action and the desert environment, and without replacements from Germany, the *Luftwaffe* in North Africa was overwhelmed.

On 18 November 1941, the British offensive against Tobruk began. The British fielded more than 1000 planes against the *Luftwaffe's* 120 (plus an additional 200 Italian machines). More fighters were sent from *Luftflotte* 2 – at the expense of the Eastern Front – but even these were disabled through a lack of fuel and parts. The British took a leaf out of the German book and attacked airfields and aircraft on the ground, further dwindling the *Luftwaffe*

inventory. The battle was going against Rommel's *Afrikakorps*.

New cannon

An initial answer for the quantitative superiority of the Allies was better armament for the *Luftwaffe* fighters. By April 1941, the MG 151/15 aerial cannon complemented the two MG 17s in the nose of the Bf 109F-series aircraft. The MG 151/15 was a 15mm (0.59in) auto-cannon produced by Mauser, its higher cyclic rate (680 rounds per minute) and increased capacity making the Bf 109F-2 a powerful weapon. In the proper hands, it was deadly. Pilots like Hans-Joachim Marseille scored well in the

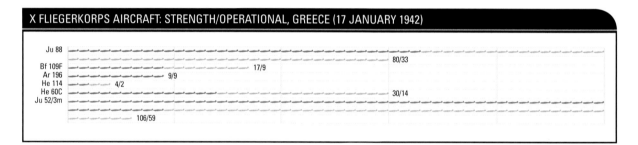

X FLIEGERKORPS AIRCRAFT: STRENGTH/OPERATIONAL, GREECE (17 JANUARY 1942)

Ju 88	80/33
Bf 109F	17/9
Ar 196	9/9
He 114	4/2
He 60C	30/14
Ju 52/3m	106/59

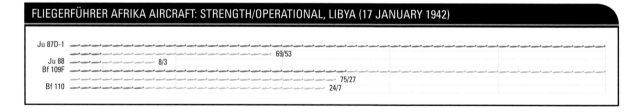

FLIEGERFÜHRER AFRIKA AIRCRAFT: STRENGTH/OPERATIONAL, LIBYA (17 JANUARY 1942)

Ju 87D-1	69/53
Ju 88	8/3
Bf 109F	75/27
Bf 110	24/7

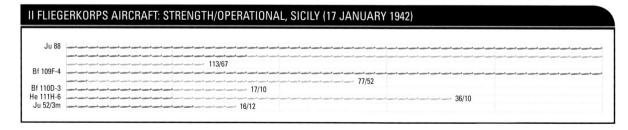

II FLIEGERKORPS AIRCRAFT: STRENGTH/OPERATIONAL, SICILY (17 JANUARY 1942)

Ju 88	113/67
Bf 109F-4	77/52
Bf 110D-3	17/10
He 111H-6	36/10
Ju 52/3m	16/12

desert campaign. Marseille himself recorded 151 'kills' in North Africa, earning him the name of 'Star of Africa'. He was killed in North Africa when his engine caught fire (in a non-combat event) and he struck the vertical stabilizer as he sought to escape from the stricken plane.

Supply problem

The war in North Africa hinged on getting supplies to the *Afrikakorps*. The Germans were having a difficult time with logistics; the British were savaging German and Italian shipping from their base on Malta. In response, the *Luftwaffe* proposed a

technological solution. To solve the transport issue, Willi Messerschmitt offered a new heavy-lift airframe to overcome poor logistics. The Me 323 Gigant was an improvement on the Me 321 glider, a massive heavy-lift airframe. Late in 1942, the Me 323 was finally ready for operations, in limited numbers. It was a huge six-engine transport that could carry some 12.2 tonnes (12 tons) of cargo. However, the plane was slow and vulnerable, and losses quickly mounted. In one illustrative example, on 22 April 1943, 27 Me 323s took off with supplies for

North Africa. They were escorted by Bf 109s from JG 27 but faced seven squadrons of Spitfires and P-40s. The escorts claimed three P-40s shot down, but the *Luftwaffe* lost 21 of the 27 transports. The giant plane stayed in service, but the Allied efforts still strangled the *Afrikakorps*. With little resupply from air or sea, the weight of Allied materiel was now crushing the Axis in North Africa. Something had to be done about Malta.

II FLIEGERKORPS, SICILY (20 AUGUST 1942)

Type	Strength	Operational
Ju 88	132	60
Bf 109F-4	60	38

FLIEGERFÜHRER AFRIKA, LIBYA/EGYPT (20 AUGUST 1942)

Type	Strength	Operational
Ju 87D-1	107	74
Ju 88	24	6
Bf 109F	109	66
Bf 110	19	10
Do 17Z	7	4

X FLIEGERKORPS, GREECE/CRETE (20 AUGUST 1942)

Type	Strength	Operational
Ju 88	85	34
Bf 109F	5	2
Bf 110	46	24
He 111H-2	5	4
Ar 196	11	9
He 114	27	11
Bv 222	5	1
Ju 52/3m	192	116

MESSERSCHMITT ME 321/323 GIGANT

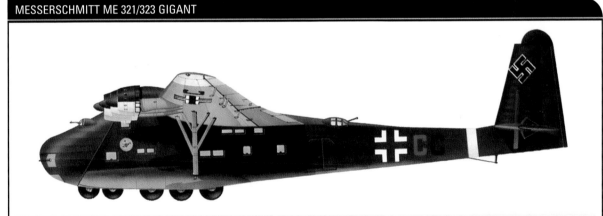

Specifications

Length: 28.2m (92ft 4in)
Wing span: 55.2m (181ft)
Max speed: 270km/h (170mph)

Powerplant: 6 x Gnome-Rhône 14N, air-cooled, 14-cylinder (two rows of 7) radial aircraft engine, 784kW (1045 hp) each. Built in occupied France, it did not tax German aircraft engine industry

Capacity: 130 troops or up to 12.2 tonnes (12 tons) of equipment. The clamshell doors in the nose could be opened to load/unload large equipment such as trucks or tanks

Malta

In early 1942, the Luftwaffe *intensified its bombing campaign against the Allied eastern Mediterranean outpost of Malta. The heightened pounding was intended as a prelude to an Axis invasion of the island, codenamed Operation* Herkules *(Hercules).*

From the time the Italians entered the war (10 June 1940) and 1942, the Italian Air Force (*Regia Aeronautica*) and the *Luftwaffe* conducted over 3000 bombing sorties to reduce the island fortress. The Axis attacked the British airfields and ports but could not defeat the garrison. It was an epic battle between the Axis and Allies, but the latter maintained control of the island and continued to resupply it from the sea. The initial Allied air contingent included obsolete Gloster Gladiators but was quickly restocked with Hurricane Mk Is and IIs, and eventually Spitfires and P-40s made their way to the Malta, both for its protection and for the harassment of German shipping. The Allies also maintained surface ships and submarines to hamper the German SLOCs between Italy and North Africa. Although Allied losses were heavy, Churchill and the British

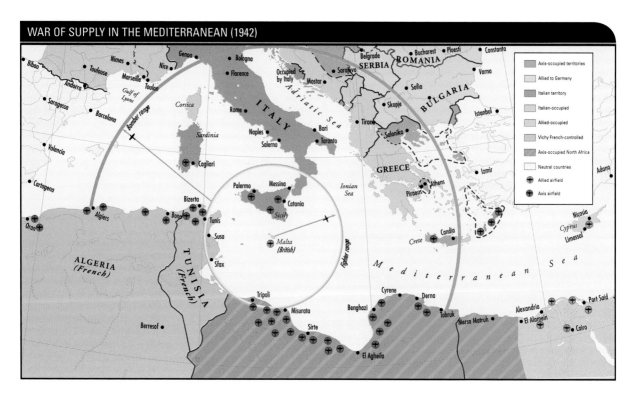

WAR OF SUPPLY IN THE MEDITERRANEAN (1942)

■The map above clearly indicates the precarious position of Malta during the battles of 1942, sandwiched between German airbases of *Luftflotte* 2 scattered across North Africa, Sicily and the Balkans. Once the Allies began to push German ground forces back westwards in North Africa, however, the airbases there were steadily lost, and were then used by Allied squadrons that progressively established air superiority across the Mediterranean.

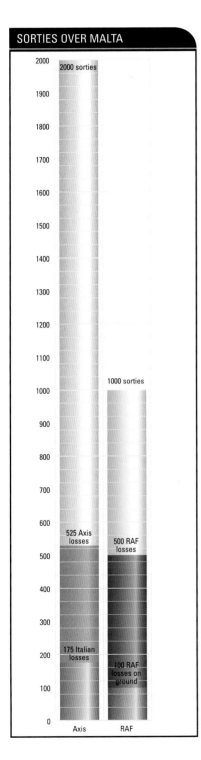

SORTIES OVER MALTA

2000 — 2000 sorties

1000 sorties

525 Axis losses

500 RAF losses

175 Italian losses

100 RAF losses on ground

Axis   RAF

were determined to maintain the strategic outpost. Following the costly Crete aerial invasion, Hitler was unwilling to drop paratroopers onto Malta, for fear of losing heavily to a much better organized resistance. The invasion (Operation *Herkules*) was continually postponed until it was finally cancelled; Hitler focused elsewhere. In the final analysis, the Germans did not take Malta seriously enough while the Allies recognized the importance of their strategic outpost.

Losses on both sides

By the end of the campaign for Malta, the figures tell the tale of Axis woe. The British were able to maintain adequate numbers of aircraft on the island, in addition to the port facilities, to disrupt German logistics. The RAF cycled over 1000 aircraft through the base, losing almost 400 to enemy action (and another 100 destroyed on the ground), in a desperate effort to maintain a fighting force of around 700. The Axis lost heavily, flying over 2000 sorties (both Italian and German) to the continual attacks but losing more than 525 (over 350 German and 175 Italian) over Malta alone.

But the real butcher's bill was in what the Allies prevented. During the course of the Mediterranean campaign, Allied forces from Malta sank over 70 per cent of the Italian transport fleet and destroyed 23 per cent of the Axis merchant fleet, cutting off the lifeline to North Africa. Had the Germans defeated Malta – what Churchill called the 'unsinkable aircraft carrier' – the war in the Mediterranean would have had a very different outcome.

Operation Torch

After the United States joined the war in late 1941, there was an ongoing debate about how and where to strike the Axis powers. The Americans was concerned about Japanese expansion in the Pacific but had already promised action against the Germans.

US President Franklin Delano Roosevelt assured British Prime Minister Winston Churchill that an attack was imminent against the Nazis. It was decided to attack into North Africa to secure a strategic foothold for the eventual invasion of Europe. Operation *Torch* was the plan. With the Americans working in combination with British and Commonwealth troops, and hoping for Free French assistance, the Allies planned a seaborne invasion of western North Africa to put the beleaguered Germans and Italians between two converging forces – one from the west and the remaining Allied troops fighting their way out of

Egypt. The landings in western North Africa came on 8 November 1942.

The landings in the eastern Mediterranean (the Americans in Morocco and the British in Algeria) added another two air forces to the fight against the Germans in North Africa. The US Army Air Forces contingent was commanded by Major-General Jimmy Doolittle, and added about 500 aircraft to the fight. It comprised mostly bombers (B-17s, B-25s and B-26s) but also included fighters (P-40s, P-39s and P-38s) as well as transport and liaison aircraft. At the time, the Americans also flew British Spitfires in combat. This US contingent was designated the Twelfth Air Force, broken off from the Eighth Air Force for the campaign. The British component, meanwhile,

was the Eastern Air Command, under Air Marshal Sir William Welsh, based in Algeria. The British, flying Hurricanes and Spitfires, added another 200 aircraft to the campaign.

The initial concern was the French forces in the area. Their loyalties were in question; they were ordered by the Vichy government to resist the Allied advance, and for the first few days they did. American and British pilots were forced to shoot down French fighters, accounting for about a dozen French aircraft (mostly Dewoitine D.520s) on the first two days. However, the French quickly capitulated, declared themselves 'Free French' and joined the Allied cause against the Axis in North Africa. Thus by the end of November, the Axis, with only about 160 combat

aircraft (80–100 operational), faced more than 800 Allied combat aircraft, not to mention transports.

Casablanca Conference
Allied materiel weight played an important role in the destruction of the Axis in North Africa. Early in the new year, President Roosevelt and Prime Minister Churchill met at Casablanca to discuss the war face to face. General Charles de Gaulle, who had been in exile in London, represented the Free French. At the conference, which took place from 14 to 24 January 1943, the Mediterranean and North African air commands were combined under Air Marshal Sir Arthur Tedder into the Mediterranean Air Command, for ease of command and control. The Allies turned their attention on the remaining Axis forces in North Africa, leading to a showdown at Tunis.

The Axis and *Luftwaffe* showed signs of operational effectiveness in battles but were being overwhelmed strategically. They were able to bloody the Allies at Kasserine Pass, but even though it was a German victory, lack of supplies and stretched lines of communications forced Rommel to retreat back to Tunisia. With growing Allied air superiority, the *Luftwaffe* could not compete in the attrition war in the air. In the opening months of 1943, the *Luftwaffe* lost heavily. In January, facing increasing Allied opposition, the *Luftwaffe* lost 282 aircraft in the Mediterranean theatre to combat, and the number increased over the next few months. By May, the *Luftwaffe* had lost another 1000 aircraft in the

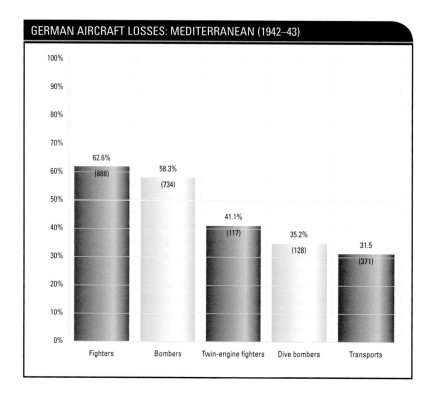

GERMAN AIRCRAFT LOSSES: MEDITERRANEAN (1942–43)

- Fighters: 62.6% (888)
- Bombers: 58.3% (734)
- Twin-engine fighters: 41.1% (117)
- Dive bombers: 35.2% (128)
- Transports: 31.5 (371)

NORTH AFRICAN CAMPAIGN FIGHTER AIRCRAFT COMPARED

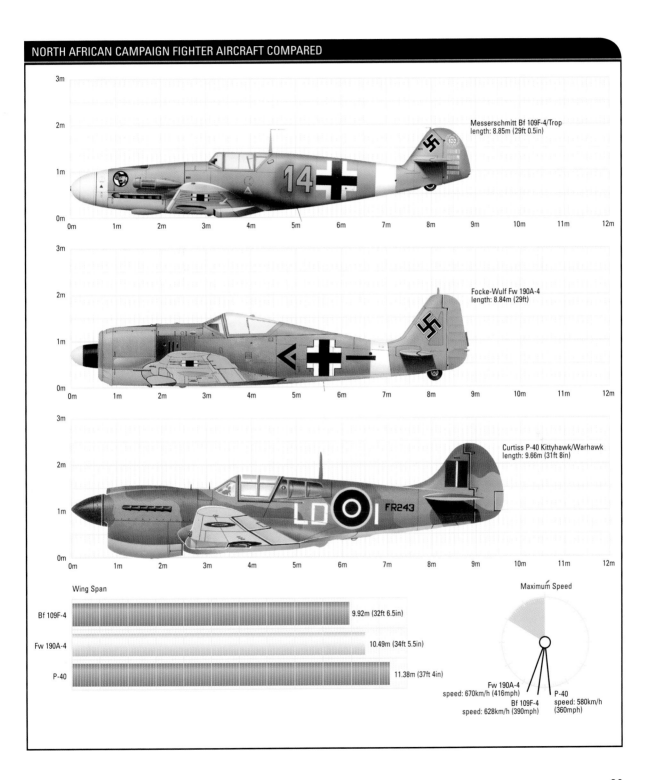

Messerschmitt Bf 109F-4/Trop
length: 8.85m (29ft 0.5in)

Focke-Wulf Fw 190A-4
length: 8.84m (29ft)

Curtiss P-40 Kittyhawk/Warhawk
length: 9.66m (31ft 8in)

Wing Span

Bf 109F-4	9.92m (32ft 6.5in)
Fw 190A-4	10.49m (34ft 5.5in)
P-40	11.38m (37ft 4in)

Maximum Speed

Fw 190A-4
speed: 670km/h (416mph)

Bf 109F-4
speed: 628km/h (390mph)

P-40
speed: 580km/h (360mph)

campaign, compounding their losses in all theaters. *Luftwaffe* production was increasing in Germany, but the additional weight of the American entry into the war was felt in North Africa and would soon impact Germany as well. Further, the lack of transport and logistics to North Africa had a cumulative effect on the Axis forces there; while the Allies could get supply, the Germans could not, forcing the latter to expend precious resources in the contest.

By May, the struggle had come to a head. Axis forces were surrounded at Tunis, and had little by way of supply. Their requirements of an estimated 142,250 tonnes (140,000 tons) per month were reduced to a trickle of a mere 23,370 tonnes (23,000 tons) in April. The Allies had effectively cut the *Afrikakorps* off in North Africa – 60,000 men with 100 operational tanks and only 75 combat aircraft faced 300,000 Allied soldiers, with 1400 tanks and over 1000 combat aircraft.

The Allies proceeded to bomb the Axis stronghold and destroyed the *Luftwaffe* on the ground and in the air, achieving absolute air superiority. The only *Luftwaffe* fighter group left in North Africa by this point was JG 77, commanded from April by *Oberstleutnant* Johannes Steinhoff. Flying their Bf 109s, the pilots faced increasingly heavy odds against the Allied air forces, and attempted to hold their own. Although they had some successes, losses mounted; the *Geschwader* was relocated to Sicily on 8 May. The Germans surrendered Tunis on 13 May; the Axis forces were led into captivity. The war had begun to turn against the Germans; the Allies focused on their next step.

Sicily

With North Africa secured, the Allies began planning for Operation Husky*, the invasion of Sicily. With new airfields in North Africa, the Allies began bombing raids against Axis airfields in Sicily and Italy, in order to destroy the ability of the Italian Air Force and* Luftwaffe *to repel Allied attacks.*

Allied bombers focused on airfields on Sicily as well as the airfield on Pantelleria, forcing the *Luftwaffe* to respond to their advances. The Allies bombed for 10 days, flying more than 1100 sorties, and dropping 1525 tonnes (1500 tons) of bombs. The heavy bombers of Mediterranean Air Command pounded Axis airfields, forcing the fighters to move back to Italian bases, extending the distances they would need to fly and decreasing their efficiency. The *Luftwaffe*, already savaged by the North African campaign, was ineffective and turned most of the aerial fighting over to the Italian Air Force. The Italians were poorly suited to fighting the Allies;

their effectiveness decreased while the Allied efforts increased.

Husky
On 9 July, *Husky* kicked off. The Allies were confident that the airfields had been destroyed and launched the invasion of Sicily, dropping paratroops and landing on the beaches. Air superiority won the day, as the Allies landed seven assault divisions on the island, pushing the defences back through ground assaults, supported from the sea by naval gunfire and coordinated air attacks. Italian and *Luftwaffe* torpedo-bombers tried to stem the tide of Allied naval attacks, and a few

got through, but the Allied material superiority was beginning to show; the battle of attrition swayed in the Allies' favour. By 1 August, Kesselring, commander of the German forces in Italy, decided that Sicily was a loss and ordered evacuation. Without air cover from the *Luftwaffe*, and with overwhelming Allied material superiority, he decided that the best course of action was to retreat to Italy and set up a series of defensive lines. In a stunning series of evacuations (between 1 and 17 August), some 60,000 German troops and an equal number of Italians, and most of their equipment, were successfully evacuated from Sicily.

JG 77, still under Steinhoff, continued backtracking. From Sicily in May, they were relocated to Foggia in southern Italy in June and moved back further with Allied advances. Two *Gruppen* then returned to Germany for refit; the remaining two *Gruppen* were the only *Luftwaffe* fighter groups in Italy.

Defence of Italy

Allied intentions now focused on Italy. Operation Avalanche *was the codename for the main invasion. Like* Husky, *the operation against Sicily,* Avalanche *was to be an invasion by air and sea, focusing on overwhelming material superiority to gain both air and land advantages.*

The Germans prepared lines of defence while the Allies planned their invasion. Unfortunately for the Germans, *Luftwaffe* assets continued to dwindle throughout the campaign due to needs in other theatres; the Eastern Front and the air defence of the Reich took increasing precedence over the Italian campaign. Thus, as the Allies increased their numbers, the *Luftwaffe* lost ground in a heavy battle of attrition.

There were four *Luftwaffe Geschwader* represented in Italy. JG 3 was represented by II *Gruppe* (about 30 planes), JG 27 was based in Greece but had victories in the theatre, JG 53 was present for the initial battles but was relocated to Germany in October 1943 and JG 77 fought a retreating battle as the Allied forces drove up the Italian peninsula. In all, the *Luftwaffe* had 300 combat aircraft in the northern Mediterranean, facing increasing numbers of US and British aircraft. The Allies attacked Italy on 3 September 1943. With overwhelming air superiority, they landed successfully and began their drive north.

Luftwaffe claims for the month of September were 82 aircraft, including an impressive 21 on the first day of the attack. Numbers dwindled during the remainder of the month, as *Luftwaffe* losses increased. To further complicate matters, the Italians surrendered on the first day of the Allied attack, reducing the available manpower and materiel still more, as well as putting increasing pressure on Germany to protect its southern flank.

The Allies drove on quickly, while the Germans retreated up the peninsula. The Allies swiftly established an advance airbase at Foggia, recently evacuated by JG 77, and began bombing operations. From that location, American B-24s were

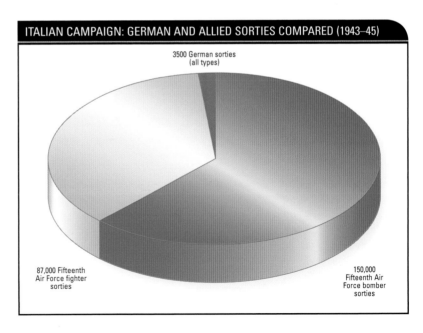

ITALIAN CAMPAIGN: GERMAN AND ALLIED SORTIES COMPARED (1943–45)

3500 German sorties
(all types)

87,000 Fifteenth Air Force fighter sorties

150,000 Fifteenth Air Force bomber sorties

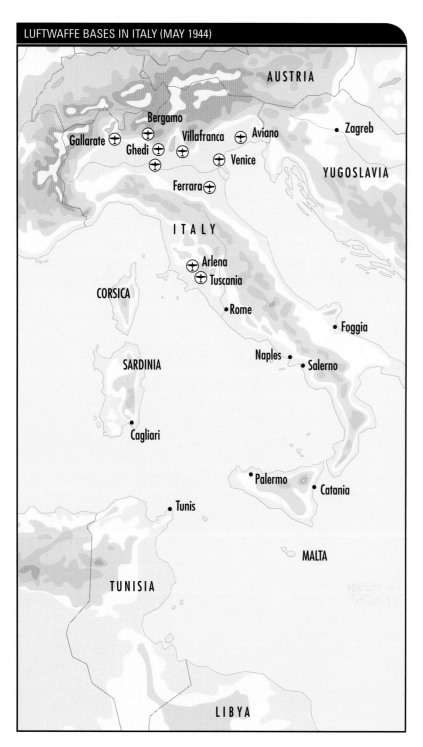

LUFTWAFFE BASES IN ITALY (MAY 1944)

AUSTRIA

Bergamo
Gallarate
Ghedi
Villafranca   Aviano   • Zagreb
Venice
Ferrara

YUGOSLAVIA

ITALY

Arlena
Tuscania

CORSICA

• Rome

• Foggia

SARDINIA

Naples •
• Salerno

• Cagliari

• Palermo
• Catania

• Tunis

MALTA

TUNISIA

LIBYA

■ *Luftflotte* 2 airbases in 1943–45
were concentrated throughout Sicily
and mainland Italy, although many of
these bases were of course lost as
the Allies advanced progressively
northwards. Furthermore, Allied
engineers built nine airbases around
Catania alone, overwhelming the
German operating capability. On
mainland Italy, the airbases were also
scattered. There were concentrations
around the Gulf of Taranto, and three
airbases around Naples and Salerno
caused some problems for Allied
landings at the latter location on
9 September 1943. There was a further
cluster around Foggia in the east, but
by the end of 1943, *Luftwaffe* strength
in Italy was negligible.

able to reach vulnerable oil fields in
Romania, including the impressive
raid on Ploesti in August, as well as
into the heart of southern Germany.
With attacks from the south,
increasingly effective bombing raids
from British bases in the north and
heavy pressure from the Soviets in
the east, Germany, and the *Luftwaffe*
by extension, were locked into a war
of attrition that consumed German
resources at an increasing rate. The
Luftwaffe was forced to prioritize, and
the Italian front suffered.

On the back foot

Over the next year, Kesselring's
command continued its retreat up the
peninsula. While the *Luftwaffe* fought
on, the Germans were forced to
concede the southern half of Italy, up
to and including Rome. *Luftwaffe*
units were reassigned to the defence
of the Reich as Allied bombing
intensified; only JG 77 was retained in

Italy. As the Allies increased the weight of their attacks, it became clear that the *Luftwaffe* was simply outnumbered. From the Italian surrender to the end of the war (VE Day) in May 1945, the *Luftwaffe* flew only 3500 sorties in the theatre, and lost heavily. In the same time, the US Fifteenth Air Force (established on 1 November 1943) flew almost 150,000 bomber and 87,000 fighter sorties, dropping over 305,000 tonnes (300,000 tons) of bombs on Italy, southern Germany and additional targets. Planes of the Fifteenth Air Force were credited with destroying (or at least heavily damaging) all of the aircraft factories and industrial targets within their range, and claimed more than 6000 enemy aircraft destroyed – most on the ground, but many in the air as well.

Because of frequent transfers and incomplete histories, the Mediterranean theatre is the most difficult for specific numbers. It is clear that the *Luftwaffe* was hampered by other events, such as the Combined Bomber Offensive over Germany and the requirements of the Eastern Front, and was a distant concern to Hitler and the German high command. Thus there was a constant lack of supply and coordination in the theatre. Regardless, some of the finest German commanders, such as Rommel, made their mark on the North Africa campaign. The Allies also benefited, in the long run, from fighting the Axis in North Africa. The Americans gained valuable experience in amphibious landings, paratroop landings, supply and logistics and were tested in battle against very good Axis forces. The specific numbers are difficult to discern, but it can be summarized that the *Luftwaffe* was always outnumbered by British forces, and was later overwhelmed when the Americans joined the fight.

The *Luftwaffe* in North Africa, and later over Sicily and Italy, posted about 10 per cent of the sortie rates of the Allies, and lost significant numbers of aircraft as well as experienced veterans in the greater campaign. Pilots like Marseille never returned to the Fatherland; the *Luftwaffe* lost a number of ace fighter pilots in the contest. And significantly, as *Luftwaffe* strength began its decline, Allied strength in the air emerged, allowing the Allies more freedom of action as they battled the Germans on the southern front. Using air power, against an increasingly beleaguered *Luftwaffe*, the Allies gained ground against the Germans and forced an Italian surrender. Allied airpower was in the ascendant.

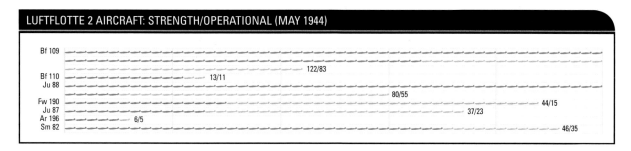

LUFTFLOTTE 2 AIRCRAFT: STRENGTH/OPERATIONAL (MAY 1944)

Bf 109	122/83
Bf 110	13/11
Ju 88	80/55
Fw 190	44/15
Ju 87	37/23
Ar 196	6/5
Sm 82	46/35

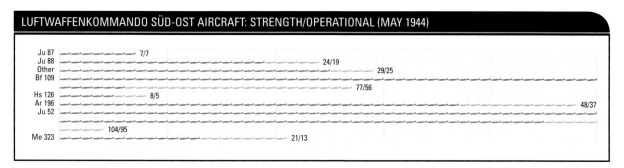

LUFTWAFFENKOMMANDO SÜD-OST AIRCRAFT: STRENGTH/OPERATIONAL (MAY 1944)

Ju 87	7/7
Ju 88	24/19
Other	29/25
Bf 109	77/56
Hs 126	8/5
Ar 196	48/37
Ju 52	104/95
Me 323	21/13

CHAPTER 6

The Eastern Front

Hitler's ultimate goal was the destruction of the Soviet Union. With the Western Front secure – with only a minor nuisance from the British – he turned his armies and his attention east. Intent on the Lebensraum (living space) of the defeated Poland, the wheat fields of the Ukraine, and the plains leading to Moscow, Hitler unleashed his dogs of war on the Soviets.

The initial planning for the conquest of the Soviet Union was named Operation Barbarossa. Planning began in late 1940 for the largest operation in military history; Hitler was confident that his war machine could defeat the Soviet Union in a matter of weeks. He based this premise on two main factors: first, his armies had been successful against all other land opponents with amazing swiftness and decision; and two, he underestimated Soviet resolve and ability. The campaign followed previous tactical and operational planning; the Germans would once again employ Blitzkrieg, this time against a new foe.

▥ Many Europeans saw the invasion of the Soviet Union as an anti-communist crusade. Here, a Croatian bomber crew drink a toast before flying a mission in

Operation Barbarossa

Operation Barbarossa *was launched in the early hours of the morning of 22 June 1941. The initial results of the offensive completely exceeded German expectations, as all three army groups made deep penetrations into Soviet Russia.*

The operation had three moving parts. Army Group North was headed by *Generalfeldmarschall* Wilhelm Ritter von Leeb, and was composed of 26 divisions; its target was Leningrad to the north. Leeb had at his disposal the aircraft of *Luftflotte* 1, the entire air contingent of fighters, bombers and ancillary aircraft, for the attack. Army Group Centre, commanded by *Generalfeldmarschall* Fedor von Bock, was the main thrust, aimed at Moscow, fighting with 49 divisions of ground troops and supported by the aircraft of *Luftflotte* 2.

Army Group South was led by *Generalfeldmarschall* Gerd von Rundstedt and comprised 41 divisions supported by *Luftflotte* 4; its initial objective was Kiev. In all, 4.3 million German troops faced 3.3 million underequipped and poorly located Soviet troops. The Germans were able to muster 4400 aircraft for the attack, against more than 11,000 Soviet planes.

However, these numbers are deceptive; most of the Soviet planes were obsolete and the vast majority were quickly outclassed by the experienced German pilots. In addition, the German battle plan was spectacularly successful: the *Luftwaffe* destroyed a large portion of the Soviet Red Air Force on the ground in the first few days. It is important to note, however, that the *Luftwaffe* still had not developed an operational heavy (four-engine) strategic bomber, and the lack of a strategic capability restricted German capabilities.

Order of battle

On the opening day of the campaign, the German air component's order of battle included the following: 3904 aircraft of all types (3032 operational), with 952 bombers, 965 single-engine fighters, 102 twin-engine fighters and 456 Stukas. Their task was to find and destroy the forward-based Red Air Force on the ground and in the air, secure air superiority and lead the German Army's ground-based offensive into the Soviet Union.

Meanwhile, to the rear, German aircraft production churned. By summer 1941, the Germans were producing over 230 single-engine fighters per month, with the new Focke-Wulf Fw 190 in production by August. In addition, the *Luftwaffe* could count on more than 350 twin-engine aircraft (heavy fighters and bombers) added to the inventory. In the early stages of the attack on the Soviet Union, the *Luftwaffe* was still able to replace losses, while it seemed as if the Soviets could not.

Invasion of the Soviet Union

Operation *Barbarossa* kicked off on 22 June 1941. Stalin's armies were quickly overrun by the German *Blitzkrieg*. The experienced and well-equipped German troops destroyed everything in their path, killing and capturing the bulk of the Soviet front-line forces. The *Luftwaffe* was equally successful. On the first day, the *Luftwaffe* lost only 35 aircraft but claimed over 1800 aircraft destroyed on the ground and in the air.

A number of *Luftwaffe* pilots achieved 'ace' status in the opening days of the campaign, shooting down obsolete Soviet types, specifically Spanish Civil War-vintage Polikarpov I-15s and I-16s. The Germans claimed 3100 aircraft destroyed in the first three days of *Barbarossa*; Soviet records reveal that the

Type	Total
Single-engine fighters	898
Twin-engine day-fighters	105
Night-fighters	148
Fighter-bombers	124
Dive-bombers	260
Twin-engine bombers	931
Four-engine bombers	4
Long-range reconnaissance aircraft	282
Short-range recce/army cooperation	388
Coastal and maritime aircraft	76
Transport aircraft	212
Total	3428

LUFTWAFFE STRENGTH: ALL THEATRES (24 JUNE 1941)

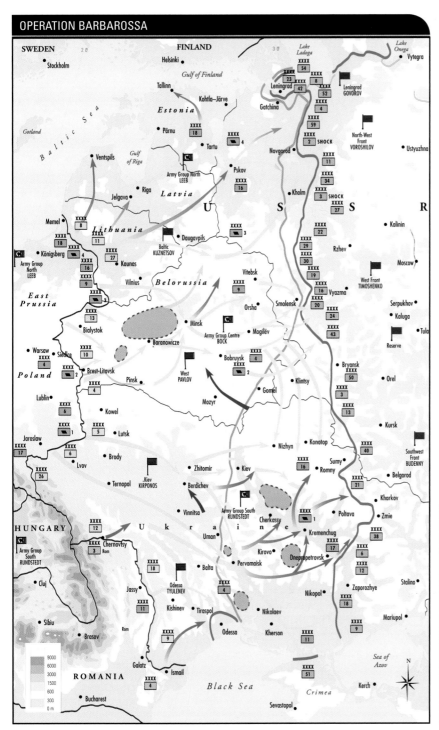

OPERATION BARBAROSSA

SWEDEN
FINLAND
Lake Ladoga
Lake Onega
Stockholm
Helsinki
Vytegra
Baltic Sea
Gulf of Finland
Tallinn
Kohtla–Järve
Ustyuzhna
Gotland
Estonia
Pärnu
Tartu
Novgorod
North-West Front VOROSHILOV
Ventspils
Gulf of Riga
Pskov
Leningrad
Leningrad GOVOROV
Kalinin
Memel
Riga
Jelgava
Latvia
Kholm
Rzhev
Moscow
Lithuania
Daugavpils
Baltic KUZNETSOV
Army Group North LEEB
Königsberg
Kaunas
Belorussia
Vitebsk
West Front TIMOSHENKO
East Prussia
Vilnius
Orsha
Smolensk
Vyazma
Serpukhov
Kaluga
Bialystok
Minsk
Mogilëv
Army Group Centre BOCK
Tula
Baranowicze
Reserve
Warsaw
Siedlce
Bobruysk
West PAVLOV
Bryansk
Orel
Poland
Brest-Litovsk
Pinsk
Gomel
Klintsy
Lublin
Mozyr
Kursk
Kowel
Lutsk
Jaroslaw
Nizhyn
Konotop
Southwest Front BUDENNY
Lvov
Brody
Zhitomir
Kiev
Sumy
Romny
Belgorod
Ternopol
Kiev KIRPONOS
Berdichev
Kharkov
HUNGARY
Vinnitsa
Army Group South RUNDSTEDT
Cherkassy
Poltava
Zmie
Uman
Kremenchug
Army Group South RUNDSTEDT
Chernovtsy
Rom
Kirovo
Dnepropetrovsk
Cluj
Balta
Pervomaisk
Stalino
Jassy
Odessa TYULENEV
Zaporozhye
Sibiu
Kishinev
Tiraspol
Nikolaev
Mariupol
Brasov
Rom
Odessa
Kherson
Nikopol
Galatz
Ismail
Sea of Azov
ROMANIA
Black Sea
Crimea
Kerch
Bucharest
Sevastopol

U S S R

9000
6000
3000
1500
600
300
0 m

■ The German plan involved three army groups (Army Group North, Army Group South and Army Group Centre), with the bulk of the attacking forces concentrated in Army Groups North and Centre.

Army Group North targeted Leningrad, while Army Group Centre, which contained around half the German armour, was to shatter Soviet forces in Belorussia before heading for the Soviet capital, Moscow. Army Group South, meanwhile, was to deal with Soviet forces in the Ukraine.

The great problem for this operation was the sheer length of the front and the elongation of supply lines as the Germans advanced deeper and deeper into a seemingly limitless land. For the *Luftwaffe*, these stretched supply lines led to difficulties in obtaining everything from fuel to basic engine parts, and the replenishment issues became even more extreme during the Russian winter.

Operation *Barbarossa*
22 June – early October 1941

German attack

Soviet positions 22 June

Soviet units encircled

Soviet counterattacks

German front line, end of August

German front line, early October

Soviet positions, early October

number was closer to 3900. By concentrating on airfields – as in the Polish and French campaigns – the *Luftwaffe* savaged the Red Air Force.

Initial German successes were spectacular. On land and in the air, the Germans advanced across the open steppes of Russia. The *Luftwaffe* was forced to fly from improvised fields, which added problems of supply and logistics, and also increased accidents, but its record in the air was unsurpassed. Yet despite their success against the Red Air Force, *Luftwaffe* pilots were concerned that the Soviet pilots kept coming in significant numbers every day. The Soviets seemed to have an endless supply of aircraft and men, even as the Germans continued their three-prong approach.

Poorly prepared

The Soviets' first mistakes stemmed from their lack of preparation. Stalin had not heeded warning signs of German aggression, and the Soviet planes were lined up on their airfields. The Germans took advantage of the situation and were able to destroy Soviet forces at will. Further, when the Soviets did counter, it was with inexperienced pilots flying outdated aircraft, which provided easy marks for the experienced *Luftwaffe* aggressors. Initial successes were fleeting, though; within a few weeks, the Soviets were able to counter with planes that were comparable to the German aircraft, and flown by pilots who had survived the initial attacks.

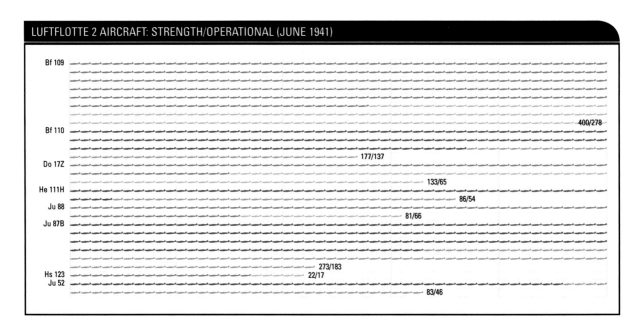

LUFTFLOTTE 1 AIRCRAFT: STRENGTH/OPERATIONAL (JUNE 1941)

Bf 109   213/176
Ju 88   270/210
Ju 52   44/8

LUFTFLOTTE 2 AIRCRAFT: STRENGTH/OPERATIONAL (JUNE 1941)

Bf 109   400/278
Bf 110   177/137
Do 17Z   133/65
He 111H   86/54
Ju 88   81/66
Ju 87B   273/183
Hs 123   22/17
Ju 52   83/46

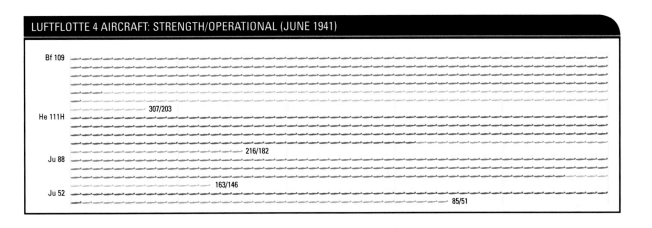

LUFTFLOTTE 4 AIRCRAFT: STRENGTH/OPERATIONAL (JUNE 1941)

Bf 109

He 111H — 307/203

Ju 88 — 216/182

Ju 52 — 163/146

— 85/51

Into the Soviet Union

On land, the Germans were seemingly unstoppable. Army Group North had advanced quickly on Leningrad, and the city was besieged. Army Group Centre was racing across the plains, and approached Moscow.

Army Group South passed Kiev, and continued to advance. In all, the Soviets lost the bulk of their front-line forces in the opening months of the campaign, with over one million men killed or captured. It seemed as if Hitler's predictions were coming to fruition; Soviet resistance crumbled. However, Soviet industry was saved and relocated deeper inside the Soviet Union; the lack of a *Luftwaffe* strategic bombing force meant that the Germans had no realistic way to destroy Soviet industry.

Furthermore, as the Germans advanced, their supply lines lengthened, leading to logistics complications. Finally, German losses continued to mount in a heavy attritional battle; losses that were not easily replaced. German industry,

already working at maximum output, was barely replacing losses, whereas Soviet industry was recovering, and producing better aircraft. The Soviets replaced lost I-15s and I-16s with new types like the Yakovlev Yak-9 and Lavochkin LaGG-3. The new fighter types were supplemented with a new ground-attack airframe, the Ilyushin Il-2, as well as Lend-Lease aircraft from the United States, specifically the Bell P-39 Airacomet. Between July and December 1941, Soviet production plus American assistance equated to over 15,000 additional aircraft for the Soviet inventory.

'General Winter'
The Germans faced another problem, beginning on 8 October. Fierce snowstorms and the onset of the

Russian winter grounded planes. The snow fell, and the Germans did not have adequate supplies or resources to overcome the harsh climate. Captured Soviet aircraft mechanics taught the Germans how to respond; one solution was to add (highly flammable) aviation fuel to the oil crankcase of the plane to thin the oil so that the planes could be started. As the engines warmed, the fuel would burn off and the planes could fly.

However, the rate of more than 1000 sorties a day at the beginning of the campaign was reduced to fewer than 300 sorties with the onset of winter. Although the *Luftwaffe* attempted to continue operations, the harsh conditions, added to poor logistics and primitive airfields,

GERMAN AND SOVIET FIGHTERS COMPARED

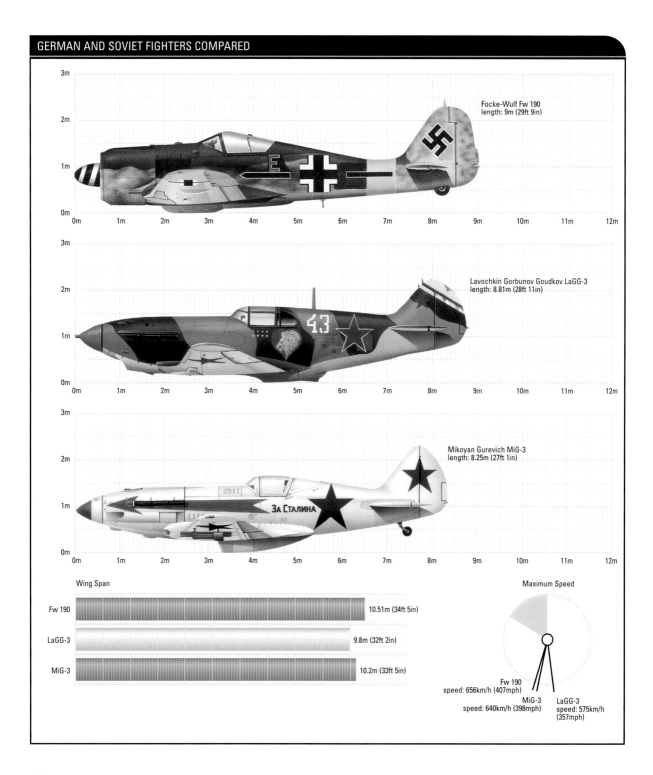

Focke-Wulf Fw 190
length: 9m (29ft 9in)

Lavochkin Gorbunov Goudkov LaGG-3
length: 8.81m (28ft 11in)

Mikoyan Gurevich MiG-3
length: 8.25m (27ft 1in)

Wing Span

Fw 190 — 10.51m (34ft 5in)

LaGG-3 — 9.8m (32ft 2in)

MiG-3 — 10.2m (33ft 5in)

Maximum Speed

Fw 190
speed: 656km/h (407mph)

MiG-3
speed: 640km/h (398mph)

LaGG-3
speed: 575km/h (357mph)

constrained offensive operations. The German lines became static; the offensive was halted.

On 5/6 December 1941, the Soviet forces counterattacked, compelling a German withdrawal to more secure supply lines. The Soviets were acclimatized to the savage weather, whereas the Germans were not, and were able to push back the German advance. A desperate battle of attrition began in the air and on the ground; Soviet industry emerged as one of the key variables in the new year.

1942: Fall Blau and Stalingrad

The new year brought new plans. The Germans, although turned back at the gates of Moscow, planned for a new series of offensive operations in spring 1942.

Fall Blau (Case Blue) was designed as a renewed attack into the south of the Soviet Union, aimed at Stalingrad and on to the Caucasus oil fields, to secure their vital resource for the German war machine. In the meantime, the *Luftwaffe* fought on, in a war of attrition, against the Soviet Red Air Force.

The Soviets benefited from higher production figures added to the American Lend-Lease programme. Soviet aircraft production increased unhindered by German strategic attack on the relocated industries. The Red Air Force accepted over 2000 planes in January, a figure that increased every month. By the end of the year, the Soviets had produced over 25,000 aircraft, almost double German production for the period. And as explained above, the new Soviet planes were increasingly better against the *Luftwaffe*.

The *Luftwaffe* did attempt strategic attacks on Soviet targets. German He 111 and Ju 88 bombers carried out raids against Soviet cities, concentrating first on industrial targets within range of the advance, and later targeting Leningrad and Moscow. The capital was bombed in 87 missions (76 night and 11 day) to defeat resistance in the city. Bombers from KG 2, 3 and 53 of *Luftflotte* 2 and KG 4 of *Luftflotte* 1 bombed the city from late autumn 1941 up until the last raid in April 1942. The first mission against Moscow included 195 sorties, but subsequent raids averaged fewer than 50. But even with this bombing campaign, and the similar attacks on Leningrad, the cities refused to capitulate. With no real decision achieved, the bombers were withdrawn in the spring and used elsewhere; later they were concentrated on Stalingrad farther to the southeast.

The Soviet defences grew stronger. *Luftwaffe* losses began to mount early in 1942 and hampered German efforts in the wide skies of Russia. *Luftwaffe* aircraft casualties in the spring were indicative of dangers ahead, with losses outstripping production as the Soviets contested air superiority. By late spring 1942, the Germans found themselves in a three-front war against Allied material superiority. In

■ **Opposite: The Soviets' main strength was always their fighters, which were simple, robust aircraft designed to deal with the rigours of combat on the Eastern Front. The LaGG-3 and MiG-3, although both inferior to the Fw 190 and Bf 109, proved popular with Soviet pilots because of their durability.**

LUFTFLOTTE 4 STUKAS (JULY 1942)			
Luftwaffe Unit	*Type*	*Strength*	*Serviceable*
III/StG 2	Ju 87	31	28
Stab/StG 77	Bf 110/Ju 87	8	5
I/StG 77	Ju 87	37	24
II/StG 77	Ju 87	32	21
III/StG 77	Ju 87	34	21

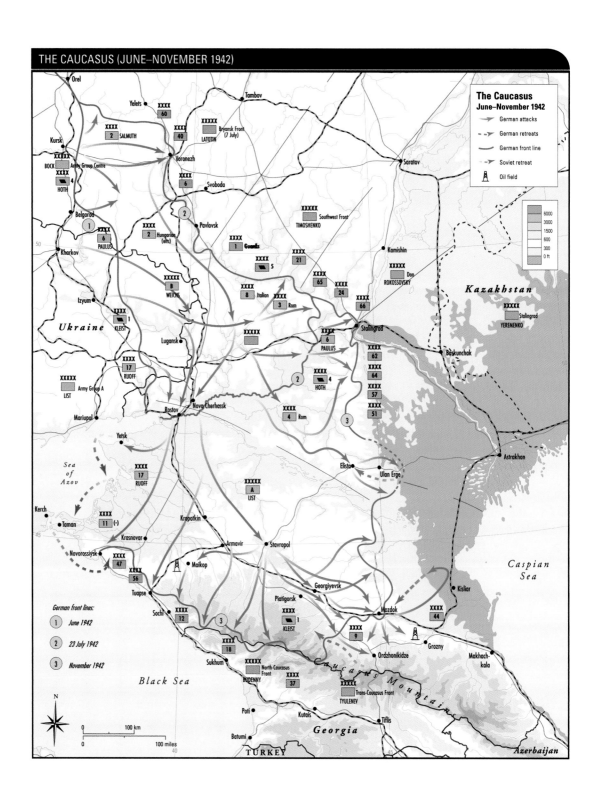

THE CAUCASUS (JUNE–NOVEMBER 1942)

The Caucasus
June–November 1942

→ German attacks
- → German retreats
— German front line
- → Soviet retreat
⛏ Oil field

6000
3000
1500
600
300
0 ft

Orel
Yelets
XXXX
60
Tambov
XXXX
2 SALMUTH
XXXX
40
LATOTIN
XXXXX
Bryansk Front
(7 July)
Kursk
XXXXX
BOCK Army Group Centre
XXXX
4 HOTH
Voronezh
XXXX
6 Svoboda
Belgorod
1
XXXX
6 PAULUS
XXXX
2 Hungarian
(elts)
Pavlovsk
2
Saratov
XXXXX
Southwest Front
TIMOSHENKO
XXXX
1 Guards
XXXX
21
Kamishin
Kharkov
XXXXX
B WEICHS
XXXX
8 Italian
XXXX
5
XXXX
3 Rom
XXXX
65
XXXX
24
Don
ROKOSSOVSKY
Izyum
XXXX
1 KLEIST
Ukraine
Lugansk
XXXXX
XXXX
66
XXXX
6 PAULUS
Stalingrad
XXXXX
Stalingrad
YEREMENKO
Baskunchak
Kazakhstan
XXXX
62
XXXX
64
XXXX
57
XXXX
51
XXXX
17 RUOFF
XXXXX
Army Group A
LIST
XXXX
2
XXXX
4 HOTH
2
Rostov
Nova Cherkassk
XXXX
4 Rom
3
Mariupol
Yetsk
XXXX
17 RUOFF
Sea of Azov
XXXXX
A LIST
Elista
Ulan Erge
Astrakhan
Kerch
XXXX
11 (-)
Taman
Krapotkin
Krasnovar
XXXX
47
XXXX
56
Novorossiysk
Tuapse
Armavir
Maikop
Stavropol
Caspian Sea
Kisliar
German front lines:
1 June 1942
2 23 July 1942
3 November 1942
Sochi
XXXX
12
3
XXXX
18
Sukhum
Piatigorsk
XXXX
1 KLEIST
Georgiyevsk
Mozdok
XXXX
44
XXXX
9
Grozny
Ordzhonikidze
Makhach-kala
Black Sea
XXXXX
North-Caucasus Front
BUDENNY
XXXX
37
Caucasus Mountains
XXXXX
Trans-Caucasus Front
TYULENEV
Poti
N
0 100 km
0 100 miles
Kutais
Batumi
Georgia
Tiflis
TURKEY
Azerbaijan

■ **Opposite: The main objective of** *Fall Blau* **was the capture of the Caucasian oil fields around the Caspian Sea and further south in Azerbaijan and Armenia. For this operation to work, Stalingrad had to be captured to secure the flank of** *Generaloberst* **Hermann Hoth's Fourth Panzer Army as it thrust south.**

the Mediterranean on the Eastern Front and against the Reich itself, the Allies began to turn the tide against the German war machine.

Summer offensive

However, in southern Russia, the Germans once again began to roll. The German advance, spearheaded by *General der Panzertruppe* Friedrich von Paulus' Sixth Army, gained ground. The initial thrust was aimed at Stalingrad, in order to secure the German flanks, at which point the rest of the offensive turned south towards the Caucasus oil fields.

The *Luftwaffe* once again supported the offensive, deftly playing its part in combined arms operations against the Soviet foe. Operational command of the *Luftwaffe* in theatre was reorganized after *Luftflotte* 2 was sent to the Italian front to support Mediterranean operations. *Luftflotte* 5 flying from Finland coordinated with *Luftflotte* 1 against Leningrad; *Luftwaffenkommando Ost* commanded assets in the central region; and *Luftflotte* 4 was in charge of the Don–Caucasus sector. In the south, the *Luftwaffe* employed 1500 aircraft in the offensives and for logistics. While this figure is impressive, the Soviets mustered even more aircraft in defence; more than 2000 were available from the Americans and increasing numbers were produced in Soviet factories.

German gains were impressive. Stalingrad was 90 per cent in German hands by November, though Paulus was not able to fully secure the city, and German forces were nearing the coveted oil fields as winter once again hampered operations. But the toll was heavy. In June, the *Luftwaffe* lost 350 aircraft on the Eastern Front;

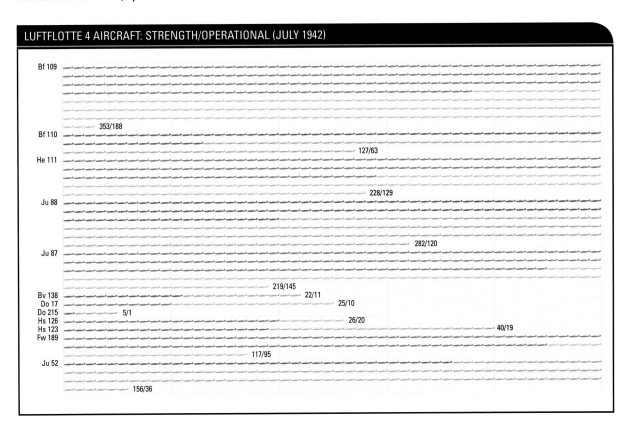

LUFTFLOTTE 4 AIRCRAFT: STRENGTH/OPERATIONAL (JULY 1942)

Aircraft	Strength/Operational
Bf 109	353/188
Bf 110	127/63
He 111	228/129
Ju 88	282/120
Ju 87	219/145
Bv 138	22/11
Do 17	25/10
Do 215	5/1
Hs 126	26/20
Hs 123	40/19
Fw 189	117/95
Ju 52	156/36

■ Ju 87 Stuka dive-bombers on their way to a target on the Eastern Front, winter 1942. The Ju 87 was outclassed from 1941, but continued to see action on the Eastern Front in the ground-support role. The last of more than 4000 Stukas came off the production line in September 1944.

losses increased to more than 430 in July and again in August. By October, the *Luftwaffe* on the Eastern Front had lost more than 90 per cent of the total aircraft that had been available in January. Indeed, in terms of single-seat fighters, losses ran at 115 per cent: 1734 were lost on the Eastern Front in 1942; 1500 had been available at the start of the year. Moreover, in 1942, German single-engine fighter production totalled only 800 machines. Across the board, the *Luftwaffe* was losing in the battle of attrition against the Soviets.

Stalingrad

Stalingrad was an important city to Stalin – and not just because it bore his name – and he ordered that the city not fall. Hitler also perceived the city's importance, and ordered it to be taken at all costs. What emerged was a death struggle between the two armies, resulting in a conflagration beyond measure. Although the Germans occupied nearly all of the city by the onset of winter, the Soviets fought on. German aircraft pummelled the city while the army fought house to house on the ground. The city was devastated in

the meantime, creating for its people a hell on earth.

Soviet counterattack

When the Soviets launched their winter counterattack, codenamed Operation *Uranus*, the Germans had the opportunity to escape and leave the devastated city behind. Hitler refused to allow a retreat, and turned to his trusted air commander Göring for advice. Göring replied that the trapped armies could be supplied by airlift, and Hitler decided to hold Stalingrad. The trapped German forces required a minimum of 610 tonnes (600 tons) of resupply per day, which led to a transport crisis almost immediately. The first consideration was the weather. As winter descended, sortie rates declined, hampering resupply efforts. The second concern was the lack of transport aircraft to carry out the mission. Historian Richard Muller points out that the *Luftwaffe* had only limited resources on hand to carry out the operation – resources that dwindled further due to the third concern: Red Air Force action.

By January, the situation was dire. Only 529 aircraft were on hand to bring

in supplies for the beleaguered forces: 317 Ju 52s, 181 He 111s (converted), 20 Fw 200 maritime reconnaissance aircraft, 10 prototype He 177s and a single Ju 290. The minimum figure of 610 tonnes (600 tons) was never achieved as the delivery dwindled to a mere 51 tonnes (50 tons) by January. Operational availability never exceeded 170 aircraft (8 December); sorties exceeded 150 on only one day (31 December) and averaged only 70, with a number of zero-sortie days.

The trapped forces slowly starved; newly promoted *Generalfeldmarschall* Paulus surrendered on 2 February 1943. It was the first major reversal for the Germans and was attributed directly to a lack of transport and loss of air supremacy. The Germans lost more than 1000 transport aircraft – including almost 300 Ju 52s and another 170 He 111s – in the campaign, losses that were even more difficult to replace than fighters.

LUFTWAFFE AIRCRAFT LOSSES: STALINGRAD CAMPAIGN	
Type	Total
Ju 52	266
He 111	165
Ju 86	42
Fw 200	9
He 177	5

LUFTWAFFE AIRLIFT AT STALINGRAD (24 NOVEMBER – 31 DECEMBER 1942)

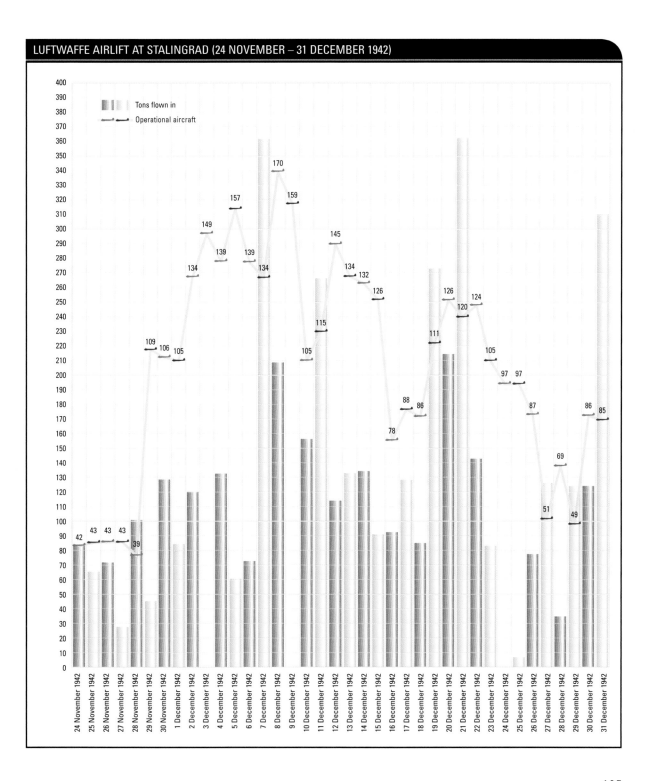

Tons flown in

Operational aircraft

LUFTWAFFE AIRLIFT AT STALINGRAD (1 JANUARY – 3 FEBRUARY 1943)

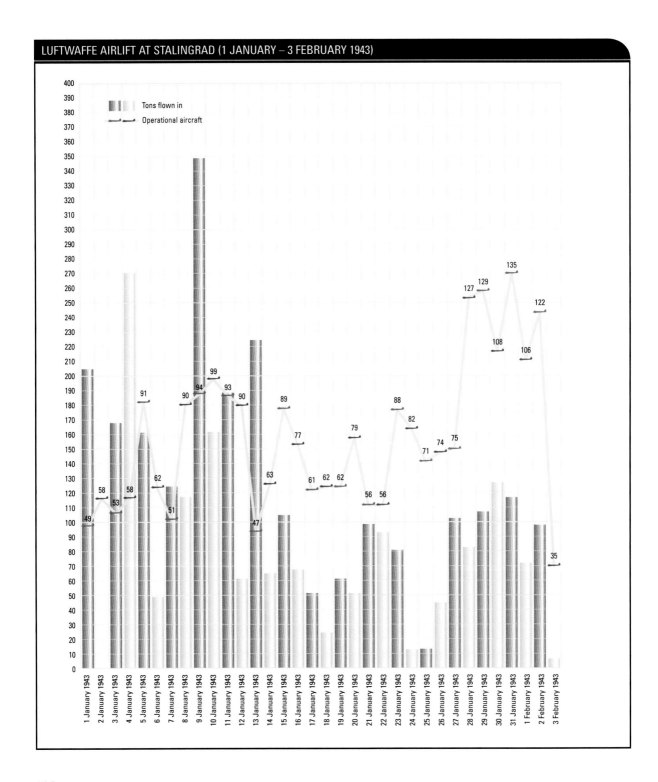

THE FINAL BATTLE FOR STALINGRAD (JANUARY 1943)

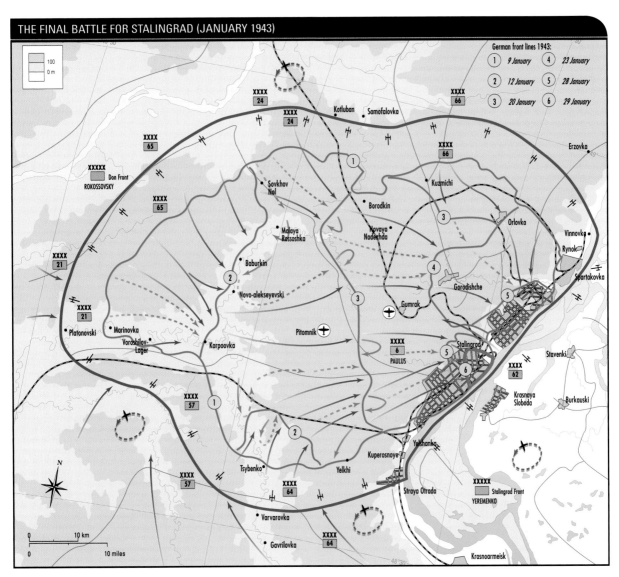

German front lines 1943:
1. 9 January
2. 12 January
3. 20 January
4. 23 January
5. 28 January
6. 29 January

The Battle for Stalingrad
January 1943

→ Soviet attacks
→ German counterattacks
- → German retreats
— German front line
— Limit of Soviet artillery
≈ → Soviet air support

■ Marshal Georgi Zhukov launched Operation *Uranus* on 19 November 1942, and within days a massive Soviet pincer movement had isolated the German Sixth Army fighting in Stalingrad. All attempts to relieve the trapped German soldiers failed, and the *Luftwaffe* was never able to make good Hermann Göring's boasts that he would sustain the city from the air. As January progressed, the noose around Stalingrad was tightened. The German forces retreated to the city, losing control of important airfields. The fighting was less fierce than it had been in September and October: the Soviets could let cold, starvation and disease do most of the work. Stalin ordered the pocket eliminated in January, and by the end of the month the surviving Germans were pressed into two small pockets on the Volga.

1943: Year of the Last Offensive

The reversal at Stalingrad put the Germans on their heels in early 1943. It also translated into operational initiative for the Soviets across the entire front. In an effort to consolidate their losses, the Germans withdrew to defensive positions, but the Soviets continued to harass and push them back.

The extended war of attrition continued; the Germans continued their retreat. They lost operational initiative, and by the spring of 1943, the Allies were harassing German-held territory in the south, the east and from Britain in the north. By not defeating the Soviets, the Germans had placed themselves in a very precarious position, ultimately surrounded by foes. While German industry increased output, the mounting war of attrition chewed up resources, material and manpower. By spring 1943, German

aviation production had increased to its highest levels thus far, and continued to rise.

Production of single-engine fighters is indicative: output rose from an average of 435 fighters per month in the second half of 1942 to more than 750 per month by the first half of 1943. The figure continued to rise: according to post-war reports, the Germans produced 850 fighters per month by the second half of 1943. Furthermore, these were the most advanced fighters in combat at the time; by summer 1943, Messerschmitt

was producing the Bf 109G-6, and Focke-Wulf the Fw 190A-4. More than a match for any Allied fighter, these planes still contested air superiority well into 1944.

Green pilots

The main problem the *Luftwaffe* faced was a lack of experienced pilots. Whereas Allied pilots' training time increased throughout the war, German pilot training was on the decline. The need for fighter pilots forced the *Luftwaffe* to commit men to combat well before their Allied

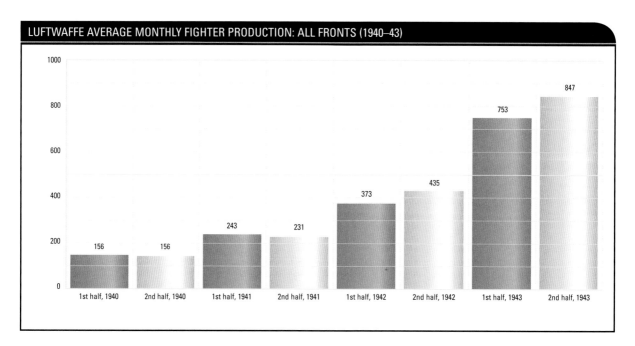

LUFTWAFFE AVERAGE MONTHLY FIGHTER PRODUCTION: ALL FRONTS (1940–43)

counterparts were deemed ready. By 1943, German pilot training hours had been cut from 250 hours' training to 200 hours, and hours continued to decrease as the war dragged on.

By summer 1943, *Luftwaffe* pilots received only half as many training hours as comparable American and British pilots. Training hours for Soviet pilots was even lower, at only 20–50 hours of training before being pressed into combat. In general, the Soviets tended to throw pilots (as well as ground and tank troops) into the fray with even less training than the Germans, in order to overwhelm the Germans with numbers rather than experience. Thus a divide grew in the *Luftwaffe* between the very experienced pilot cadre and the inexperienced newcomers. The experienced *Luftwaffe* pilots became better (and gained more kills), but inexperienced German pilots became easy targets.

Continual losses

With the hectic pace of warfare on the Eastern Front, the *Luftwaffe* continued to lose heavily during late 1942 and early 1943. The debacle at Stalingrad accounted for the loss of over 1900 aircraft (mostly transports) to the Soviet Red Air Force. And though losses decreased after the fall of Stalingrad, the *Luftwaffe* continued to lost significant numbers of aircraft.

The figures tell their own tale: the *Luftwaffe* lost 314 aircraft in March (including 100 fighters); there was a decline to 238 (67 fighters) in April; then an increase to 331 (110 fighters) in May. Added to the total butcher's bill were the planes lost in the Mediterranean theatre as well as in renewed attacks on Germany. With the Soviet push in the East, the *Luftwaffe* was in trouble.

Operation Zitadelle

By July 1943, the German high command knew they needed to halt the Soviet offensive; they decided to make a stand at Kursk. Soviet forces created a salient around the city of Kursk, and the Germans decided to attack there to shorten their lines and halt the ongoing Soviet advance.

Operation *Zitadelle* (Citadel) gathered all of the best and freshest German land and air forces for a concentrated attack against the Soviets. On the ground, the Germans committed 50 divisions, with some of the Panzer divisions equipped with the new Panther and Tiger tanks, arguably the finest of the war. The Soviets countered with over 1.3 million men, 3500 tanks (mostly T-34s) and a heavy concentration of 20,000 artillery pieces. As well, the Soviet position was protected with a series of fortifications and anti-tank defences, a million landmines and a web of barbed wire. The German ground attack was designed as a pincer manoeuvre, simultaneous attacks from the north and south to defeat the Soviet defences. The Soviets added almost 2800 aircraft to the fight, including Il-2 Shturmoviks for anti-tank operations and new fighters for air supremacy. The new Soviet types included Yak-1s, Yak-7Bs and La-5s in great numbers; they were comparable to the German fighters in capability but with inexperienced pilots.

The *Luftwaffe* countered the Soviet air threat with over 2000 planes of their own, with *Luftflotte* 6 supplying the northern attack, and *Luftflotte* 4 the southern advance. The northern attack was supported by a variety of aircraft, including single-seat and heavy fighters, medium bombers and a *Geschwader* of Stukas. JG 51 and JG 54 flew the latest Fw 190s – A-4/5s and A2s respectively. In the south, the air contingent included Bf 109Gs of JG 3 and JG 52 and bombers from five *Geschwader*. In addition, new Henschel Hs 129 tank-busters joined in the action.

Collision of armour

Zitadelle opened on 5 July, and immediately emerged as the largest armoured battle in history. German aerial attacks focused on Soviet armour, but the *Luftwaffe* found out very quickly that the Soviet ground-to-air defences and fighters were a worthy foe.

The *Luftwaffe* flew 3000 sorties on the first day and was able to break through the Soviet front lines, knocking out over 100 tanks. But the Soviet defences were formidable; they immediately countered on land and in the air to deny a German advance. *Luftwaffe* attacks on Soviet airfields were also successful; the *Luftwaffe* destroyed hundreds of Soviet aircraft on the ground and in the air. But the Soviets kept coming. With more reserves than the Germans, and with unbreakable defensive lines, the Soviets successfully defended Kursk, though the costs were high. By the end of the operation, both sides had suffered tremendous losses. After two weeks, the Germans were exhausted from the pace of the battle, with little to show for their efforts. The Soviets were able to pour men and materiel into the battle; the Germans were running short of both. As the tide of the battle turned, the Soviets emerged victorious; the Germans were spent.

By the end of the campaign, each side had lost about 500 tanks, but the Soviets were producing about that number per month, whereas the Germans were only producing about 50 each month. The Soviets lost about 1600 aircraft at Kursk but were able to make up these losses more quickly as well. The *Luftwaffe* lost less than half that number – 681, including at least 200 fighters – but were no longer able to keep up the pace of attritional warfare against the USSR's military and industrial muscle.

When the Allies invaded Sicily on 9 July, Hitler intervened. By the 17th, forces were withdrawn to support Italian operations, and operations on the Eastern Front were doomed. The Soviets, flush with victory, began a series of offensives that continued to push the Germans back towards their borders. As the German retreat continued, the *Luftwaffe* was harassed on the ground as well as in

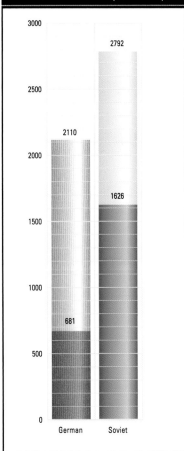

AIRCRAFT DEPLOYED AND LOSSES: KURSK (JULY 1943)

FLIEGERFÜHRER NORD (OST), UNDER LUFTFLOTTE 5 (30 NOVEMBER 1943)				
Unit	Base	Type	Strength	Operational
Stab JG5	Petsamo	Bf 109G2	2	–
Stab III./JG5	Petsamo	Bf 109G2	2	–
7., 8., 9./JG5	Petsamo	Bf 109G2	25	–
		Bf 109F4	3	–
13.(Z)/JG5	Kirkenes	Bf 110G0	1	–
		Bf 110G2	11	–
		Bf 110G4	2	–
		Bf 110F2	2	–
14.(Jabo)/JG5	Petsamo	Fw 190A	13	–
Jagdkdo Nord	Altengard	Bf 109G	1	–
1.(F)/124	Kirkenes	Ju 88D1	13	–
		Ju 88D5	1	–
		Ju 88A	4	–
		Bf 109G4	4	–
Westa 6	Banak	Ju 88D	–	–
3.(F)/SAGr130	Billefjord	Bv 138	8	–
1.(H)/32	Alakurti	Fw 189	12	–
I./SG5	Nautsi	Ju 87D	13	–
TrStFlFhrN	Rovaniemi	Ju 52/3m	5	–
4./TGr20	Kemi	Ju 52/3m	12	–
Sanflugber8	Kemi	Ju 52/3m	3	–
		Fi 156C	4	–

the air. Sortie rates plummeted because of equipment breakdowns and a lack of supplies. Individual *Geschwader* were forced to relocate monthly, then weekly, in the constant retreat. With the increasing tempo of the Combined Bomber Offensive, *Luftwaffe* units were recalled for the defence of the Reich. And at the same time, the Soviets increased their industrial output and were able to commit increasing numbers of aircraft to the front. In 1943, the Soviets produced more than 34,000 aircraft, compared with the German figure of 24,000 – and the Soviets were only fighting on one front. *Luftwaffe* losses declined after Kursk but were still beyond the capabilities of German industry to make up; after the massive destruction at Kursk, the *Luftwaffe* went on to lose a further 1300 aircraft, including 300 fighters.

1944 – Turn of the Tide

By 1944, the tide had turned; the Germans continued their 'strategic withdrawal' across the entire Eastern Front. They were slowly but surely losing the battle of attrition against the superior production capabilities of the Allies.

The Allies were gaining air superiority and initiated plans for the final destruction of Germany. In the spring, the Soviets continued to whittle away at German power, using superior production to overcome the *Luftwaffe*. *Luftwaffe* ground troops (specifically paratroopers) were organized into emergency ground divisions to fight on the ground on the Eastern Front, while their pilot compatriots tried to stem the Soviet tide. But it was never enough.

By summer, the Allies had coordinated a sequence of attacks designed to overwhelm German defences. In the south, having invaded Italy in September 1943, the Allies liberated Rome on 4 June. In the west, they landed in Normandy on 6 June in the largest amphibious assault in history. On the Eastern Front, the Soviets began Operation *Bagration* on 22 June, designed to liberate German-occupied Belorussia and eastern Poland.

Army Group Centre destroyed

Operation *Bagration* saw more than 1.2 million Soviet soldiers oppose fewer than 500,000 German troops. In the air, the Soviets mustered more than 5000 aircraft, which in the end overwhelmed the remaining 600 *Luftwaffe* aircraft in theatre.

FLIEGERFÜHRER 1 (HQ AT MINSK), UNDER LUFTFLOTTE 6 (JUNE 1944)			
Unit	*Base*	*Type*	*Strength*
12/NAGr 12	Mogilev	Bf 109	12
2/NAGr 5	Budsslav	Bf 109	5
4/NAGr 31	Budsslav	Fw 190	6
Stab/NSGr 2	Lida	Ju 87, Ar 66	2
1/NSGr 2	Bobruysk	Ju 87	14
3/NSGr 2	Lida	Ju 87	21
4/NSGr 2	Mogilev	Ju 87	17
1 Ostfliegerstaffel (Russia)	Lida	Go 145, Ar 66, U2	9
1, 2/NSGr 1	Kovno	in transition	–
Stab/JG 51	Orsha	Bf 109, Fw 190	5
Stab/StJG 51	Orsha	Bf 109, Fw 190	12
I/JG 51	Orsha	Bf 109	35
III/JG 51	Bobruysk	Bf 109	31
IV/JG 51	Mogilev	Bf 109	17
III/JG 11	Dokudovo	Bf 109	19
Stab I/NJG 100	Baranovichi	Ju 88	51
1, 3/NJG 100	Biala-Podlaska	Do 217, Fw 190	–
4/NJG 100	Puchovichi	Ju 88	4

IV FLIEGERKORPS, UNDER LUFTFLOTTE 6 (JUNE 1944)

Unit	Base	Type	Strength
1(F)/100	Pinsk	Ju 88	14
Stab/NAGr 4	Piala-Podlaska	Bf 109, Fw 189	3
3/NAGr 4	Kobbryn	Hs 126	5
12/NAGr 3	Brest-Litovsk	Bf 109, Hs 126, Fw 189	8
Stab/KG 4	Bialystok	He 111, Ju 88	8
II/KG 4	Baranovichi	He 111	34
III/KG 4	Baranovichi	He 111	40
Stab/KG27	Krosno	He 111	1
III/KG 27	Krosno	He 111	41
III/KG 27	Mielec	He 111	35
Stab/KG 53	Radom	He 111	1
I/KG 53	Radom	He 111	36
II/KG 53	Piastow	He 111	37
III/KG 53	Radom	He 111	36
Stab/KG 55	Deblin-Irena	He 111	1
I/KG 55	Deblin-Ulez	He 111	35
II/KG 55	Deblin-Irena	He 111	35
III/KG 55	Grojek	He 111	36

LUFTFLOTTE 6 (JUNE 1944)

Unit	Base	Type	Strength
Stab/FAG 2, 4(F)/11	Baranovichi	Ju 88, He 111	2
4(F)/14	Baranovichi	Ju 188, Do 217	15
NSt 4	Bobruysk	Ju 88, Ju 188	7
14(Eis)/KG 3	Puchevichi	Ju 88	13
Stab/KG 1	Prowehren	Ju 88	1

4 FLIEGERDIVISION, UNDER LUFTFLOTTE 6 (JUNE 1944)

Unit	Base	Type	Strength
Stab/NAGr 10	Tolochin	Bf 109, Fw 189, Hs 126	3
2/NAGr 4	Orsha	Fw 189, Hs 126	18
13/NAGr 14	Tolochin	Bf 109, Fw 189	7
I/SG 1	Tolochin	Ju 87	44
II/SG 1	Vilna	Fw 190, Ju 87	73
10(Pz)/SG 1	Bojari	Ju 87	20
10(Pz)/SG 3	Tolochin	Ju 87	22
Stab/SG 10	Dokudovo	Fw 190	3
III/SG 10	Dokudovo	Fw 190	39

The history of *Bagration* includes the sad tale of the collapse of *Luftflotte* 4, destroyed by the Red Air Force.

By the summer of 1944, the operational status of the remaining *Luftwaffe* planes on the Eastern Front stood at less than 50 per cent, because of the effects of combat, relocation and a lack of qualified pilots; by that time, the aircraft were also suffering from a lack of fuel and spare parts. As the Soviet behemoth rolled on, the German defences crumbled. The best troops and fighter squadrons were relocated to the west to fight the Americans and British – strength that was desperately needed on the Eastern Front. The collapse was slow and painful but inevitable.

By the time it ended on 19 August, *Bagration* had destroyed the remaining German defences on the Eastern Front. The Germans had lost 400,000 men, Army Group Centre had been destroyed and *Luftflotte* 4 had lost over 800 aircraft. By the end of the campaign season, with the onset of winter, the Soviets were poised to re-enter Poland and continue their drive on Berlin in the spring.

Losses
Accurate figures for *Luftwaffe* losses on the Eastern Front during 1944 are extremely difficult to obtain, mainly because systems of administration were in meltdown. In June and July 1944, however, despite reinforcement from some 150 fighters, 325 aircraft were lost in combat, and those that could fly were rapidly running out of fuel and supplies. The *Luftwaffe* was being totally overrun by the Allied air

forces on all fronts.

Total collapse was just months away, made inevitable by Soviet the industrial machine pushing more and more aircraft out into action. In total during World War II, the Soviet Union built over 125,600 combat aircraft alone, and total aircraft production in 1944 rose to over 40,000 aircraft.

The battle for the Eastern Front had become as impossible to sustain for the *Luftwaffe* as it had for the ground forces, and by the end of 1944 the Soviet front line ran in a line

1 FLIEGERDIVISION, UNDER LUFTFLOTTE 6 (JUNE 1944)			
Unit	*Base*	*Type*	*Strength*
Stab/NAGr 4	Urezhcye	Fw 189	2
I/NAGr 4	Bobruysk	Fw 189	12
II/NAGr 11	Urezchye	Fw 189	9
II/NAGr 12	Urezchye	Fw 189	7
Stab/SG 1	Pastovichi	Fw 190	5
III/SG 1	Pastovichi	Fw 190	38
I/SG 10	Bobruysk	Fw 190	10

that roughly (from north to south) tracked through Warsaw, Budapest and Belgrade. With the Allies also pressing in from the west, the *Luftwaffe*'s focus was now on defending the homeland.

1945 – Collapse and Retreat

Early in 1945, the Soviets initiated new offensives. They entered Warsaw in January, and continued their drive into Germany. Königsberg (modern-day Kaliningrad) fell in April as the German front collapsed.

The Soviets aligned 2.3 million men on the front, with over 7500 aircraft, for the final drive to Berlin. As the German front collapsed, Hitler ordered a suicidal defence of the city against overwhelming Soviet strength. The fighting was bitter, but in the end the Germans were defeated. While no reliable figures exist to validate Soviet air claims in the final months of the war, it is sufficient to say that the remaining *Luftwaffe* forces facing the Soviets were completely destroyed.

A few *Luftwaffe* pilots flew to the American sector, to be captured by the Western Allies, but for the most part *Luftwaffe* pilots died in combat or were captured by advancing

Soviet forces. Among those taken by the Soviets was *Major* Erich Hartmann. Hartmann, who flew Bf 109s and was a holder of the Knight's Cross with Diamonds, remains the highest-scoring ace of all time with 352 victories, all on the Eastern Front. He was eventually repatriated to Germany in 1955.

Whys and wherefores

The collapse of the *Luftwaffe* on the Eastern Front can be directly attributed to two factors. First and foremost, the Soviets survived the initial onslaught in 1941, moved their factories behind the Ural mountains and were able to continue production on a massive scale. Without a

strategic bombing force, the *Luftwaffe* could not disrupt Soviet aircraft production and thus faced increasing numbers of effective Soviet planes. During the war, the Soviets produced more than 150,000 aircraft, which the Germans had to face in the air because they did not have a way to destroy the Soviet factories. The Soviets' production capabilities meant that in a war of attrition, they were eventually able to overwhelm the *Luftwaffe* with sheer numbers, which they did beginning in the summer of 1943.

Second, the coordination of the Allies, as loose as it was, meant that the *Luftwaffe* had to face threats from every direction, especially after the summer of 1944. The combined weight of Allied materiel production operated in concert, forcing the Germans to defend everywhere, which they could not do. The collapse of the *Luftwaffe* on the Eastern Front can be attributed to the overwhelming Allied material superiority on all fronts of the war. German production simply could not keep pace with Allied resources in an ongoing war of attrition.

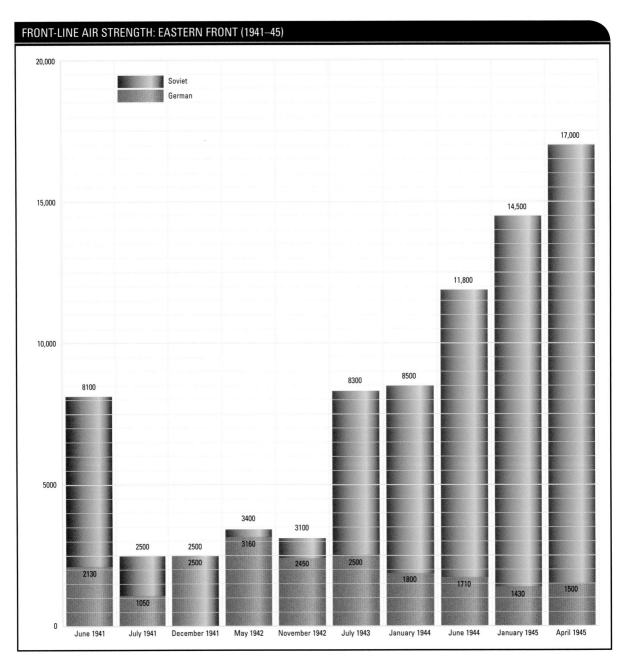

FRONT-LINE AIR STRENGTH: EASTERN FRONT (1941–45)

ERICH HARTMANN

Known as the 'Black Devil' to his Soviet counterparts, Erich Hartmann was the highest-scoring ace of the Luftwaffe; *indeed, he remains the highest-scoring ace of all time. Hartmann began combat operations with JG 52 in October 1942 and had shot down 352 planes in 1400 combat sorties by the end of the war. His record was unmatched; he shot down 345 Soviet aircraft and another seven US fighters flying missions into Romania.*

A full 260 victories were against Soviet fighter aircraft, which by the end of the war were comparable to his own Messerschmitt Bf 109G. In March 1944, he was considered so dangerous that Stalin personally placed a 10,000-rouble bounty on his head. At the end of the war, Hartmann was captured by the Soviets and spent almost 11 years in Soviet POW camps before being repatriated to Germany. He was recommissioned into the West German Air Force (Bundesluftwaffe), *where he commanded JG 71 until his retirement in 1970.*

■ **Hartmann (left) examines a map before an operation.**

BIRTH:	19 April 1922
DEATH:	20 September 1993
PLACE OF BIRTH:	Weissach, Würtemberg, Germany
FATHER:	Doctor Alfred Erich Hartmann
MOTHER:	Elisabeth Wilhelmine Machtholf
SIBLINGS:	Alfred Hartmann (younger brother – also in the *Luftwaffe;* a rear gunner in a Ju 87, was shot down in North Africa and taken POW by the British)
PERSONAL RELATIONSHIPS:	Ursula Paetsch, married September 1944. Erich-Peter (son, born 1945, died 1948 without ever seeing his father, who was a Soviet POW); Ursula Isabel (daughter, born 23 February 1957)
MILITARY SERVICE:	1 October 1940: Flying Cadet with the 10th Flying Regiment
	1 March 1941: promoted to *Luftkriegschule* 2 at Berlin-Gatow
	10 October 1942: posted to JG 52 on the Eastern Front
	29 October 1943: awarded *Ritterkreutz* (Knight's Cross of the Iron Cross) for his 148 kills
	March 1944: awarded *Eichenlaube* (Oak Leaves) to his Knight's Cross
	1 July 1944: promoted to *Oberleutnant* (First Lieutenant; RAF Flying Officer)
	2 July 1944: awarded Crossed Swords to his Knight's Cross
	17 August 1944: became top-scoring ace of the *Luftwaffe,* surpassing squadron-mate Gerhard Brakhorn, with his 274th victory
	24 August 1944: shot down 11 enemy aircraft in two sorties
	1 September 1944: promoted to *Hauptmann* (Captain; RAF Flight Lieutenant)
	September 1944: awarded Diamonds to his Knight's Cross
	8 May 1945: promoted to Major (Major; RAF Squadron Leader)
	9 May 1945: Captured by the US 90th Infantry Division
	24 May 1945: under agreement, handed over to the Soviets by his American captors
	Late 1955: released from Soviet POW camp and repatriated

CHAPTER 7

Late War Innovations and X-planes

By 1944, the Germans had the finest equipment in the world. Although the bulk of their military hardware was dated, their best designers had built prototypes and operational examples of the best technology available.

From land weapons like the Tiger and Panther tanks, as well as anti-tank and other infantry equipment, to the revolutionary Type XXI submarine of the Kriegsmarine, the German technical lead was impressive. But in the air the Germans were on the cusp of war-winning technology, and it was approaching operational status against the Allies.

A Messerschmitt Me 163B-1a launches at Bad Zwischenahn, home of the trials unit *Erprobungscommando 16, which accepted*

Late War German Aircraft Development

The increasingly urgent need to counter the Allied bombing campaign spurred German designers to produce fighters that were technologically far ahead of their time, but they were too few in number and too late to affect the outcome of the air war.

Besides state-of-the-art fighters, Germany also developed the so-called *Veregeltungswaffen*, or retaliation weapons; that is, weapons designed to wreak revenge for Allied bombing of Germany. The first, the Fieseler Fi 103, better known as the V-1, was a pilotless pulse-jet drone, packed with explosives – the first cruise missile. Known to the Allies as the 'Doodlebug' (among other things), the V-1 was launched from ramps in northern France and the Low Countries and aimed mostly at southern England and Antwerp. It was designed to fly a determined path, and when it ran out of fuel for the pulse-jet motor it would fall to the ground and explode.

The second of the retaliation weapons was the V-2 rocket, which, although an aerial weapon, fell under the jurisdiction of the army. The V-2 was aimed at London and, once again, Antwerp with the aim of knocking the British out of the war and denying important ports to the Allied effort in northwest Europe. More than 10,000 V-1s were launched in the closing months of the war plus over 3000 V-2s. Germany even built a manned (single-seat) version of the V-1, the Fi 103R Reichenberg IV. Prototypes did fly, but the manned V-1 never saw combat.

New airframes

The *Luftwaffe* made extensive use of German high-tech weapons in the last year of the war. By 1944, there were jet and rocket airframes in service, as well as experimental piston-engine and other prototypes, designed to turn the tide of the Allied air effort.

The most successful, the Messerschmitt Me 262, was built in significant numbers and was operational, in a trials unit, as early as July 1944. Other airframes included the Arado Ar 234 jet bomber, the Dornier Do 335 *Pfiel* (Arrow) and the Messerschmitt Me 163 *Komet* (Comet). Additional experimental aircraft will be addressed below.

The Me 262 was a game-changing aircraft that was the brainchild of legendary aircraft designer Willi Messerschmitt. Originally designed as an air-superiority fighter, it had a very turbulent history. Messerschmitt and his main rival, Ernst Heinkel, had sponsored jet engine development before the war; Heinkel had the first jet aircraft with the He 178, which flew a week before the attack on Poland in 1939.

Continued development

However, at the start of the war Hitler ordered the cancellation of all development programmes for aircraft that would not be in production within six months. Expressly ignoring this order, both Messerschmitt and

ADVANCED FIGHTER PRODUCTION								
Type	1939	1940	1941	1942	1943	1944	1945	Total
Dornier Do 335	–	–	–	–	–	23	19	42
Focke-Wulf Ta 152	–	–	–	–	–	34	46	80
Focke-Wulf Ta 154	–	–	–	–	–	8	–	8
Heinkel He 162	–	–	–	–	–	–	116	116
Heinkel He 219	–	–	–	–	11	195	62	268
Messerschmitt Me 163	–	–	–	–	–	327	37	364
Messerschmitt Me 262	–	–	–	–	–	564	730	1294
Messerschmitt Me 410	–	–	–	–	271	629	–	910

■ **Opposite: Although the Me 262 was employed in only relatively small numbers, its high speed proved very effective against bomber formations, especially compared with the head-on attacks used by conventional fighters. The He 162, on the other hand, was inadequately developed when rushed into service and only 116 were built. Even so, it had the potential to become a very good interceptor.**

JET FIGHTERS COMPARED

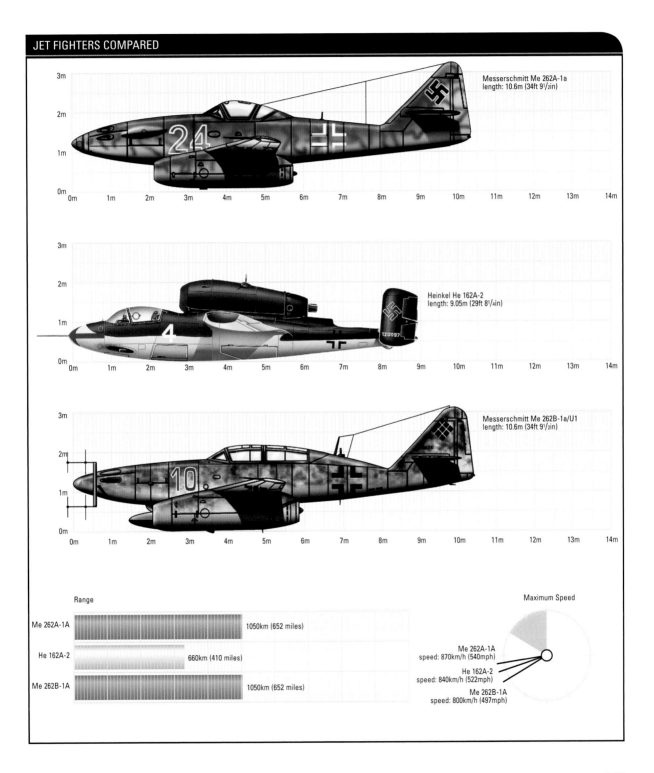

Messerschmitt Me 262A-1a
length: 10.6m (34ft 9¹/₂in)

Heinkel He 162A-2
length: 9.05m (29ft 8¹/₄in)

Messerschmitt Me 262B-1a/U1
length: 10.6m (34ft 9¹/₂in)

Range

Me 262A-1A — 1050km (652 miles)

He 162A-2 — 660km (410 miles)

Me 262B-1A — 1050km (652 miles)

Maximum Speed

Me 262A-1A
speed: 870km/h (540mph)

He 162A-2
speed: 840km/h (522mph)

Me 262B-1A
speed: 800km/h (497mph)

MESSERSCHMITT Me 262 VARIANTS	
Type	Description
Me 262A-1a *Schwalbe*	The main production version, built as both a fighter and fighter/bomber
Me 262A-1a/R-1	Modified to carry R4M air-to-air rockets
Me 262A-1a/U1	A single prototype fitted with six nose-mounted cannon – two 20 mm (0.79in) MG 151/20, two 30mm (1.18in) MK 103 and two 30mm (1.18in) MK 108
Me 262A-1a/U2	A single night-fighter prototype equipped with FuG 220 Lichtenstein SN-2 radar
Me 262A-1a/U3	An unarmed reconnaissance version produced in small numbers, with two Reihenbilder RB 50/30 cameras mounted in the nose
Me 262A-1a/U4	An experimental bomber destroyer version fitted with a single nose-mounted 50mm (1.97in) MK 214 (or *Bordkanone* BK 5) anti-tank gun
Me 262A-1a/U5	A bomber destroyer armed with six 30mm (1.18in) MK 108 cannon
Me 262A-2a *Sturmvogel*	The definitive bomber version fitted with two 30mm (1.18in) MK 108 and external racks for one 500kg (1100lb) or two 250kg (550lb) bombs
Me 262A-2a/U2	Two prototypes with glazed nose position for a bomb aimer
Me 262A-5a	The definitive reconnaissance version, small numbers of which were in service by the end of the war
Me 262B-1a	A two-seat advanced trainer
Me 262B-1a/U1	Me 262B-1a trainers converted as interim night-fighters, equipped with FuG 218 *Neptun* radar

Heinkel continued development of the revolutionary systems, Messerschmitt working on an airframe and Heinkel developing both airframe and engines.

By 1943, both had working twin-jet-engine prototypes: the Heinkel He 280 and the Messerschmitt Me 262. Hitler once again stepped in to foil production by denying Heinkel the contracts and giving the green light to Messerschmitt on the condition that the aircraft be developed as a fast jet bomber.

Messerschmitt Me 262

A continuing misconception surrounds this decision by Hitler; it is commonly recounted that it cost the Germans jet aircraft in time to confront the Allied landings at Normandy. In fact, based on new research, it is clear that the plane was not ready anyway, regardless of the 'jet order'.

In reality, Me 262 production was hampered by a lack of engines from the Junkers Motorenwerke (Jumo) factory, which was responsible for the development of the Jumo 004 jets for the aircraft. And as airframes rolled off the production lines and as engines became available, Messerschmitt expressly disregarded the Hitler order once again – the Me 262 was actually produced as a fighter, belatedly equipped with an add-on bomb rack to assuage the *Führer*'s conditions. By the time Hitler rescinded the order in September 1944, the plane was finally becoming ready for series production and operations with combat units.

The key point was that the new technology – especially the engines – were very primitive and temperamental; they were the limiting factor in the successful production of the jet aircraft. Little could be done to increase production of the airframes or engines in the final days of the collapsing Reich.

Turning point

The turning point for the German jet programme came in the summer of 1944, when the tide was already turning against Germany. That summer, the *Luftwaffe* High Command could have put more resources into the development of both the Messerschmitt and Heinkel jet fighters, but there were serious snags. On the one hand, the necessary materials for the engines – high-temperature substances such as chromium and tungsten – were no longer available, which in turn led to substitute materials being used with consequent short operational lifespans for the engines.

Furthermore, production of the jets would have cut into production of existing types, planes that were already in short supply for the defence of the Reich. Finally, it has been argued persuasively that additional jets would not have mattered in the end; Allied aircraft production (specifically American production) would have still overwhelmed German jet production and efficacy; and the air war would have still ended in the Allies' favour.

That said, the story of the *Luftwaffe*'s jets remains an interesting episode in history. With the Allies ashore in Normandy and starting to move on the Reich, the *Luftwaffe* began to accept operational jets and quickly organized them into squadrons. The first jet squadrons were recce units, taking advantage of the jets' amazing speed. Further squadrons were organized using the jets as point interceptors and air-superiority fighters. By the end of the war, there were three operational fighter squadrons flying the jet, as well as two additional recce squadrons and a training unit.

The most famous fighter unit was *Jagdverband* (JV) 44, also known as the 'Squadron of Experts'. Adolf Galland, now a *Generalleutnant*, had fallen foul of Göring and been relieved of his post. Galland had been *General der Jagdflieger* (General of Fighters), but Göring was angry that Galland's aircraft had not protected the Reich from incessant Allied bomber attacks. He was removed from the position, much to his chagrin, and replaced by *Oberst* (Colonel) Gordon Gollob.

However, Galland was one of Hitler's favorites, and after a meeting with the *Führer* he was given a reprieve. Galland was not reinstated but instead was made squadron commander of the most prestigious unit in the *Luftwaffe* – JV 44.

Jagdverband 44

Galland was given permission to gather Germany's top aces, train them on Me 262s and form an elite air defence unit. Based initially at Munich-Riem, JV 44 flew to protect important industrial centres in southern Germany. Galland recounts in his post-war memoir, 'I was to set up a small unit to demonstrate that the Me 262 was the superior fighter that I had always claimed. A small

unit only in *Staffel* strength was to be organized ... I would have to find the aircraft myself ... The unit would not be under the command of any division, corps or airfleet – I was to be totally independent.'

Galland instructed his new pilot volunteers to stop at Leipheim and commandeer factory-fresh jets for the new unit, an action that faced resistance from the beginning; the Messerschmitt workers had not even

LUFTFLOTTE REICH, DAY-FIGHTERS			
Unit	Type	Strength	Serviceable
I/JG 2	Fw 190	5	3
II/JG 2	Fw 190	8	4
III/JG 2	Fw 190	12	9
Stab/JG 4	Fw 190	6	4
II/JG 4	Fw 190	50	34
III/JG 4	Bf 109	61	56
Stab/JG 7	Me 262A-1	5	4
I/JG 7	Me 262A-1	41	36
II/JG 7	Me 262A-1	30	23
Stab/JG 26	Fw 190	4	3
I/JG 26	Fw 190	44	16
II/JG 26	Fw 190	57	29
III/JG 26	Fw 190	35	15
I/JG 27	Bf 109	29	13
II/JG 27	Bf 109	48	27
III/JG 27	Bf 109	19	15
I (J.)/KG 54	Me 262A-1	37	21
Stab/JG 301	Ta 152H	3	2
I/JG 301	Fw 190	35	24
II/JG 301	Fw 190	32	15
II/JG 400	Me 163B	38	22
JGr. 10	Fw 190	15	9
Jagdverband 44	Me 262A-1	approx. 30	approx. 15

LUFTWAFFENKOMMANDO WEST, DAY-FIGHTERS AND BOMBERS			
Unit	Type	Strength	Serviceable
Stab/JG 53	Bf 109	1	1
II/JG 53	Bf 109	39	24
III/JG 53	Bf 109	40	24
IV/JG 53	Bf 109	54	27
I/KG 51	Me 262A-2	15	11
II/KG 51	Me 262A-2	6	2
Stab/KG 76	Ar 234B	2	2
II/KG 76	Ar 234B	5	1
III/KG 76	Ar 234B	5	1

heard of *Jagdverband* 44. Among Galland's pilots were some of the most decorated *Luftwaffe* flyers, including Günther Lützow, Johannes Steinhoff, Gerhard Barkhorn, Walter Krupinski and Heinrich Bär. These men represented the core of the *Luftwaffe*; all had years of experience and, between them, many hundreds of 'kills'.

The main problem for JV 44 was finding planes and parts. Facing incessant Allied aerial attacks, the 'Experts' flew to protect the shrinking Reich. Galland recounted after the war that they were fighting a losing battle, but that it was important to fly for Germany nonetheless. In the final months of the war, JV 44 was responsible for as many as 55 victories against Allied aircraft; Galland increased his record by 12 in combat with the Me 262.

Obstacles overcome

A number of factors combined to conspire against the jet pilots. In addition to the lack of planes and parts, they also faced harassment from Allied fighters. The Me 262 had a long, slow take-off and landing pattern; American P-51s and P-47s quickly adapted to take advantage of this vulnerability. While the Me 262s could not be caught easily in the air, the 'Rat Catcher' tactic was very successful in catching them closer to the ground. Galland decided to employ Fw 190s to provide cover for the jets while they took off and landed; Fw 190D-9s (known as *Würgers,* or Butcher-birds) protected the vulnerable jets. The other, insurmountable, problem was production. There were simply not

enough jets to stem the tide of Allied production capabilities.

One example is illustrative: on the most active day of jet combat, in March 1945, a total of 55 Me 262s faced more than 800 Allied bombers and 1200 fighters. The Me 262, while good, was not enough to turn the tide of the air war over Germany.

By the end of the war, JV 44 had lost 53 planes in combat in gaining its 55 credited victories. Overall, almost 1300 Me 262s were produced before the conflict's end, only about 400 being used in combat in operational squadrons. The Allies had destroyed German aircraft manufacturing and transport networks, defeating the bulk of the *Luftwaffe* on the ground.

As discussed above, it was commonly argued after the war that Hitler had disrupted jet production with an often cited order to turn the jet fighter into a bomber. In fact, the Me 262 programme was hindered by a lack of engines from Jumo; the Hitler order did not, in the end, matter. And, as one historian argues, neither the airframes nor the engines could have been produced earlier or in greater numbers than they were, due to the lack of raw materials in the shrinking Reich and the embryonic state of the technology. The German jets were actually ahead of their time; it is a credit to German design and manufacturing that the *Luftwaffe* had any jets at all.

Other jets

Additional high-technology aircraft made their debut in the closing months of the war. At the Arado factory, efforts were put into a jet bomber, the Ar 234. Deliveries of the

twin-engine (later four-engine) high-speed bomber began in mid-1944, and recce and bomber squadrons were incorporated to use the new weapon. Recce missions commenced in the autumn, but bomber operations did not start until Christmas. Then, in a series of missions in March 1945, Me 262s and Ar 234s attacked the bridge at Remagen. This was the first example of an all-jet aerial attack. Approximately 200 Ar 234s were built before the end of the war.

One other jet aircraft began production in the final days of the war, the Heinkel He 162 *Volksjäger* (People's Fighter), which was also known as the Salamander – the creature with the mythical ability to live through fire. A marvel of ingenuity, the He 162 was conceived, designed, built, tested and put into production in a matter of weeks. It was intended to be a disposable plane, built from non-scarce materials – mostly plywood – and easy to fly.

The He 162's jet engine, attached to the top of the airframe, was one of the first BMW jets – the BMW 003. Although it is unclear if it made it into combat, the He 162 was envisaged as

■ **Opposite: Four late-war** *Luftwaffe* **developments are compared here; high-speed, high-altitude air-superiority fighters to combat the Combined Bomber Offensive. The Do 335 was the fastest piston-engine aircraft of the war; the Me 609 was a projected day-fighter. The He 219 was a twin-engine night-fighter, and the Ta-152 was an evolution of the Fw 190 developed late in the war by master aircraft designer Kurt Tank.**

PISTON-ENGINED FIGHTERS COMPARED

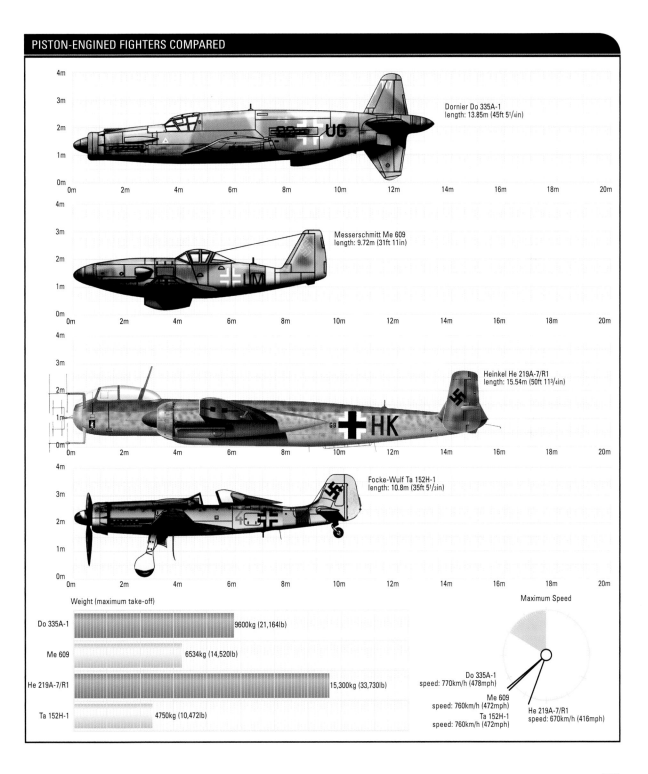

Dornier Do 335A-1
length: 13.85m (45ft 5¹/₄in)

Messerschmitt Me 609
length: 9.72m (31ft 11in)

Heinkel He 219A-7/R1
length: 15.54m (50ft 11³/₄in)

Focke-Wulf Ta 152H-1
length: 10.8m (35ft 5¹/₂in)

Weight (maximum take-off)

Do 335A-1	9600kg (21,164lb)
Me 609	6534kg (14,520lb)
He 219A-7/R1	15,300kg (33,730lb)
Ta 152H-1	4750kg (10,472lb)

Maximum Speed

Do 335A-1
speed: 770km/h (478mph)

Me 609
speed: 760km/h (472mph)

He 219A-7/R1
speed: 670km/h (416mph)

Ta 152H-1
speed: 760km/h (472mph)

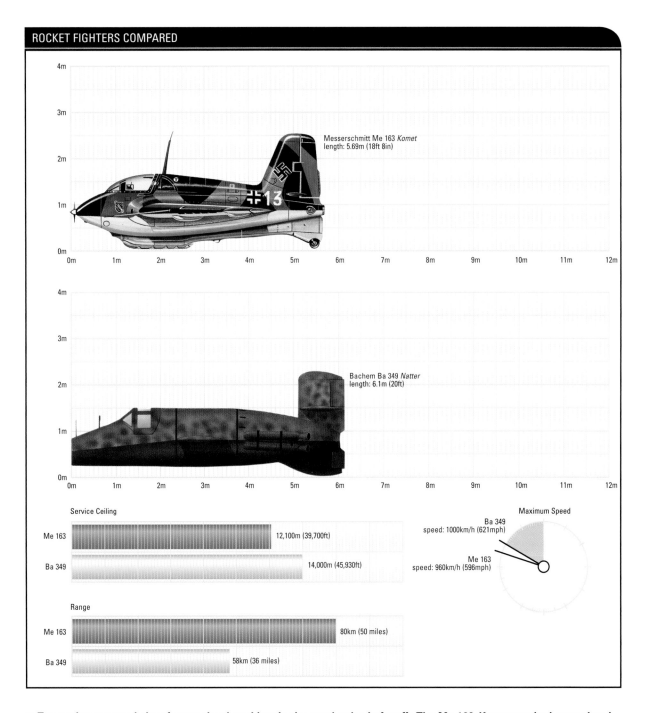

ROCKET FIGHTERS COMPARED

Messerschmitt Me 163 *Komet*
length: 5.69m (18ft 8in)

Bachem Ba 349 *Natter*
length: 6.1m (20ft)

Service Ceiling

Me 163 — 12,100m (39,700ft)

Ba 349 — 14,000m (45,930ft)

Maximum Speed

Ba 349
speed: 1000km/h (621mph)

Me 163
speed: 960km/h (596mph)

Range

Me 163 — 80km (50 miles)

Ba 349 — 58km (36 miles)

■ Two rocket-powered aircraft were developed late in the war by the *Luftwaffe*. The Me 163 *Komet* reached operational status with more than 300 produced. The tempestuous Ba 349 *Natter* killed its first test pilot, and the project was quickly abandoned, with only 11 examples built.

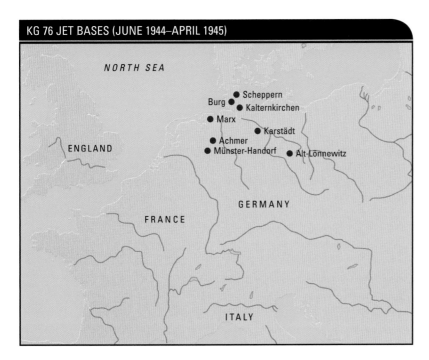

KG 76 JET BASES (JUNE 1944–APRIL 1945)

NORTH SEA

ENGLAND

FRANCE

GERMANY

ITALY

Scheppern
Burg
Kalternkirchen
Marx
Karstädt
Achmer
Münster-Handorf
Alt-Lönnewitz

KG 76 JET BASES (JUNE 1944–APRIL 1945)		
Unit	Date	Base
Stab	Jun 1944	Alt-Lönnewitz
	Feb 1945	Achmer
	Mar 1945	Karstädt
II/KG 76	Aug 1944	Burg
	Mar 1945	Scheppern
III/KG 76	Jun 1944	Alt-Lönnewitz
	Dec 1944	Burg, Münster-Handorf
	Jan 1945	Achmer
	Mar 1945	Marx
	Apr 1945	Kalternkirchen
IV/KG 76	Oct 1944	Alt-Lönnewitz

■ *Kampfgeschwader* (KG) 76 began conversion to the Arado Ar 234 in June 1944. By December 1944, the unit had 51 of these aircraft. III./KG 76 operated over France and the Low Countries until the end of the war. It flew some of the first jet bomber missions in history on 24 December 1944 against rail targets in Namur, Belgium.

a quick and cheap solution to Allied air superiority.

Rocket aircraft

Even more radical were the *Luftwaffe*'s rocket planes. The Messerschmitt factory produced one of these, the Me 163 *Komet*. This revolutionary aircraft was a liquid-rocket-fuelled interceptor, designed specifically for point interception of American heavy bombers.

The Me 163 was incredibly fast but also incredibly dangerous to fly. Taking off from a wheeled trolley, it jettisoned the wheel unit for a breathtakingly fast climb to altitude

with the aid of its rocket motor. The six minutes of liquid fuel (a mixture of *T-Stoff,* or hydrogen peroxide, with *C-Stoff,* hydrazine hydrate and methanol) powered the little plane to altitude at which point it became a glider. It would fight, then return to earth as a glider to land on a skid. The aircraft's landing speed was high – about 220km/h (140mph) – and the pilot had only one shot at putting the plane down, a factor that resulted in numerous accidents. Also, the flammable liquids had the potential to catch fire at any time, presenting a further danger to the plane and the lone pilot of the vehicle.

Armed with two 30mm (1.18in) cannons, the Me 163 was intended to be an effective fighter against the American daytime bomber streams. However, the aircraft's record was not as impressive as predicted. The *Komet* arrived with the *Luftwaffe* early in 1943 for familiarization, and in May the following year the first *Komet* operational unit began to form. The aircraft went into action on 16 August 1944 and achieved its first 'kill' some days afterwards. Even so, the *Komet* had only nine confirmed 'kills' (possibly as many as 16 'kills' from all Me 163s) before the end of the war. Organized into a single unit – *Jagdgeschwader* 400 – the planes flew from an airfield at Leipzig. More than 300 were eventually built, but only a few dozen reached the operational unit.

Vertically launched

One other rocket plane, the Bachem Ba 349 *Natter* (Adder), was tested in Germany during the war. This aircraft was designed to be launched vertically from a gantry, also for point interception of incoming enemy bombers. The intention was that once the *Natter* had rocketed to 14,000m (45,930ft), it would start to dive earthwards into the attack; the *Natter*'s pilot would launch the 24 unguided rockets in the plane's nose, then bail out before the aircraft, designed to be expendable, reached the ground. Development of the *Natter* was hampered by pilot deaths; only 11 examples of the aircraft were built, fewer were tested and none ever saw combat.

Long-range bomber

Development of other planes continued in the closing stages of the war. Work on heavy bombers went on, even after operational reasons no longer pertained. The Messerschmitt Me 264, a four-engine long-range bomber designed to put the United States in reach, was finally cancelled in 1944, but the idea resurfaced. A Horten 'flying wing' design, the jet-powered P. 18, was chosen for

development but too close to the war's end. Horten had already had one of their flying wing jet designs, the Ho IX/Go 229, built in prototype, but that project never got any further either. More projects sat uncompleted as the Allies overran the German aircraft factories.

One final aircraft project deserves mention. The Dornier company fielded an interesting aircraft in the closing phases of the war, a twin-piston-engine fighter/interceptor with the designation Do 335 *Pfiel* (Arrow). The plane had engines in the front and rear of the aircraft, turning two propellers, one that pulled and one that pushed. With a maximum speed of 765km/h (474mph), the Do 335 was comparable to late-war Allied fighters in speed and armament. However, only 42 were built; not enough to impact the air war.

The technology gatherers

In the closing days of the war, the Allies (specifically the Americans but to a lesser extent also the British and

French) saw the development of German aircraft and were determined to gather as much German equipment and aircraft designers as possible. Under the codename Operation *Paperclip* (and later Operation *Lusty*), the Americans roamed conquered Europe for examples of German aircraft technology and the designers who had built them.

By the end of the war, the Americans had collected flying examples of *Luftwaffe* aircraft for return to the United States for flight-testing and examination, and much of the technology was incorporated into post-war American designs. Post-war American aircraft built on German swept-wing design, jet engine technology and other specific aviation advances. In certain cases – Alexander Lippisch, for example – German aircraft designers were spirited away to the United States to continue aviation design work there.

Many of the captured German aircraft are still on display; a wide variety of *Luftwaffe* aircraft can still

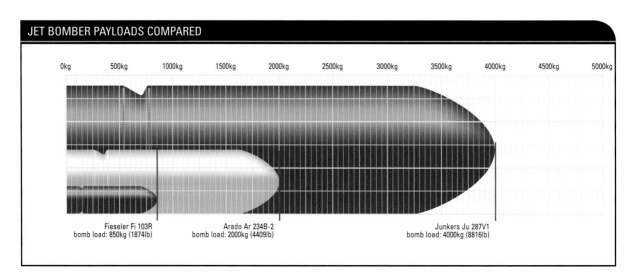

JET BOMBER PAYLOADS COMPARED

| 0kg | 500kg | 1000kg | 1500kg | 2000kg | 2500kg | 3000kg | 3500kg | 4000kg | 4500kg | 5000kg |

Fieseler Fi 103R
bomb load: 850kg (1874lb)

Arado Ar 234B-2
bomb load: 2000kg (4409lb)

Junkers Ju 287V1
bomb load: 4000kg (8816lb)

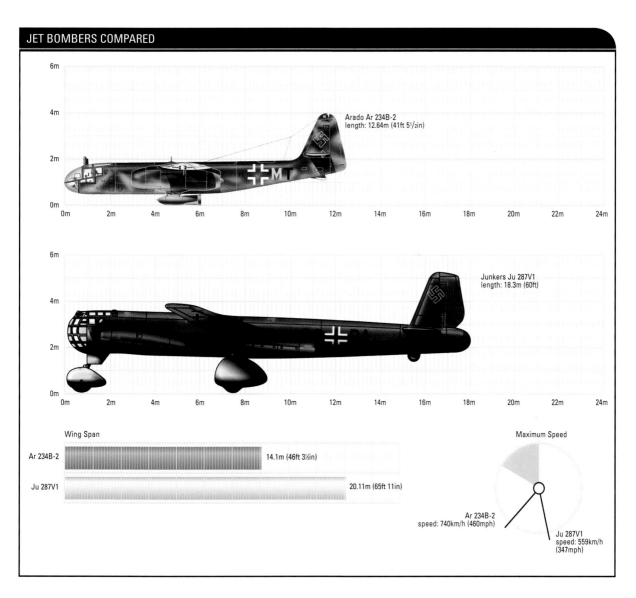

JET BOMBERS COMPARED

Arado Ar 234B-2
length: 12.64m (41ft 5½in)

Junkers Ju 287V1
length: 18.3m (60ft)

Wing Span

Ar 234B-2   14.1m (46ft 3½in)

Ju 287V1   20.11m (65ft 11in)

Maximum Speed

Ar 234B-2
speed: 740km/h (460mph)

Ju 287V1
speed: 559km/h
(347mph)

be seen at the National Museum of the United States Air Force in Dayton, Ohio, as well as in other venues in the United States, Britain and elsewhere around the world.

Interestingly, the Me 262 has even found a cult following in the United States. Beginning in the mid-1990s, and continuing to this day under the name of the Collings Foundation, a small number of Me 262s have been reproduced from World War II plans and built for investors. The new Me 262s fly with upgraded engines and avionics but represent an effort to keep the history of the air war alive. Fans can see history come to life at a number of air shows every year.

■ **Two late-war jet bombers are represented above. Deliveries of pre-production Arado Ar 234s began in the summer of 1944, and the type saw service in both the bomber and reconnaissance roles. The Junkers Ju 287, with forward-swept wings, was in prototype development at the end of hostilities.**

CHAPTER 8

Defence of the Reich

*From the end of the Battle of Britain to the
beginning of the Normandy campaign, the Luftwaffe
forces in the west of Europe were starved of resources.
Even with the intensification of the Allied bomber war
against the Reich in 1943 and 1944, which often involved
overflights of France and the Low Countries, German
fighter strength in those countries was relatively low.
Despite the development of some superb new
technologies, such as the Me 262 jet fighter, the Luftwaffe
was unable to come close to matching the numerical
superiority of the Allies from 1943 onwards.*

*Even had the Luftwaffe been developed as a truly
strategic air force earlier in the war, it is hard to see how
the outcome of the air war would have been different
once Germany had committed itself to fight the combined
industrial might of the United Kingdom, the United States
and the Soviet Union.*

The Focke-Wulf Fw 190A demonstrated immediate superiority over its Allied
fighter adversaries when it entered service in 1941, and it was employed as an

Theory and Practice

At the close of World War I, theorists made predictions about the effectiveness of air power in future wars. Building on the limited experiences of the Great War, and the potential of aircraft evolution, air-power advocates argued that future wars could be fought entirely with aircraft, and be over in a matter of hours, or days at most.

An Italian theorist, Giulio Douhet, predicted that fleets of bombers would always get through and that the destruction of enemy cities would bring capitulation. In his opus, *The Command of the Air* (published in 1921; available in English by 1942; translated into German in the early 1930s), he forecast fleets of bombers flying over national boundaries,

avoiding all defences and attacking enemy cities and industry in preemptive attacks. He theorized that a nation could be brought to its knees and would surrender through bombing alone, obviating the need for navies and armies. Indeed, he went still further, suggesting that the threat of an air attack could promote peace through deterrence.

The Germans considered and rejected these ideas, eventually settling on combined operations, with air power as a support component of *Blitzkrieg*. The Americans and British, though, not only explored these theories but the latter attempted to put them into practice against military targets from the opening phases of World War II. In Britain, Hugh

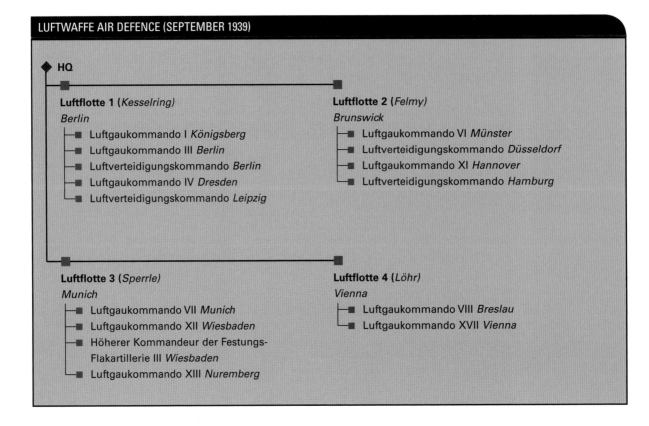

LUFTWAFFE AIR DEFENCE (SEPTEMBER 1939)

◆ HQ

Luftflotte 1 (*Kesselring*)
Berlin
- Luftgaukommando I *Königsberg*
- Luftgaukommando III *Berlin*
- Luftverteidigungskommando *Berlin*
- Luftgaukommando IV *Dresden*
- Luftverteidigungskommando *Leipzig*

Luftflotte 2 (*Felmy*)
Brunswick
- Luftgaukommando VI *Münster*
- Luftverteidigungskommando *Düsseldorf*
- Luftgaukommando XI *Hannover*
- Luftverteidigungskommando *Hamburg*

Luftflotte 3 (*Sperrle*)
Munich
- Luftgaukommando VII *Munich*
- Luftgaukommando XII *Wiesbaden*
- Höherer Kommandeur der Festungs-Flakartillerie III *Wiesbaden*
- Luftgaukommando XIII *Nuremberg*

Luftflotte 4 (*Löhr*)
Vienna
- Luftgaukommando VIII *Breslau*
- Luftgaukommando XVII *Vienna*

Trenchard, the 'Father of the RAF', became an outspoken proponent of strategic bombing, as the British built a bomber force to fulfil the theory. In the United States, Billy Mitchell, the 'Father of the US Air Force', emerged as the main advocate of the new technology and the benefits it could (potentially) provide.

Offence and defence
In the inter-war period, aircraft evolution seemed to justify the theory. In the United States and Britain, efforts went into the development and production of heavy bombers for strategic bombing. At the same time, defensive measures improved, and fighter defences and the complementary radar and signals technologies threatened the viability of bombers. However, in both the United States and Britain, the defence was seen as weaker, and each country's air service (the RAF in Britain and the United States Army Air Forces – USAAF – after 1941 in the United States) continued the development of strategic bombing forces. No one seriously questioned the premise that an enemy population would buckle under bombing attacks; this prediction was taken for granted.

Strategic bombing in practice
When the Germans began their bombing campaign over Britain in the summer of 1940, they were convinced that they could knock the British out of the war by bombing RAF airfields and later British cities. However, the British did not surrender during or after the Battle of Britain; if anything, they grew more resistant. The British argued that the campaign was unsuccessful because the Germans simply did it wrong, and that Britons were more stout; they insisted that British strategic bombing would be more effective. Indeed, Britain had already begun its bombing campaign over Germany in 1940.

Defensive strength
It must be noted, however, that defences were able to combat, if not defeat, bombing offensives. The Germans were defeated over the skies of Britain through attrition and an effective defensive network. The British defences were strong enough, and additionally British morale remained high; the British outlasted the German offensive. The Germans, meanwhile, prepared their own defences against the widening British onslaught from the air.

Like the British, the Germans had excellent fighter interceptors to defend against incoming bombers. The ubiquitous Messerschmitt Bf 109 was the main bomber interceptor for the first half of the war, and improvements continued. The Germans also had radar, searchlights and barrage balloons protecting cities and important industrial centres, connected to fighter *Geschwader* for protection of targets. The British had launched bombing raids immediately after the declaration of war, beginning a bombing campaign that lasted throughout the war.

Bombing Raids, 1939–1941

The British launched their first bomber raid on Germany on 4 September 1939. That day, 15 Bristol Blenheim and 14 Vickers Wellington bombers took off from their bases to attack German Navy targets at Wilhelmshaven.

A combination of bad weather and poor navigation hindered the raid, and only 10 Blenheims and eight Wellingtons found their target, the 'pocket battleship' *Admiral Sheer*. Attacking at low level, the bombers attacked the ship, but their bombs failed to explode. The Blenheims suffered heavily; four were shot down by flak. The Wellingtons directed their anger at German capital ships docked at Brunsbüttel, the *Scharnhorst* and *Gneisenau*. Their performance was equally dismal; two Wellingtons did not return and no targets were destroyed. In that raid, Bf 109s claimed the victories, but it is still unclear if the Wellingtons were lost

ADOLF GALLAND

Adolf Galland lives on in modern memory as one of the most successful fighter pilots of all time. Galland flew from the birth of the Luftwaffe to the very final days of the war, amassing kills and sorties, as well as awards for his proficiency.

BIRTH:	19 March 1912
DEATH:	9 February 1996
PLACE OF BIRTH:	Westerholt, Westphalia
FATHER:	n/k
MOTHER:	n/k
SIBLINGS:	Three brothers, inlcuding Paul Galland (17-victory ace; shot down and killed, 31 October 1942), Wilhelm-Ferdinand Galland (54-victory ace; shot down and killed, 17 August 1943)
PERSONAL RELATIONSHIPS:	Sylvinia von Dönhoff, married February 1954; Hannelies Galland, married 1963 – two children: Andreas Hubertus and Alexandra; Heidi Horn, married 1984

■ **Adolf Galland enjoys the company of his pet dog between missions.**

MILITARY SERVICE:
1932: Accepted into pilot training with Lufthansa civilian training programme
1933: Joins (illegal) *Luftwaffe*
1935: Posted to JG 2 at Berlin
1936: Spanish Civil War; assigned as *Staffelkapitän* of 3 Squadron, Condor Legion
1939: Promoted to *Hauptmann* (Captain; RAF Flight Lieutenant)
February 1940: Transferred to JG 27
June 1940: Appointed *Gruppenkommandeur* of III./JG 26
29 July 1940: Awarded Knight's Cross
22 August 1940: Appointed *Geschwaderkommodore* of JG 26
24 September 1940: Awarded Oak Leaves to his Knight's Cross (for 40 victories)
End of 1940: Promoted to *Oberstleutnant* (Lieutenant-Colonel; RAF Wing Commander – 58 victories)
21 June 1941: Awarded Swords to his Knight's Cross
November 1941: Appointed *General der Jagdflieger* at age 29
28 January 1942: Awarded Diamonds to his Knight's Cross
February 1945: Forms JV 44, an all-jet fighter unit composed of his fighter pilot friends
26 April 1945: Shot down for the last time, surrenders to Americans at the close of the war

to aircraft or flak. British Bomber Command, although stunned, decided that raids simply needed to be flown at higher altitudes. German opinion was equally misguided; commanders perceived initial successes as proof of effective defences. That day began the seesaw battle of offensive versus defensive air warfare in the strategic bombing campaign.

In the opening phases of the war, equipment limited British effectiveness. The Vickers Wellington was adequate as a medium bomber but was not sufficient as the backbone of Bomber Command. It was slow, underarmed and ill-equipped for large-scale strategic bombing. Unfortunately for Bomber Command, it was also the best aircraft in the inventory. Building on what they thought were lessons learned from the first raid, the RAF dispatched 11 Handley Page

Hampdens on 29 September to bomb Wilhelmshaven again. The planes were savaged by a 'hornet's nest' of German fighters; five failed to return. Undeterred, Bomber Command continued raids against convenient German targets but continued to lose aircraft as tactics were developed. When a major raid with 24 Wellingtons returned virtually unscathed on 3 December, Bomber Command was convinced that it finally had the answer. The Wellingtons flew higher – at 3050m (10,000ft) – and avoided fighter interception but did not hit their targets. Thus although the aircraft returned successfully, Bomber Command failed to realize that the bombing was thus far ineffective. The RAF persisted, and continued to send bombers into the fray to test doctrine and tactics. The Germans responded as quickly, developing tactics to counter the bombers.

Battle of Heligoland Bight

On 18 December 1939, Bomber Command launched its largest raid to date, which was later named the Battle of Heligoland Bight. Flying at 3050m (10,000ft), as ordered, 22 Wellingtons from Nos. 9, 37 and 149 Squadrons targeted ships in Wilhelmshaven harbour. The clear day was unhelpful to the attacking force; it was spotted from the ground. As well, both naval and *Luftwaffe* radars spotted the raiders, allowing the German pilots to muster for a counterattack.

Having been commanded not to drop bombs too close to civilians, the bombers turned for home without releasing their weapons. As they

turned, they were attacked by *Luftwaffe* fighters, Bf 109s and 110s. In a melee involving as many as 40 German defenders, the British lost 12 bombers in return for three German planes. The British began to question their abilities to bomb Germany, and a decision was made to shift to night attacks. The Germans were confident that they could turn back bomber attacks, and continued with their methods. Both sides faced difficult issues in the new year.

District Commands

In 1940, the *Luftwaffe* had an opportunity to bask in the glory of the Polish campaign, and the time to reassess the role of fighter defence. The decision was made to separate fighter defence units from attack squadrons and create a specific command. The air defence of the Reich and occupied territories had been placed under the command of *Luftgaukommandos* (Air District Commands), who were put in charge of planes, flak and other defensive measures to protect airspace from enemy bombers. The organization was effective but could be confusing; squadrons assigned to protection could be pulled away for offensive operations, as air support trumped defence.

Another shortcoming was that defence was not comprehensive (as in Britain) but local; commanders had control over specific sectors for the protection of specific targets. Compared with the British, who had a central control for the defence of the whole country, the *Luftwaffe* decentralized control to specific regions, and the planes could be

Squadron	Unit	Defence Area
III–IV	I./JG 27	Berlin
XI	Stab JG 1	Heligoland Bight
XI	I./JG 54	Heligoland Bight
XI	II./ZG 76	Heligoland Bight
VI	III./JG 3	Ruhr region
Holland	II./JG 52, I./JG 1	Holland

LUFTGAUKOMMANDO FIGHTER SQUADRONS ASSIGNED TO AIR DEFENCE (JANUARY 1941)

called away from defensive operations for offensive missions. Thus with the outbreak of war with Poland, while *Luftflotte* 2 fighters stood in a defensive role, *Luftflotte* 1 and *Luftflotte* 4 fighters were flying offensive operations against the Poles. When the Western Offensive started in 1940, most of the fighters were pulled from the defensive posture for attacking operations. As the war progressed, the defensive would become more important, but at the beginning of the war it was convoluted. The significance was that the Germans downplayed the role of the defensive (as they had strategic bombing in general) in the formation of commands and operations. And the lack of concern led to neglect and dislocation when significant Allied bombing offensives began in 1942.

A permanent solution emerged when the British began city raids in 1940. At the height of the Battle of Britain, Bomber Command launched a raid on Berlin to destroy the airfield at Tempelhof. Ninety-five British bombers raided the capital to start with, and five more raids followed over the next two weeks. Göring, who famously stated that his *Luftwaffe* would not allow Berlin to be bombed, went into action. That autumn, he consolidated *Luftgaukommandos* III and IV, based on Berlin and Dresden, under the command of *General der Flakartillerie* Hubert Weise. With increased British attacks in 1941, the command was further expanded to become *Luftwaffenbefehlshaber Mitte* (Central Air Force Command) and eventually *Luftflotte Reich*.

Night bombing

By the start of 1940, the British had shifted to night bombing. In order to protect their bombers and aircrew, Bomber Command decided it would be safer to attack at night. The sacrifice was accuracy; darkness was safer but hampered navigation and target identification. British tactics, technology and doctrine did evolve, but the prophesies of Douhet and Trenchard were shattered in the night skies over Germany; bombing did not end the war for either side. A devastating war of attrition for air supremacy began.

One immediate concern for the British was the development of a new airframe to increase the efficiency of strategic bombing. The Avro aircraft company submitted a design for a new heavy bomber, which became the four-engine Lancaster. The premier bomber of the RAF, it did not fly until 1941, and reached full production only in early 1942. The first RAF squadron to refit with Lancasters was No. 44.

The Lancaster was a vast improvement on all contemporary two-engine designs, and even outclassed the Handley Page Halifax, the other heavy bomber in service.

20ᴍᴍ (0.79ɪɴ) MG 151/20 & MG FF/M AERIAL CANNON EFFECTIVENESS

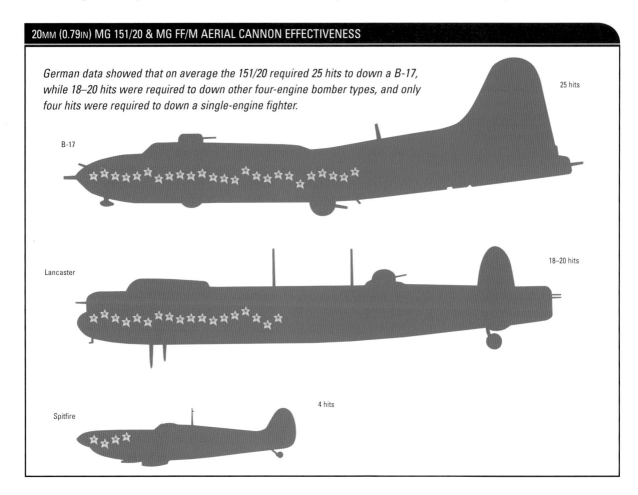

German data showed that on average the 151/20 required 25 hits to down a B-17, while 18–20 hits were required to down other four-engine bomber types, and only four hits were required to down a single-engine fighter.

B-17   25 hits

Lancaster   18–20 hits

Spitfire   4 hits

Capable of carrying 6350kg (14,000lb) of bombs, it could easily reach Berlin and return. Its one drawback was its limited ceiling of 7315m (24,000ft), well within the operating range of German 88mm (3.46in) anti-aircraft fire. More than 7300 Lancasters were eventually built at a variety of factories, including 430 constructed in Canada as the Lancaster B X.

The Germans countered the British bombers with increasingly effective aircraft. Because of the slow speed of the British bombers, the Bf 110 found a new role and moved easily into the job of heavy night-fighter. The Bf 110 was better suited to the bomber destroyer role than the Bf 109; the former had more guns and could carry more munitions. When Bomber Command shifted to night operations, its bombers were forced to forgo escorts; Spitfires and Hurricanes did not have the range in the first place. This in turn meant that the Bf 110s did not have to worry about a British fighter threat, and the *Luftwaffe* was able to concentrate the vulnerable aircraft against the bombers.

Aerial cannons

The Bf 110 was equipped with the 20mm (0.79in) MG FF/M aerial cannon, which proved very effective against the bombers. Whereas the bombers could withstand multiple hits from the 7.92mm (0.31in) MG 17 machine gun, they were more vulnerable to the cannon. And while the Bf 109 had only one 20mm (0.79in) cannon and just 60 rounds, the Bf 110 had two and could carry multiple 60-round canisters, which could be reloaded by the rear gunner/radio operator. Also, the Bf 110 could be fitted with radar for finding and firing on the bombers at night.

The 20mm (0.79in) aerial cannon was plagued by a low cyclic rate (only 540 rounds per minute) and low muzzle velocity (580–700 metres per second/1900–2295 feet per second), but was devastating when firing high explosive (HE) shells. A Lancaster

AERIAL WEAPON RATES OF FIRE COMPARED (IN ROUNDS PER MINUTE; RPM)

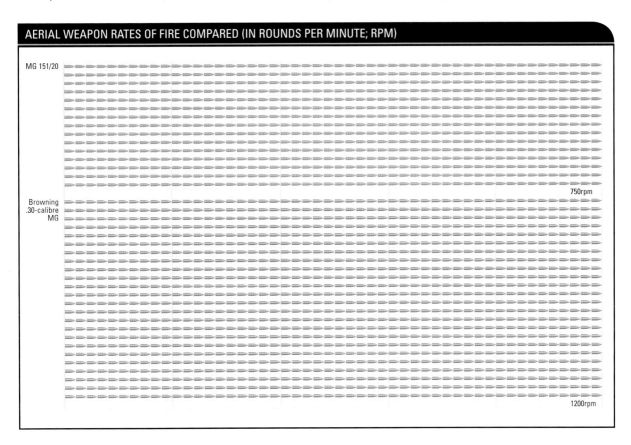

MG 151/20

750rpm

Browning .30-calibre MG

1200rpm

could be brought down with only 18 to 20 accurate hits, compared with a requirement for hundreds of 7.92mm (0.31in) rounds. A major drawback was that the German fighter had to get very close to the target, and have very accurate shot placement, but it could often disable the aircraft before British gunners could respond and return fire.

An interesting development by spring 1941 was the *Schräge Musik* (Jazz Music) configuration of a single or twin MG FF/M in a Bf 110 (and later added to other night-fighter variants). The weapons were placed amidships in the aircraft, firing upwards at an angle. The pilot would manoeuvre under the bomber and fire into the unprotected belly of the plane. German night-fighter pilots became very adept at bringing down bombers by using this new set-up.

New strategy

In 1940, RAF bombers flying at night had trouble finding anything smaller than a city, and changed their bombing doctrine. Focusing on industrial cities, and with frequent raids on the capital, their new concept was to disrupt German industry with a 'dehousing' campaign. The British surmised that if they bombed German workers in their beds, the workers would not be able to work, crippling German industry.

Furthermore, after Dunkirk the British were off the Continent and bombing was the one tool available to try to counter German strength. With operations restricted to the hours of darkness, and with incredibly poor accuracy, the area bombing of cities was a logical and singular option.

HEINZ-WOLFGANG SCHNAUFER

■ **Schnaufer was one of the greatest fighter aces in history.**

Heinz-Wolfgang Schnaufer was the highest-scoring and most decorated Luftwaffe *night-fighter pilot of World War II. Born near Stuttgart in February 1922, he became known as the 'Night Ghost of St. Trond'. Schnaufer learned to fly before the war in gliders, then joined the* Luftwaffe *in 1939. In 1941 he was assigned to II./NJG 1, his first night-fighter unit. Flying the night-fighter version of the Bf 110, his first victories came in June 1942, when he shot down a Handley Page Halifax four-engine RAF bomber over Belgium. Reassigned to III./NJG 1, he amassed another 35 victories the following year. By February 1944, Schnaufer had accumulated 50 victories in the night skies, and was appointed* Gruppenkommandeur *of IV./NJG 1. He had 100 victories by October 1944, and at 22 years old he became the youngest* Geschwaderkommodore. *Schnaufer was taken prisoner by the British at the end of the war but released before the end of 1945. He died in 1950, at the age of 28, after a car accident. His successes were without equal: in 164 combat missions, he shot down 121 aircraft, including 114 RAF four-engine bombers. Today, the tail fin of his last Bf 110, which shows his victory tally, is displayed at the Imperial War Museum in London.*

BIRTH:	16 February 1922
DEATH:	15 July 1950
PLACE OF BIRTH:	Calw (near Stuttgart)
FATHER:	n/k
MOTHER:	n/k
MILITARY SERVICE:	November 1939: Enters *Luftwaffe* as a pilot trainee
	April 1941: Posted to *Nachtjagdschule* 1
	November 1941: Posted to II./NJG 1
	July 1943: Promoted to *Oberleutnant* (First Lieutenant; RAF Flying Officer –17 victories)
	August 1943: Appointed *Staffelkapitän* in IV./NJG 1
	31 December 1943: Awarded Knight's Cross (42 victories)
	March 1944: Appointed *Gruppenkommandeur* of IV./NJG 1
	30 July 1944: Awarded Swords to his Knight's Cross
	16 October 1944: Awarded Diamonds to his Knight's Cross (100 victories)
	November 1944: Appointed *Geschwaderkommadore* of NJG 4

As 1941 dawned, the stage was set for a long attritional war between the pilots of Bomber Command and the night-fighter defenders of the *Luftwaffe*. Besides infrequent high-altitude, heavily escorted coastal raids, Bomber Command took the war to the Germans at night in an increasingly devastating bombing campaign. Bomber Command increased its pace from 1940 to 1941, dropping almost 2.5 times as much tonnage in the latter year – 13,210 tonnes (13,000 tons) in 1940; 31,500 tonnes (31,000 tons) in 1941. In reaction, the *Luftwaffe* committed more resources to fight the British – six groups of night-fighters and another two groups of day-fighters;

the consensus was that the *Luftwaffe* had succeeded in daylight.

The British raids were taxing but not considered more than a nuisance. German industry and the economy were in full swing as operations opened against the Soviets that summer. Berlin was raided a number of times that year, without significant successes; the British were still having trouble finding the city at night. In one large raid, on 7 November, Bomber Command sent 160 bombers to Berlin, of which 20 were shot down, a loss rate of 12.5 per cent. Little damage was done to Berlin, but the dismal record of 1941 caused a shake-up at Bomber Command in early 1942. Air Marshal Arthur

'Bomber' Harris took over as commander-in-chief, and vowed to level the German capital.

Harris is quoted as saying, 'The Nazis entered this war under the rather childish delusion that they were going to bomb everyone else, and nobody was going to bomb them. At Rotterdam, London, Warsaw, and half a hundred other places, they put their rather naive theory into operation. They sowed the wind, and now they are going to reap the whirlwind.' Already, at the end of 1941, Japan, an Axis partner of Germany, had bombed Pearl Harbor. Hitler had then declared war on the United States, bringing the industrial might of the Americans into the war.

American Intervention

By 1942, the Luftwaffe *was on the defensive in the West. Offensives in the Soviet Union and Mediterranean pulled all available bombers from the Reich and dispersed them abroad.*

German strategic bombing over England ceased. In February, Bomber Command issued a document called the Area Bombing Directive, stating '... that the primary objective of your operations should be focused on the morale of the enemy civil population and in particular the industrial workers'. Unable to fly during the day due to heavy losses, and incapable of finding anything smaller than a city at night, Bomber Command institutionalized area bombing. German cities and civilians became legitimate targets.

Type	Average Strength	In Action	Other	Total	% of Strength
Close recce	280	70	73	143	51
Long-range recce	400	236	136	372	93
Single-engine fighters	1500	868	866	1734	115.6
Twin-engine fighters	490	331	244	575	117.3
Bombers	1750	1101	648	1749	99.9
Stukas	440	315	162	477	108.4
Transport	970	250	256	506	52.2
Liaison	270	73	91	164	60.7
Coastal	230	33	40	73	31.7
Total	6330	3277	2516	5793	91.5

LUFTWAFFE AIRCRAFT WRITTEN OFF (JANUARY–OCTOBER 1942)

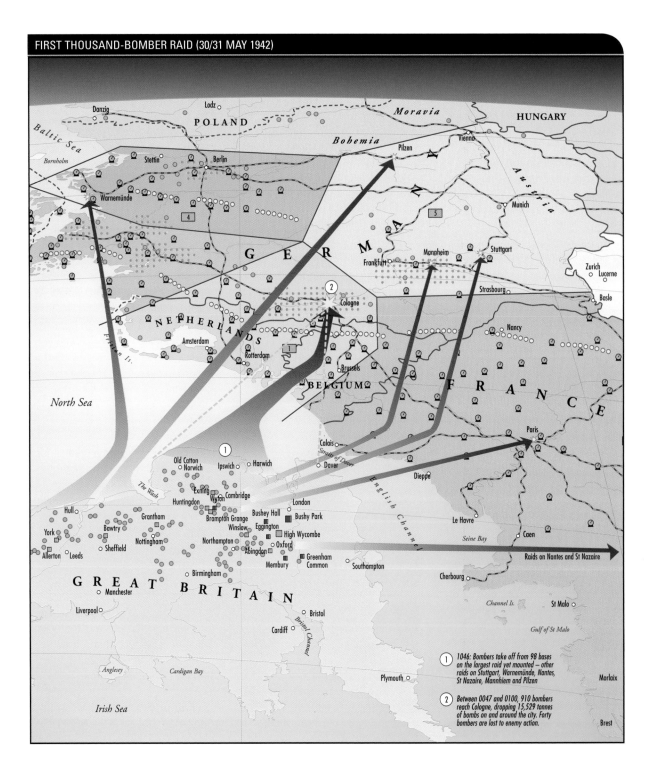

FIRST THOUSAND-BOMBER RAID (30/31 MAY 1942)

① 1046: Bombers take off from 98 bases on the largest raid yet mounted – other raids on Stuttgart, Warnemünde, Nantes, St Nazaire, Mannhiem and Pilzen

② Between 0047 and 0100, 910 bombers reach Cologne, dropping 15,529 tonnes of bombs on and around the city. Forty bombers are lost to enemy action.

The Americans began the build-up of forces in Britain, codenamed Operation *Bolero*, sending a million men and substantial equipment. The mix included 21 groups of heavy bombers, out of a total of 69 combat aircraft groups, to be in England and ready for operations over Germany by April 1943. The schedule was graduated, the first planes left the United States in May 1942 on their way to Europe. The 97th Bomb Group, with the 1st Fighter Group and 60th Troop Carriers, deployed across the Atlantic, flying the northern ferry route. The trip in itself was dangerous, the Army Air Forces

■ **Shortly after assuming command of RAF Bomber Command, Air Marshal Arthur Harris launched three raids against Cologne, Essen and Bremen, in each of which over 1000 bombers took part. To achieve this strength, Harris had to make use of aircraft from training squadrons, and it was to be some time before raids nearing this scale could be repeated.**

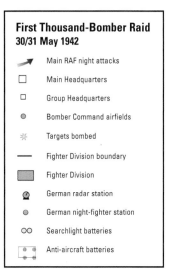

First Thousand-Bomber Raid
30/31 May 1942

↗	Main RAF night attacks
□	Main Headquarters
▢	Group Headquarters
◉	Bomber Command airfields
☀	Targets bombed
—	Fighter Division boundary
▨	Fighter Division
◉	German radar station
◉	German night-fighter station
◯◯	Searchlight batteries
▫▫▫	Anti-aircraft batteries

expected to lose 10 per cent of the planes on the trip across the ocean.

Redeployment
The initial deployment was actually more successful than expected, the American pilots successfully moving 386 aircraft to Britain by August, losing only five per cent of the planes. In July, eight planes were destroyed in bad weather over the Atlantic (the pilots survived). Forced to return to Greenland (their landing area in Iceland had fogged over), the six P-38 Lightnings and two B-17 Flying Fortresses ran out of fuel and crashed; it was the single largest loss of aircraft in the entire relocation. One of the P-38s was recovered in 1992, and was restored to flying status as 'Glacier Girl'.

The build-up was relatively slow; the Americans were not ready for combat operations in significant numbers until 1943. They did carry out minor raids on German coastal targets starting in summer, but the massive American bomber raids had to wait until the following year, when enough planes became available. The plans for mobilization and deployment of forces to Britain were continually revised. By summer 1942, the Americans promised to put 137 groups in Britain by the end of 1943.

New radar systems
In 1942, the *Luftwaffe* defensive forces facing the RAF were busy. They worked to increase their efficiency against the night bombers, as well as improving their defences. One such improvement was the Kammhuber Line, which was begun in 1940 and continually revised. By

1942, it was an important and effective series of defences against the RAF bombers. Based along the northern German border, facing Britain, it was a network of defences. The first line had overlapping Freya radars and searchlights to warn of bomber incursion. The radars were connected by landline to fighter squadrons, which were directed by radar to their targets. Before the development of radar units small enough for installation in aircraft, Ground Controlled Interception (GCI) was standard.

Another method of detection was the *Helle Nachtjagd* (Illuminated Night-Fighter) approach, where a single-engine Bf 109 (without radar) was directed to the British bomber stream by the ground-based, radar-controlled searchlights. Later improvements to the Kammhuber Line included Würzburg radars, which did not have the range of the Freya – 30km (18.6 miles) versus 100km (62 miles) – but were accurate enough for gun- and searchlight-aiming. At the same time, by mid-1942, the *Luftwaffe* began testing the new Lichtenstein radar system, a 75cm (29.5in) wavelength radar that was compact enough to be carried in aircraft. When Lichtenstein was fitted into Bf 110 and Ju 88 night-fighters, the aircraft could be guided to the general area of the bomber incursion, then find the bombers with their own airborne radar sets. This in turn increased the effectiveness of the German night-fighter force.

Technology race
One obvious outcome, similar to the history of Enigma and Ultra, was the

ALLIED BOMBERS COMPARED

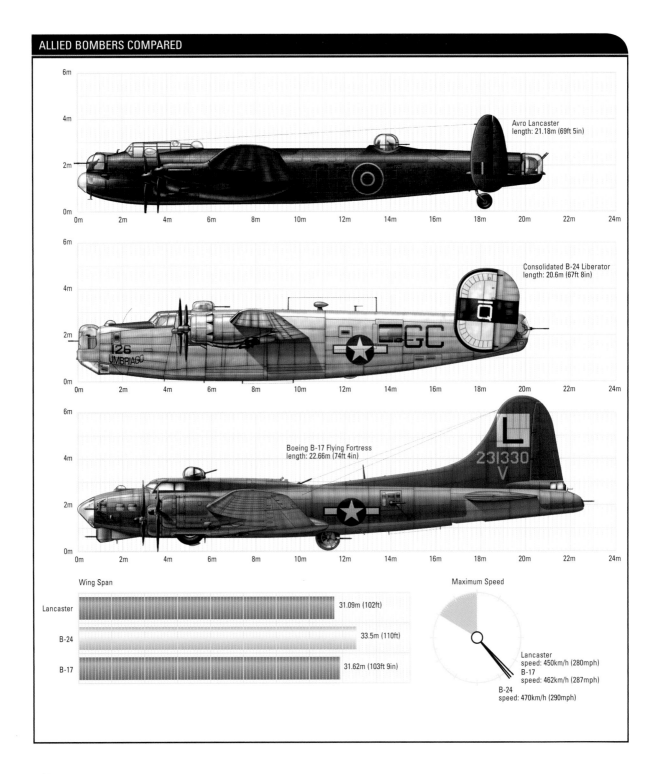

Avro Lancaster
length: 21.18m (69ft 5in)

Consolidated B-24 Liberator
length: 20.6m (67ft 8in)

Boeing B-17 Flying Fortress
length: 22.66m (74ft 4in)

Wing Span

Lancaster		31.09m (102ft)
B-24		33.5m (110ft)
B-17		31.62m (103ft 9in)

Maximum Speed

Lancaster
speed: 450km/h (280mph)
B-17
speed: 462km/h (287mph)
B-24
speed: 470km/h (290mph)

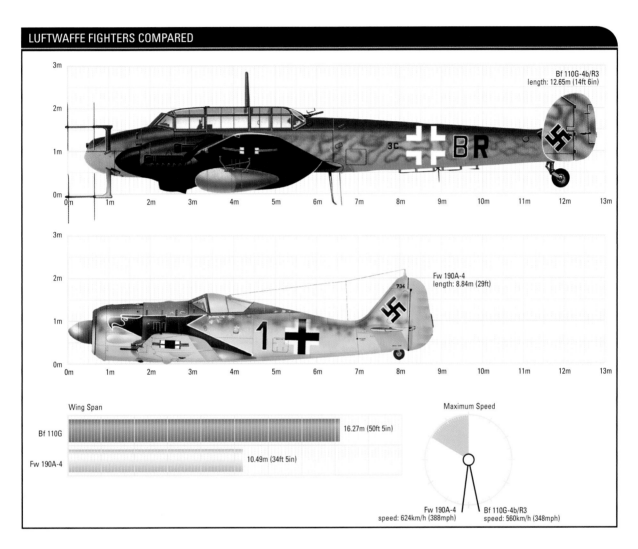

LUFTWAFFE FIGHTERS COMPARED

Bf 110G-4b/R3
length: 12.65m (14ft 6in)

Fw 190A-4
length: 8.84m (29ft)

Wing Span

Bf 110G — 16.27m (50ft 5in)

Fw 190A-4 — 10.49m (34ft 5in)

Maximum Speed

Fw 190A-4
speed: 624km/h (388mph)

Bf 110G-4b/R3
speed: 560km/h (348mph)

■ **Above: From 1941 to 1944, the Bf 110 was the *Luftwaffe*'s most numerous night-fighter, while the excellent Fw 190 was the most common air-defence day-fighter. However, as the Fw 190 was uparmed to give it more firepower against the Allied bombers, its performance suffered, and many became victims of the defensive fire that types such as the B-17 could bring to bear, which included 12 AA machine guns.**

constant struggle for supremacy in the night skies over Germany. Technological improvements were continual; the race for air superiority was also a battle for technological improvement. For the most part, it was waged in six-week to three-month increments, where the British would develop technology that was quickly overcome by the Germans. But in these windows, the battle was fierce.

The *Luftwaffe* continued improvement throughout 1942. Defensive measures were bolstered; new aircraft came online. The Junkers Ju 88, marginal as a medium bomber, had found new life as a night-fighter platform, and upgraded, radar-equipped versions were delivered. The twin-engine plane was sturdier and faster than the Bf 110, could carry more offensive armament and excelled as a night-fighter. The

Ju 88 did not completely replace the Bf 110 but instead added another effective tool to the night-fighter force. JG 1, the single day-fighter *Geschwader* assigned to air defence, also received long-awaited upgrades; their new machines were Focke-Wulf Fw 190As.

Daylight threat

With the American entry into the war, the Germans remained complacent. Göring was convinced that his fighters had driven the British from the daytime skies (they had), and that they would also drive the Americans into the darkness (they did not). He did not accept that American doctrine was 'daylight precision bombing' and did not realize the levels of US stubbornness. The Americans were going to attack during the day, and the Germans would be forced to deal with it. Göring's complacency led to another year of neglect of the daytime fighter defence forces for Germany; time sorely missed when the Americans began their heavy raids in 1943.

Fighter Harassment

By then, the first American bomber casualties had already occurred. On 6 September 1942, a force of 30 B-17s targeted the Potez aircraft factory at Meaulte in northern France. Their escort of Spitfire Mk IXs from No. 133 'Eagle Squadron' was dispersed by German fighters, and the bombers faced the defences alone.

The Americans thought that the answer to daylight precision bombing lay in bombers being able to protect each other in 'Self-Supporting Bomber Boxes'; B-17s and B-24s

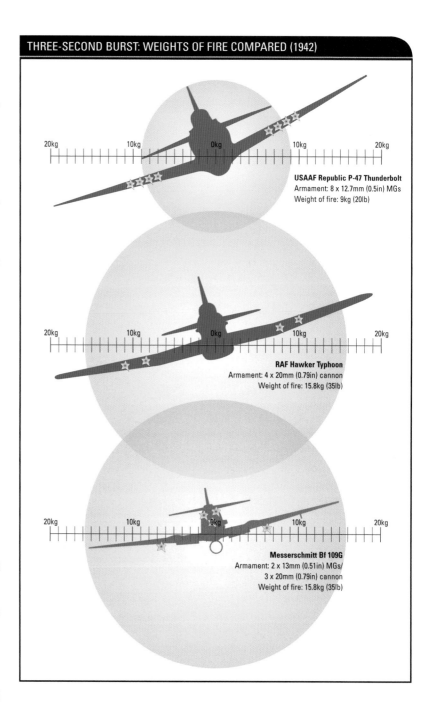

THREE-SECOND BURST: WEIGHTS OF FIRE COMPARED (1942)

20kg 10kg 0kg 10kg 20kg

USAAF Republic P-47 Thunderbolt
Armament: 8 x 12.7mm (0.5in) MGs
Weight of fire: 9kg (20lb)

20kg 10kg 0kg 10kg 20kg

RAF Hawker Typhoon
Armament: 4 x 20mm (0.79in) cannon
Weight of fire: 15.8kg (35lb)

20kg 10kg 0kg 10kg 20kg

Messerschmitt Bf 109G
Armament: 2 x 13mm (0.51in) MGs/
3 x 20mm (0.79in) cannon
Weight of fire: 15.8kg (35lb)

■ **An aircraft's weight of fire became more important as the war progressed. This diagram shows the firepower of a three-second burst from the US Republic P-47, the RAF Hawker Typhoon and the later model *Luftwaffe* Bf 109G.**

therefore bristled with defensive machine guns. The consensus was that by flying in tight formation the bombers could shield themselves without escorts – the 'Little Friends' (escort fighters) were nice but unnecessary – and would be able to drop bombs with precision in daylight, increasing damage to German industry and avoiding the moral ambiguity of area bombing.

On this day, though, the American pilots realized that there might be a hitch in their doctrine. It came in the form of JG 1 and JG 26 fighters. Fifty Bf 109s and Fw 190s attacked the American formation when it crossed into France, and harassed the planes all the way back to the Channel on their return. Nearly all of the bombers had some form of damage from the incessant fighter attacks: JG 26 had the first and second victories over American bombers; JG 1 added another two. The *Luftwaffe* also claimed three Spitfires, for the loss of two aircraft (one pilot killed).

The Americans refused to concede the daylight, while the German

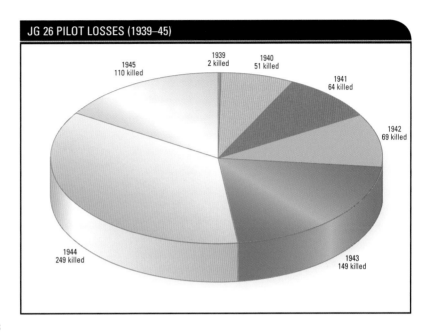

JG 26 PILOT LOSSES (1939–45)

1939 2 killed
1940 51 killed
1941 64 killed
1942 69 killed
1943 149 killed
1944 249 killed
1945 110 killed

defences continued to evolve. The American bombers were incredibly resilient; German fighters improved their destructiveness. The daytime battle for air superiority over Germany continued with (mostly) single-engine fighters taking on the Americans over the Reich. By the end of 1942, the Americans had added a mere 1525 tonnes (1500 tons) of bombs dropped on Germany but had tested their equipment, their doctrine and the German defences. With Operation *Torch* (the invasion of North Africa) and the war against the Soviet Union on the Eastern Front also in progress, the Allies prepared to close in on Germany.

1943: Combined Bomber Offensive

The new year brought significant changes to the operational practice of the strategic bombing of Germany. The British and Americans decided to combine efforts in order to reduce the Germans with air power.

The first decision came in January 1943 at the Casablanca Conference, which directed that the day (American) and night (British) efforts be coordinated as the Combined Bomber Offensive (CBO). Priority targets included the German aircraft industry and submarine facilities.

As the war had progressed, the British had continually ramped up bombing efforts over Germany; in 1942 the RAF had dropped more than 45,720 tonnes (45,000 tons) of bombs. 'Bomber' Harris, determined to crush the Germans' will to fight, had

COMBINED BOMBER OFFENSIVE (1943)

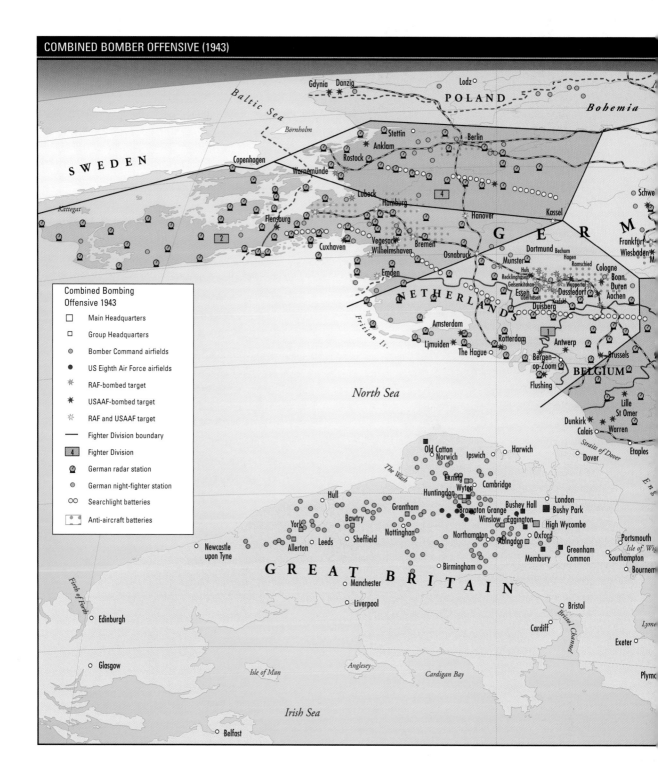

Combined Bombing Offensive 1943

- ☐ Main Headquarters
- ▫ Group Headquarters
- ● Bomber Command airfields
- ● US Eighth Air Force airfields
- ✳ RAF-bombed target
- ✱ USAAF-bombed target
- ✳ RAF and USAAF target
- — Fighter Division boundary
- [4] Fighter Division
- ⊘ German radar station
- ● German night-fighter station
- ∞ Searchlight batteries
- ⊡ Anti-aircraft batteries

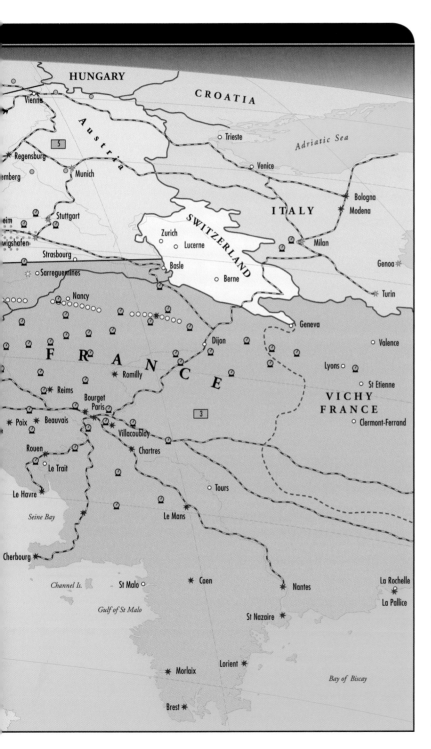

■ From 1943 onwards, strategic bombing operations against Germany and targets in occupied territories were carried out both day and night by the British and American bomber fleets. American operations were hampered by the lack of escort fighters until late in 1943, but once these were provided, they allowed effective operations against the German capital to be undertaken.

launched the first thousand-bomber raid on the night of 30/31 May 1942. Targeting Cologne, and using nearly every plane he had to achieve the numbers, Harris raised the bar for strategic bombing. That night, the 1000 bombers flew in 'bomber stream' formation, in which squadrons followed one another to the target in a continuous flow of aircraft. The first bombers released their bombs just after midnight, and the bombing continued for 90 minutes until the last of the aircraft flew over the city.

One reason for the number of bombers was to overwhelm German defences and reduce losses. Another reason was to cause as much devastation to the city as possible, hoping to prove it could be done. The RAF dropped 1480 tonnes (1455 tons) of bombs in one night (868 bombers actually made it to the target); over 12,000 non-residential buildings were damaged, including 3300 reported destroyed, while 13,000 homes were levelled and twice as many damaged. Four hundred civilians were killed, another 60 military personnel died, 5000 were injured and 45,000 were homeless. The RAF lost 44 aircraft in the raid (of an initial force of 1047), for a loss rate of 4.2 per cent; well within the margin of acceptability for Harris. Four of these were brought down by *Luftwaffe* night-fighters.

Firestorm

Yet the devastation and casualties occasioned by the RAF's 1942 Cologne raid paled by contrast with the CBO operation against Hamburg in July 1943. Operation *Gomorrah*, in which the Americans bombed by day and the British by night, was designed to destroy the city and its military industries. In addition to the shipyards, Hamburg housed submarine facilities and other military industry as well as oil refineries.

The raids began on the night of 24 July and bombing took place on eight days and seven nights until 3 August. On the first night of the campaign, RAF bombers released strips of aluminum foil, cut to specific lengths to confuse the German radars. Codenamed 'Window', the counter-measure was effective; the German radar could not see the bombers and could not target them. The 791 RAF aircraft dropped a mix of high explosive and incendiary bombs on the city; the new H2S ground-mapping radar aided accuracy.

About 1500 people were killed and the centre of the city was flattened in the first night's attack. Because of Window, only 12 RAF aircraft were lost. The next day, about 100 USAAF bombers attacked the submarine pens, followed by a similar attack the on the 26th. On the night of the 27th, 787 RAF bombers bombed the city again, targeting the centre of town with their H2S radars. Because of unusually dry conditions, a firestorm

erupted, causing more damage than the bombs. An estimated 40,000 people died in the conflagration.

On the 29th, another 777 RAF bombers visited the city, but rebombed burned-out portions,

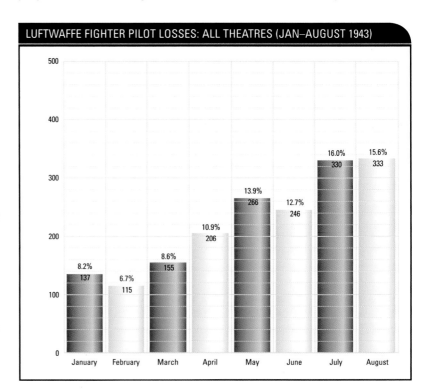

LUFTWAFFE FIGHTER PILOT LOSSES: ALL THEATRES (JAN–AUGUST 1943)

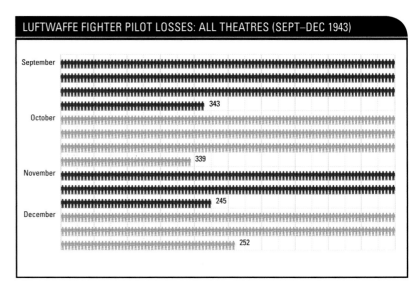

LUFTWAFFE FIGHTER PILOT LOSSES: ALL THEATRES (SEPT–DEC 1943)

causing little additional damage. However, German defences had overcome their Window problems, German night-fighter resistance was more effective and the RAF lost 28 aircraft (3.6 per cent). With no appreciable results, the RAF pilots were ready to shift targets. Harris was not. With a short pause for bad weather, Harris sent one more massive night raid at the city on 2/3 August. The raid comprised 740 RAF bombers, but the German defences had recovered; anti-aircraft flak and night-fighters shot down 30 aircraft, 4.1 per cent of the attacking force.

More than 50,000 Germans died in the attacks, mostly civilian casualties. Over one million were left homeless with the city in ruins. During the course of Operation *Gomorrah*, 3000 planes dropped 9140 tonnes (9000 tons) of bombs for a loss of 440 aircraft to flak and night-fighters. The city lay in ruins, and there was increasing concern in Berlin about the CBO, but the Germans fought on.

Schweinfurt and Regensburg
In August, the Americans targeted the ballbearing factories at Schweinfurt and Regensburg. The bombers flew unescorted, according to doctrine, as the Americans thought their bombers could defend themselves. The 230 B-17s sent to Schweinfurt had to fly the deep-incursion mission to the city, then return to England, which caused massive problems. The 146 bombers tasked for Regensburg flew a 'shuttle' mission; after bombing, they continued south to bases in North Africa. Of these, 120 made it to Tunisia, most with damage. Two

landed in neutral Switzerland with heavy damage – their crews were interned – and 24 bombers were lost.

The Schweinfurt contingent was met on its way into Germany by day-fighters from JG 1, 26 and 3, which had time to return to base and refuel after attacking the Regensburg raiders. As the massive bomber formation flew south, it was harassed constantly by more than 400 *Luftwaffe* fighters. Closer to Schweinfurt, JG 11 and 50 entered the fight, with a handful of planes from the night-fighter unit NJG 101. In addition, the bombers ran into heavy flak over the target, causing further damage. The stragglers became easy targets for the fighters.

The fighters from JG 1, 26 and 3 were able to return to base a second time and prepare for the bombers returning from Schweinfurt as they tried to get back to Britain. A number of *Luftwaffe* fighters flew three sorties that day. When it was over, 36 more American bombers had been lost to *Luftwaffe* fighters, a loss of nearly 16 per cent. On top of that, some of those that made it back to England were written off as 'damaged beyond repair'. The *Luftwaffe* lost 31 fighters and nine night-fighters. The raiders dropped

431 tonnes (424 tons) of bombs – including 127 tonnes (125 tons) of incendiaries – damaging or destroying a large portion of the Messerschmitt factory at Regensburg

LUFTWAFFE FIGHTER LOSSES (AUGUST–OCTOBER 1943)				
Type	100 %	60–100 %	40–60 %	0–40 %
Me 410	2	–	–	1
Bf 109	24	11	4	17
Bf 110	3	–	–	6
Fw 190	2	1	2	4

LUFTWAFFE NACHTJAGD NIGHT-FIGHTER ACES			
Pilot	Night	Day	Total
Maj Heinz-Wolfgang Schnaufe	121	0	121
Obst Helmut Lent	102	8	110
Maj Heinrich-Alexander zu Sayn-Wittgenstein	83	0	83
Obst Werner Streib	67	1	68
Hptm Manfred Meurer	65	0	65
Obst Günther 'Fips' Radusch	64	1	65
Maj Rudolf Schönert	64	0	64
Hptm Heinz Rökker	63	1	64
Maj Paul Zorner	59	0	59
Hptm Martin 'Tino' Becker	58	0	58
Hptm Gerhard Raht	58	0	58
Maj Wilhelm Herget	57	16	73
ObLt Kurt Welter	56	7	63
Hptm Josef Kraft	56	0	56
Hptm Heinz Strüning	56	0	56
ObLt Gustav Francsi	56	0	56
Hptm Hans-Dieter Frank	55	0	55
Ofw Heinz Vinke	54	0	54
Hptm August Geiger	53	0	53
Maj Prinz Egmont zur Lippe-Weissenfeld	51	0	51
Maj Werner Hoffmann	50	1	51
ObstLt Herbert Lütje	50	0	50
Stfw Reinhard Kollak	49	0	49
Hptm Georg-Hermann Greine	47	4	51
Hptm Johannes Hagner	47	1	48
ObLt Paul Gildner	46	2	48
Maj Paul Semrau	46	0	46
Hptm Hans-Heinz Augenstein	46	0	46
Hptm Ludwig Becker	46	0	46
Hptm Ernst-Georg Drünkler	45	2	47

as well as workshops at Schweinfurt. It was reported that the raid reduced output by 34 per cent. However, stockpiles in Germany meant that the Americans had not wiped out the targeted resource – ballbearings – and the German war machine rolled on. Nor had the Messerschmitt works been completely destroyed; fighters rolled off the production lines. But the Americans had lost dearly, above sustainable or rational losses; they would have to rethink bombing at the tactical level.

Operation *Crossbow*

One answer was to avoid the heart of Germany, which was well protected, and to focus on less central targets. Operation *Crossbow* targeted the German V-weapon site at Peenemünde, on the northern coast of Germany, where the Germans were developing the V-2 long-range rocket and the V-1 pulse-jet flying

bomb. On 17/18 August, the RAF launched 324 bombers to attack the German V-weapon facilities. The site was damaged and the consensus was that the raid had put back the German V-weapon programme by two months. However, the costs were high. The RAF lost 6.7 per cent of the mission (40 aircraft), mostly (29 of the 40) to night-fighters.

In October, the USAAF once again targeted Schweinfurt. In a similar raid to the August attack, another 228 bombers were sent to destroy factories. The raid, later known as 'Black Thursday', has become legendary in bomber circles. On that day, 291 B-17s were sent to Schweinfurt, and they were savaged by *Luftwaffe* fighters from six different *Geschwader*, 1, 3, 25, 26, 27 and 54. The Americans lost a total of 77 bombers (26.4 per cent), including 60 brought down by fighters. The *Luftwaffe* was able to achieve this

degree of success by its level of effort; nearly every fighter group in Western Europe was sent up against the Americans that day. The *Luftwaffe* flew a total of 833 combat sorties against the second Schweinfurt raiders. But in spite of the success, the *Luftwaffe* also paid dearly; 38 fighters were shot down. Both sides had serious rethinking to do about the course of the air war.

Long-range escorts

The Americans finally realized that they needed long-range escorts. British Spitfires could escort as far as the Channel and northern France and P-47s and P-51s could range to the German border, but once bombers were inside Germany, the escorts had to return home. The *Luftwaffe* would simply wait for the Allied fighters to turn away, then attack the bombers. After the losses in the second Schweinfurt raid, the

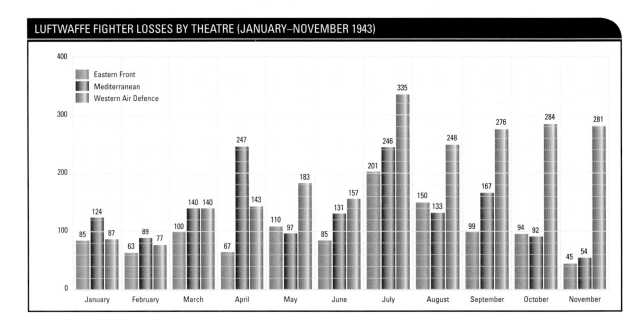

LUFTWAFFE FIGHTER LOSSES BY THEATRE (JANUARY–NOVEMBER 1943)

LUFTWAFFE FIGHTER LOSSES: ALL THEATRES (1943)

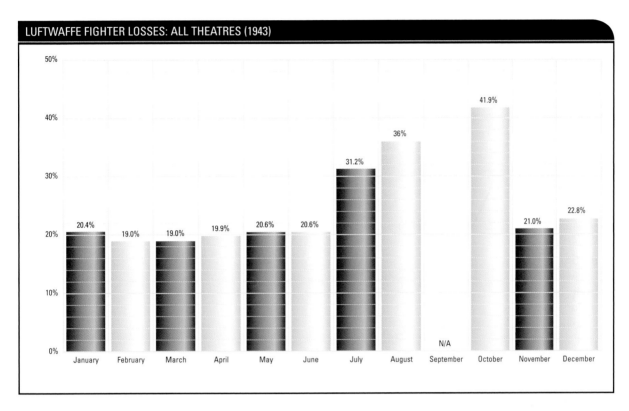

LUFTWAFFE AIRCRAFT LOSSES: ALL TYPES IN ALL THEATRES (1943)

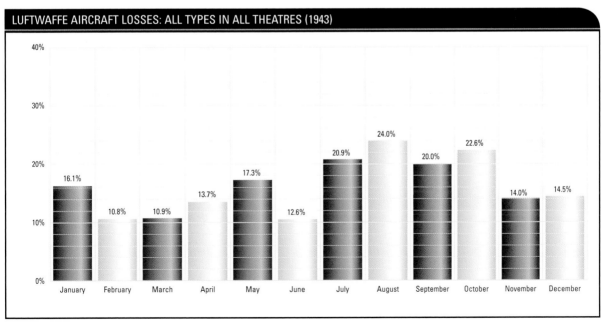

USAAF EIGHTH AIR FORCE HEAVY BOMBER CREW LOSSES (1943)

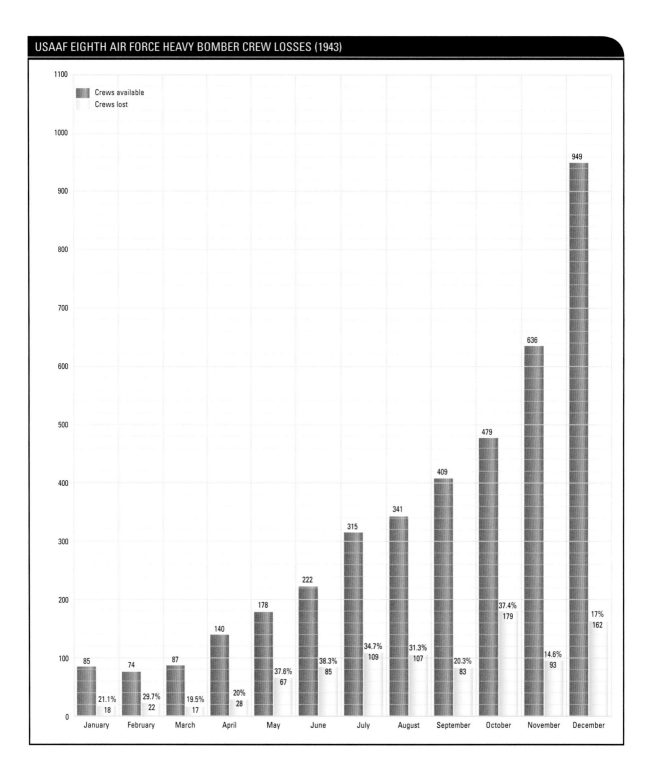

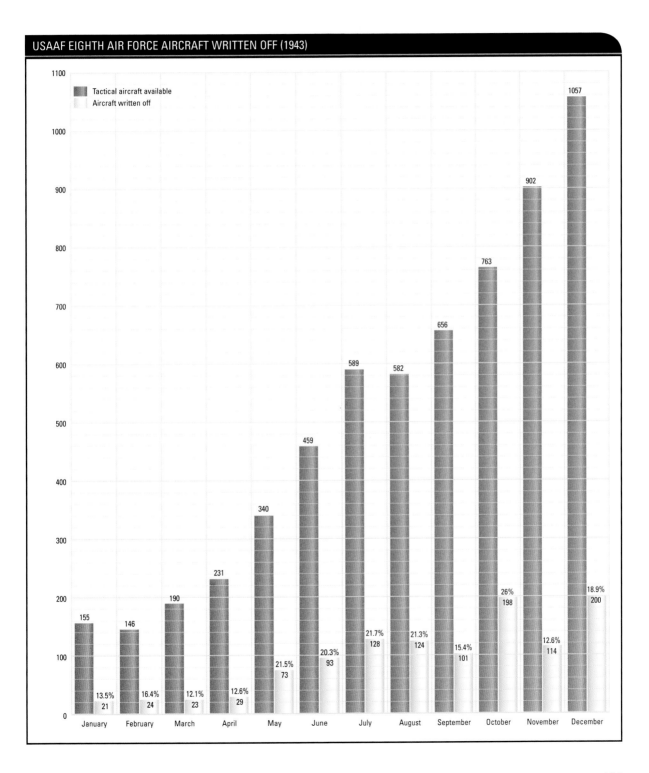

USAAF EIGHTH AIR FORCE AIRCRAFT WRITTEN OFF (1943)

Legend:
- Tactical aircraft available
- Aircraft written off

Month	Tactical aircraft available	Aircraft written off	Percentage
January	155	21	13.5%
February	146	24	16.4%
March	190	23	12.1%
April	231	29	12.6%
May	340	73	21.5%
June	459	93	20.3%
July	589	128	21.7%
August	582	124	21.3%
September	656	101	15.4%
October	763	198	26%
November	902	114	12.6%
December	1057	200	18.9%

American commander, Lieutenant-General Carl Spaatz, called off bomber missions until escorts could be organized. The reorganization proceeded quickly; the Americans resumed bombing two months later – with escorts – with a raid on Kiel on 13 December.

The Germans also revisited tactics and doctrine late in the year. *Generaloberst* Hans Jeschonnek, the Chief of the Air Staff, had committed suicide after the August Peenemünde raid. He had ordered night-fighters to Berlin to protect against what turned out to be an RAF feint, and was subsequently berated by Hitler for his incompetence. His replacement was *General der Flieger* Günther Korten, who advocated a stronger defensive stand in the skies over the Reich. His centralization of German defences was a great idea, and helped for a while, but it was a stop-gap measure as the Allies continued to increase in numbers and efficiency. In September, geographical boundaries for Reich air defence were redrawn for better efficiency against the CBO.

New rules, new discipline

The new *Jagddivisionen* of the *Reichsluftverteidigung* (RLV) focused and coordinated the fighter effort against bomber attacks, facilitating efficiency and effectiveness. New tactical rules ordered attacks on bomber formations first, to break them and defeat bombing runs. Pilots who went after stragglers and individual bombers before the formation was disrupted would face punishment. The centralization and coordination was designed to improve the *Luftwaffe*'s efficiency against bomber attacks. In October, Göring called a conference on the defensive fighter forces. He was becoming very angry with the *Luftwaffe*, and was under increasing

TOP LUFTWAFFE P-51 MUSTANG DESTROYERS

Pilot	P-51 Kills	Total
Maj Wilhelm Steinmann	12	44
Ofw Heinrich Bartels	11	99
ObstLt Heinrich Bär	10	221
Hptm Franz Schall	10	133
ObLt Wilhelm Hofmann	10	44
Hptm Emil 'Bully' Lang	9	173
Hptm Walter Krupinski	8	197
Maj Georg-Peter Eder	at least 7	78
Maj Jürgen Harder	7	65
ObLt Heinz-Gerhard Vogt	7	48
Lt Hans Fritz	7	12
Maj Erich 'Bubi' Hartmann	at least 6	352
Obst Walther Dahl	at least 6	128
Hptm Siegfried Lemke	at least 6	70

pressure from Hitler for better performance. Göring excoriated the *Luftwaffe* commanders, focusing on the poor morale of the pilot corps. However, Göring was by this point out of touch with his front-line pilots, responsible for most of the *Luftwaffe*'s failures in organization and effectiveness and his opinions were mostly ignored. His poor leadership and frequent outbursts did nothing for the benefit or detriment of the *Luftwaffe*; the pilots simply fought on as best they could.

Weight of bombs

By the end of the year, the CBO had dropped over 203,000 tonnes (200,000 tons) of bombs on Germany (British: 160,000 tonnes/157,000 tons; Americans: 44,700 tonnes/44,000 tons) in major raids on cities, industry and manufacturing. The industry raids convinced the Germans to disperse factories to more remote locations

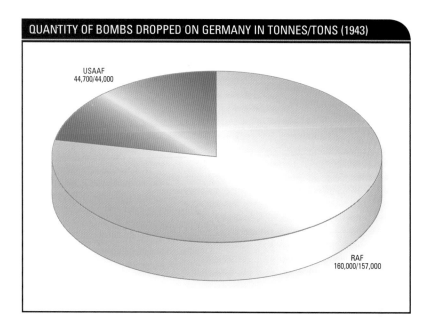

QUANTITY OF BOMBS DROPPED ON GERMANY IN TONNES/TONS (1943)

USAAF
44,700/44,000

RAF
160,000/157,000

and create smaller factories
providing the benefit of redundancy.
But the drawback was that German
industry grew more dependent on the
fragile transport network, which the
CBO targeted heavily in 1944.

By late 1943, the *Luftwaffe* was
starting to feel the weight of the
forces ranged against it. In addition
to the CBO over Germany, the war on
the Eastern Front was not going well.
The Germans had suffered severe
setbacks at Stalingrad and Kursk, as
well as in the Mediterranean. The
Allies were pressing from every side.
The *Luftwaffe* was caught in a war of
attrition against Soviet and Allied air
power; its most valuable resource at
this point was single-engine fighters.

Production war
At the end of 1943, German fighter
production was at just over 700
planes per month and rising.
However, losses mounted and the
CBO complicated the German
strategic position. By the end of
1943, the *Luftwaffe* was losing over
280 aircraft a month in the defence of
the Reich – though this was down
from a July high of 335. These losses,
combined with the other theatres,
represented over 20 per cent
operational losses per month – down
from 42 per cent in October (second
Schweinfurt raid) but still high. And it
was only getting worse for the
Germans; their industry was being
pounded but they had no way of
attacking their enemies. By the end of
1943, the Germans could not mount a
bomber raid against the British, to say
nothing of the Soviets or Americans.
The Germans would have to defeat
the CBO in the sky over Germany.

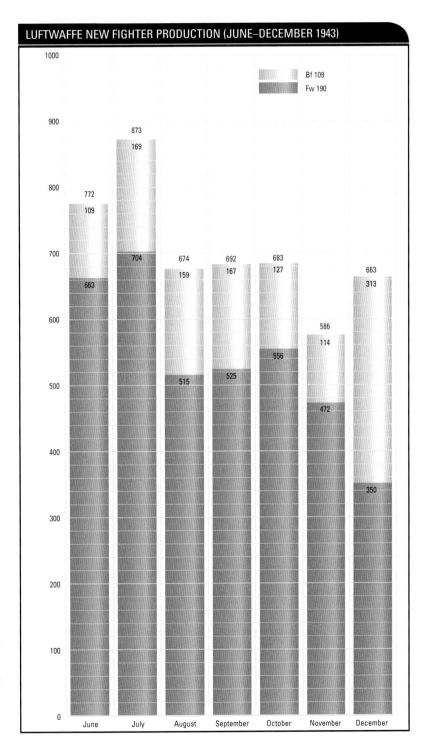

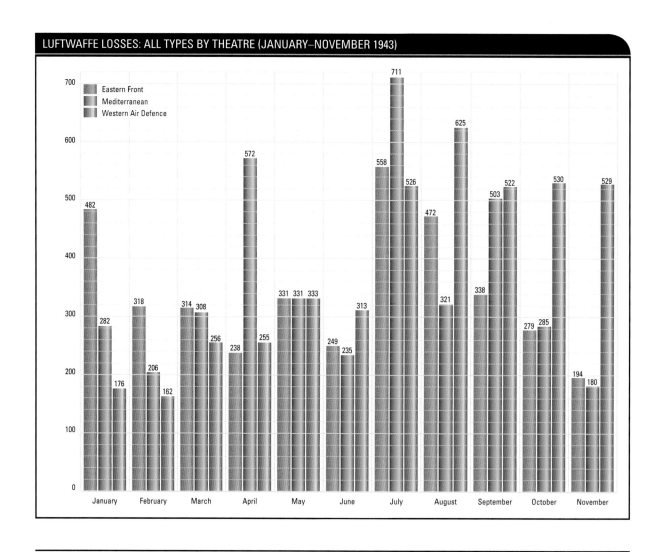

LUFTWAFFE LOSSES: ALL TYPES BY THEATRE (JANUARY–NOVEMBER 1943)

Legend:
- Eastern Front
- Mediterranean
- Western Air Defence

1944: The Decisive Year

At the beginning of the year, the Luftwaffe *was still in the fight. The service had just under 1100 fighters available for combat, with about half in the West and the other half scattered throughout other theatres: the Eastern Front, the Mediterranean and Norway.*

These fighters faced less than 900 operational American bombers (1200 aircraft but only 882 ready crews) and another 1200 British bombers of all types (including 650 Lancasters and 300 Halifaxes). The stage was set for the ultimate showdown in the skies over Germany. However, the war of attrition was in favour of the Allies.

Whereas the Germans were producing about 500 single-engine fighters per month, the Americans alone were adding 1000 bombers to their inventory. And German production was being bombed; American production was unimpeded by the war. As well, by the start of the year, the Americans had finally unlocked the secrets of long-range fighter escort with a relatively simple solution: drop tanks. The fighters (primarily P-51s) carried external fuel into combat, and jettisoned the external tanks when they entered combat. The result was that the escorts provided protection to the bombers throughout entire missions, fighting against the *Luftwaffe* defenders to, over and back from targets deep inside Germany. The addition of 1100 American fighters to the above bomber totals equalled a 4:1 ratio in favour of the US bomber offensive into Germany.

'Big Week'
American bomber raids shifted targets early in the new year. With the planned invasion of the Continent, the Americans decided that German aircraft production was the most important target, in order to destroy the *Luftwaffe* and gain air superiority. By February 1944, a massive effort was aimed at the destruction of German aircraft production. 'Big Week' (20–25 February 1944) brought massive attacks against German fighters, with the Eighth Air Force (from Britain) and the Fifteenth Air Force (from Italy) flying more than 3000 and 500 sorties respectively and dropping 10,160 tonnes (10,000 tons) of bombs. The mission was ultimately

successful; for the loss of around 200 American aircraft, most of the *Luftwaffe* twin-engine fighter groups were destroyed, and the Germans lost an additional 100 single-engine pilots and planes, plus a further 200 on the ground (at airfields or in production). To use another metric, American losses of under seven per cent destroyed almost 20 per cent of the *Luftwaffe*'s day-fighter force. And the Allies continued to dominate in the air. Allied numbers climbed while German numbers declined.

High-cost raids
In March, the RAF was pulled off a costly campaign against Berlin in which its losses were mounting.

'Bomber' Harris was determined to destroy Berlin by night but was losing aircraft at higher than anticipated rates. RAF losses went above the agreed upon five per cent, yet Harris was willing to carry on. Then the RAF bombers were given a slight reprieve when Harris was finally ordered to relent. They were retargeted in March 1944 to fulfil a counter-transportation campaign in preparation for the planned summer invasion of the Continent. Between March and May, the CBO focused its efforts on destroying the transportation network in northern France to prevent the Germans from resupplying the invasion site. At the same time, the Germans realized the

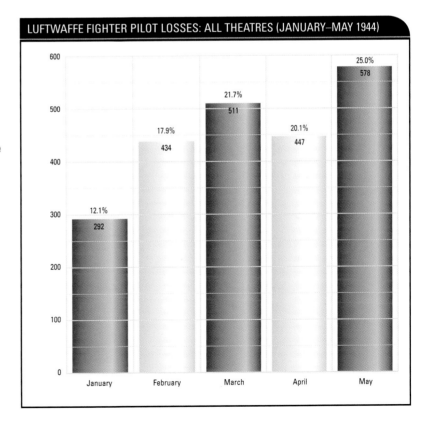

LUFTWAFFE FIGHTER PILOT LOSSES: ALL THEATRES (JANUARY–MAY 1944)

Month	Losses	Percentage
January	292	12.1%
February	434	17.9%
March	511	21.7%
April	447	20.1%
May	578	25.0%

LUFTFLOTTEN OPERATIONAL AREAS (MAY 1944)

UNITED KINGDOM

Luftflotte 5

Luftflotte 1

Luftflotte 6

GERMANY

Luftflotte Reich

Luftflotte 4

Luftflotte 3

FRANCE

ITALY

Luftwaffenkommando Süd-Ost

Luftflotte 2

■ This map shows the various areas over which the German *Luftflotten* had jurisdiction in the period immediately prior to the Normandy landings of June 1944. *Luftflotte* 3's zone covered all of France, Belgium and the Netherlands, a huge area to which the much-thinned *Luftflotte* could do little justice. It was neighboured by *Luftflotte Reich* (previously *Luftwaffenbefehlshaber Mitte*), which was responsible for the defence of Germany against the huge Allied bombing raids on its urban areas. *Luftflotte* 5 still occupied its traditional position up in Scandinavia and Finland, and would have little relevance to events following the 6 June landings. In the south, *Luftflotte* 2 (or what remained of it) covered Italy in a futile attempt to restrain the Allies' air power, and *Luftwaffenkommando Süd-Ost* defended the Balkans and the critical oil fields in Romania.

importance of the Allied strategy but continued to lose the war of attrition in the air night and day to the CBO.

By June, the Allies were pressing the *Luftwaffe* hard. At the start of the month, the Allies in the West had increased their numbers to over 2750 bombers and 1250 fighters available for combat (operational numbers were slightly lower because of pilot strength), plus another 1250 British bombers. Once again these numbers were increasing, but the important factor is that losses were declining. The Germans were simply shooting down fewer aircraft as the war dragged on. The defenders, understandably, had fewer aircraft, with only 991 fighters available on

DISTRIBUTION OF GERMAN FIGHTERS (JUNE 1944)

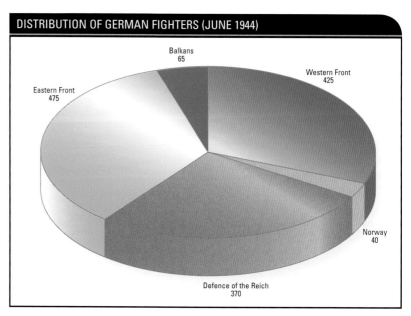

Balkans 65

Western Front 425

Eastern Front 475

Norway 40

Defence of the Reich 370

1 June 1944 to combat the Allied forces. These comprised 788 single-engine and 203 twin-engine machines, but with only 472 and 83 pilots fit for operations, respectively.

D-Day

On 6 June the Allies launched Operation *Overlord*, the invasion at Normandy. By this time, the Allies had achieved almost complete air superiority. On the day of the invasion, the Allies mounted over 15,000 sorties of all types (fighter, bomber, transport and paratroop-delivery) against the *Luftwaffe*'s 100. The tide was turning in favour of the Allied air efforts; the *Luftwaffe* was losing.

As the beachhead expanded, tactical fighters (P-47s and P-38s) were sent to forward airbases to harass the *Luftwaffe*. Meanwhile, the defenders' acquisition of further aircraft came to naught; the *Luftwaffe* lost almost 600 additional planes to Allied fighter patrols in the two weeks following the invasion. As the Allied bombers shifted their attention to oil targets, the *Luftwaffe* also began to suffer from lack of fuel for operations and training. As mentioned earlier, *Luftwaffe* pilots were given less training as the war went on, which meant that the Allies faced less experienced pilots in the skies, again increasing *Luftwaffe* losses.

Making every effort to overcome Allied material superiority, the German high command once again stepped in to fix the problem, but the measures were too little, too late. One solution was a focus on production. Fighters were given the highest priority, and materials were diverted to their manufacture. In the last half

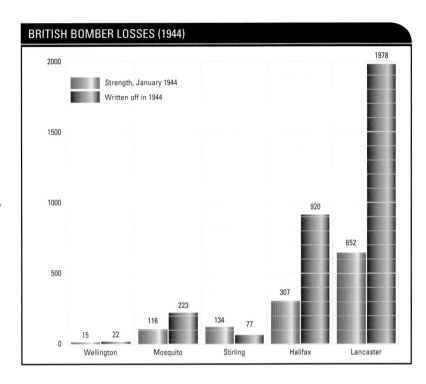

BRITISH BOMBER LOSSES (1944)

Strength, January 1944
Written off in 1944

Wellington	15 / 22				
Mosquito	116 / 223				
Stirling	134 / 77				
Halifax	307 / 920				
Lancaster	652 / 1978				

IX FLIEGERKORPS, UNDER LUFTFLOTTE 3 (JANUARY 1944)

Unit	Base	Type	Strength	Operational
Stab/KG2	Soesterberg	Do 217E	4	3
I./KG2	Eindhoven	Do 217E	37	35
II./KG2	Münster-Handorf	Ju 188E	37	31
III./KG2	Gilze Rijen	Do 217E	37	36
V./KG2	Athies	Me 410A	37	25
Stab, III./KG6	Melsbroek	Ju 88A	41	40
I./KG6	Chièvres	Ju 188A	41	37
II./KG6	Le Culot	Ju 88A	39	37
Stab, I./KG30	Eindhoven	Ju 88A	41	30
II./KG30	St Trond	Ju 88A	37	31
1./KG40	Châteaudun	He 177A	9	5
Stab, I./KG54	Marx	Ju 88A	41	28
II./KG54	Wittmund	Ju 88A	37	33
I./KG66	Montdidier	Ju 88A	37	12
		Ju 188E	?	9
4./KG66	Vannes	Ju 188E	12	?
I./KG76	Couvron	Ju 88A	37	31
I./KG100	Châteaudun	He 177A	27	21
I./SKG100	Rosières	Fw 190G	42	20

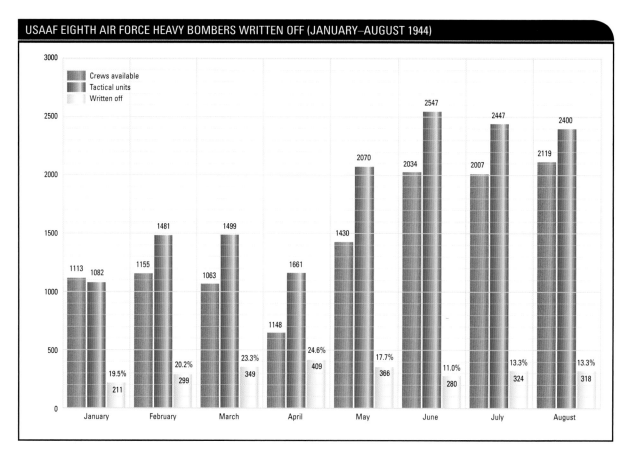

USAAF EIGHTH AIR FORCE HEAVY BOMBERS WRITTEN OFF (JANUARY–AUGUST 1944)

of 1944, fighter production actually rose, but the output was not enough to stem the Allied tide. During that period, German fighter production almost doubled, over 1943 figures, for single-engine fighters, with 12,000 Bf 109s and 4300 Fw 190s rolling off the production lines. But without experienced pilots, and with little remaining fuel, a number of these sat dormant on airfields awaiting Allied attack. German operational strength actually declined throughout the year.

New technology

The German high command's second response was high-technology

aircraft, equipment that Hitler hoped would be war-winning material. The German Army had control of the rocket programme; V-2s were launched against England and Continental port facilities. In the air war, the Germans introduced the first combat jet aircraft. The most effective and numerous was the Messerschmitt Me 262, a twin-engine air superiority fighter designed to drive American bombers from the skies. The first combat jet was plagued with engine troubles but was nevertheless an effective weapon against the bombers. Armed with four 30mm (1.18in) aerial cannons, it was a

devastating weapon in the right hands; unfortunately (for the Germans) there were not enough jets to counter the vast Allied material superiority in the air. The Me 262 (and follow-on types) were radical and novel, but the *Luftwaffe* had already conceded air superiority to the Allies.

The Allies ran rampant over the *Luftwaffe* and all of Germany as the year came to a close. In the West, the Americans and British (with a collection of other Allied forces) liberated France and pushed into Germany. In the East, the Soviets continued their drive towards Berlin, pausing briefly at Warsaw. In the air, the *Luftwaffe* struggled to combat the bombing. It could not, and the Reich collapsed around it. Losses mounted as the Allies bombed at will, further destroying German industrial targets and cities. By the end of the year, the situation seemed hopeless.

Ardennes Offensive

By December 1944, the *Luftwaffe* was on its last legs. Winter closed in, and the *Luftwaffe* counted its losses. In 1944, it had lost over 250 per cent of its operational strength. In other words, fighter defences had been destroyed two-and-a-half times over in the last full year of the war. Although numbers are lacking for the last half of the year, it is clear that *Luftwaffe* strength was all but shattered in the closing days of 1944. The Allies controlled the skies, were in the process of taking the land and stood poised to invade the Reich.

In a last-ditch effort to stop the ongoing Allied offensive in the West, Hitler planned an all-out attack. The Ardennes Offensive began on 16 December, aimed at Antwerp, to sever the Allied supply lines and drive a wedge between the Americans and British. With a fury not seen for years, the majority of the remaining German combat forces launched a winter attack. Marshalling the last of his fighters in the West, Göring promised the *Führer* 'victory or death'. Launching a massive offensive in bad weather on the 17th, *Luftwaffe* fighters from the remaining *Jagdgeschwader* (1, 2, 3, 4, 6, 26, 27, 54 and 77) attacked Allied airfields and supply depots. A number of Allied targets were hit, some with fairly significant damage, but in the end the

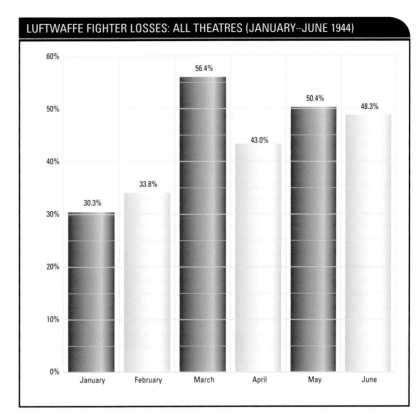

LUFTWAFFE FIGHTER LOSSES: ALL THEATRES (JANUARY–JUNE 1944)

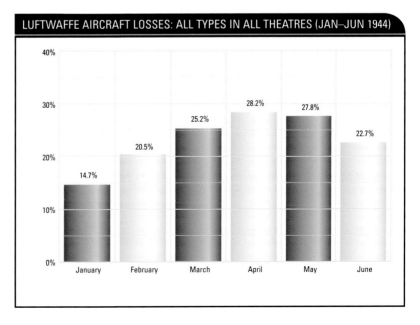

LUFTWAFFE AIRCRAFT LOSSES: ALL TYPES IN ALL THEATRES (JAN–JUN 1944)

USAAF FIGHTERS COMPARED

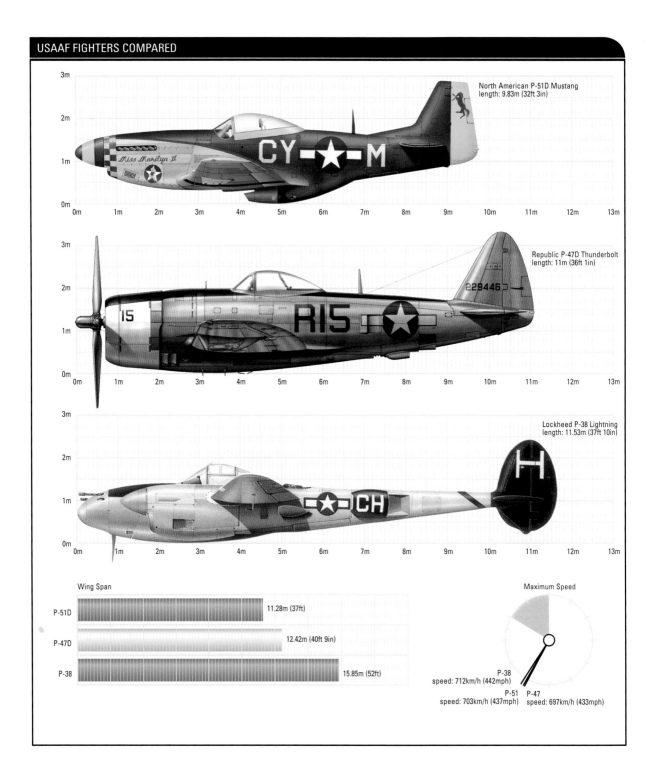

North American P-51D Mustang
length: 9.83m (32ft 3in)

Republic P-47D Thunderbolt
length: 11m (36ft 1in)

Lockheed P-38 Lightning
length: 11.53m (37ft 10in)

Wing Span

P-51D — 11.28m (37ft)

P-47D — 12.42m (40ft 9in)

P-38 — 15.85m (52ft)

Maximum Speed

P-38
speed: 712km/h (442mph)

P-51
speed: 703km/h (437mph)

P-47
speed: 697km/h (433mph)

■ The heavy cannon of the newly developed Me 410 was able to engage US heavy bombers from a distance beyond the range of the B-17s' defensive fire. The Me 262, although well armed and much faster than any equivalent Allied fighter, had only minimal imact on Allied air superiority, since production never reached significant numbers. Mostly, the Me 262 was used in the ground-attack role. The ubiquitous P-51 Mustang, on the other hand, had extra fuel tanks that allowed it to escort Allied bombers all the way to Berlin and back.

FIGHTER ARMAMENTS COMPARED

Type	Armament
Me 410A-2/U4	Armament: 1 x 50mm (2in) BK cannon; 2 x 20mm (0.79in) MG 151 cannon; 2 x 7.62mm (0.3in) MG 17
Me 262A-1a	Armament: 4 x 30mm (1.18in) cannon
North American P-51D Mustang	Armament: 6 x 12.7mm (0.5in) Browning machine guns and two wing hard points for up to 907kg (2000lb) of bombs, rockets or external fuel tanks
Republic P-47D Thunderbolt	Armament: 8 x 12.7mm (0.5in) M2 Browning machine guns and two external hard points for up to 1134 kg (2500lb) of bombs, rockets or external fuel tanks
Lockheed P-38 Lightning	Armament: 1 x Hispano M2(C) 20mm (0.79in) aerial cannon, 4 x Browning MG 53-2 12.7mm (0.5in) MGs and wing hard points for up to 2272kg (5000lb)

LUFTWAFFE FIGHTERS COMPARED

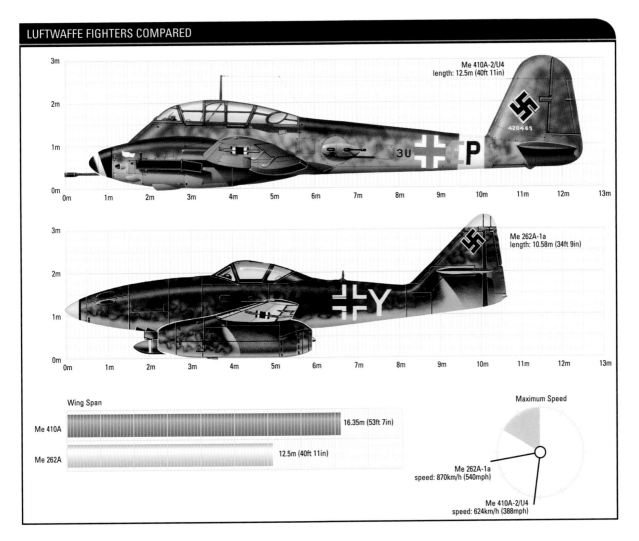

Me 410A-2/U4
length: 12.5m (40ft 11in)

Me 262A-1a
length: 10.58m (34ft 9in)

Wing Span

Me 410A — 16.35m (53ft 7in)

Me 262A — 12.5m (40ft 11in)

Maximum Speed

Me 262A-1a
speed: 870km/h (540mph)

Me 410A-2/U4
speed: 624km/h (388mph)

attack was ineffective. When the weather cleared on the 18th, American aircraft rolled out (and fresh ones were sent in from Britain) and quickly countered the land and air advance. In one day, 63 German aircraft were shot down, effectively halting the offensive as the Allies regained air superiority. At the end of the year, the *Luftwaffe* was in a death spiral. Holding materiel and air superiority, the Allies' final task was to extract a surrender from Germany.

■ In the final stages of the war, the *Luftwaffe* equipped some of its best fighters with rocket capabilities that were designed to counter the ever more heavily armed Allied bombers, such as the B-17 Flying Fortress. The use of rockets was an attampt to increase the weight of fire without having to uparm the fighters with cumbersome heavy-calibre guns. The Wgr 21 missiles were time-fused to explode 1000m (3280ft) in front of the launching aircraft. Because of the difficulty in judging this distance with accuracy, the rockets scored few kills.

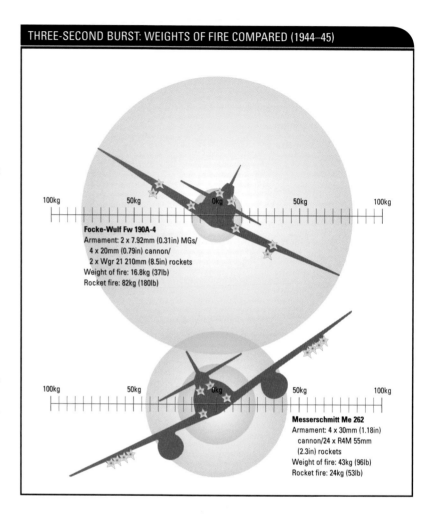

THREE-SECOND BURST: WEIGHTS OF FIRE COMPARED (1944–45)

100kg   50kg   0kg   50kg   100kg

Focke-Wulf Fw 190A-4
Armament: 2 x 7.92mm (0.31in) MGs/
4 x 20mm (0.79in) cannon/
2 x Wgr 21 210mm (8.5in) rockets
Weight of fire: 16.8kg (37lb)
Rocket fire: 82kg (180lb)

100kg   50kg   0kg   50kg   100kg

Messerschmitt Me 262
Armament: 4 x 30mm (1.18in)
cannon/24 x R4M 55mm
(2.3in) rockets
Weight of fire: 43kg (96lb)
Rocket fire: 24kg (53lb)

Operation Bodenplatte: the Final Offensive

On 1 January 1945, Göring launched a final offensive to destroy Allied air power. With the last of his air strength, including every aircraft from factories, training facilities and operational units, he launched Operation Bodenplatte *(Baseplate).*

In about 1000 sorties, the *Luftwaffe* planes knocked out about 200 Allied aircraft but in turn lost 300. Again, it was a case of short-term gain for long-term loss. The attack achieved tactical success for strategic sacrifice; the *Luftwaffe* could not replace its losses, whereas the Allies could, and did. *Luftwaffe* strength in the West was sacrificed in a few days, and the service was no longer effective against Allied air superiority.

Following the failed *Luftwaffe* offensive, the Allies continued to pound Germany. After the first few weeks of January, the Allies had complete air supremacy and bombed and attacked at will. German

■ **Taken in the summer of 1944, this photograph shows an Me 262A-1a from *Erprobungskommando* (EKdo) 262, the operational test detachment established the previous year.**

LUFTWAFFENKOMMANDO WEST (JANUARY 1945)

Unit	Type	Strength	Operational	Unit	Type	Strength	Operational
Stab/JG1	Fw 190	5	4	Stab/JG53	Bf 109	4	1
I./JG1	Fw 190	27	22	II./JG53	Bf 109	46	29
II./JG1	Fw 190	40	30	III./JG53	Bf 109	39	25
III./JG1	Fw 190	40	35	IV./JG53	Bf 109	46	34
Stab/JG2	Fw 190	4	3	III./JG54	Fw 190D	47	31
I./JG2	Fw 190	28	23	IV./JG54	Fw 190	50	39
II./JG2	Fw 190	3	2	Stab/JG77	Bf 109	2	1
III./JG2	Fw 190	19	6	I./JG77	Bf 109	43	24
I./JG3	Bf 109	31	22	II./JG77	Bf 109	32	20
III./JG3	Bf 109	32	26	III./JG77	Bf 109	10	7
IV.(St)/JG3	Fw 190A	35	24	Stab/LG1	Ju 88A	1	1
Stab/JG4	Fw 190A	2	1	I./LG1	Ju 88A	29	25
I./JG4	Bf 109	41	33	II./LG1	Ju 88A	34	29
II.(St)/JG4	Fw 190A	25	18	Stab/KG51	Me 262A	1	0
III./JG4	Bf 109	13	10	I./KG51	Me 262A	51	37
IV./JG4	Bf 109	26	17	Stab/KG53	He 111H	1	1
Stab/JG11	Fw 190	7	6	I./KG53	He III/V.1	1	1
I./JG11	Fw 190	23	20	II./KG53	He III/V.1	37	25
II./JG11	Bf 109	37	31	III./KG53	He III/V.1	30	24
III./JG11	Fw 190	42	26	I./KG66	Ju 88A	29	17
Stab/JG26	Fw 190	3	3	III./KG76	Ar 234A	12	11
I./JG26	Fw 190	60	36	Stab/SG4	Fw 190F	49	17
II./JG26	Fw 190	64	26	I./SG4	Fw 190F	29	24
III./JG26	Fw 190	56	28	II./SG4	Fw 190F	40	36
Stab/JG27	Fw 190	2	2	III./SG4	Fw 190F	34	24
I./JG27	Bf 109	33	24	NSGr1	Ju 87D	44	37
II./JG27	Bf 109	25	20	NSGr2	Ju 87D	39	26
III./JG27	Bf 109	28	23	NSGr20	Fw 190	28	21
IV./JG27	Bf 109	24	22	II./TG3	Ju 52	50	48
				III./TG4	Ju 52	51	46
				TGr30	He 111H	10	5

transportation was forced to move at night; it could not move during the day because of roaming fighter-bomber attack planes. The Allies continued to bomb German cities and industry, including a controversial attack on Dresden in February. The city was burned in a series of raids similar to the firestorm in Hamburg. More than 1300 sorties, dropping 3960 tonnes (3900 tons) of bombs, burned the city; the raid was later chronicled by the American writer Kurt Vonnegut, who was a prisoner in the city at the time. The final raids against Berlin were mounted in the spring as the Soviets approached the city from the east.

LUFTWAFFE CASUALTIES: OPERATION BODENPLATTE

Unit	KIA/MIA	POW	Wounded	Aircraft Deployed	Staff Lost	Unit	KIA/MIA	POW	Wounded	Aircraft Deployed	Staff Lost
I./JG1	7	3	0			I./JG26	5	3	2		
II./JG1	10	1	1			II./JG26	4	4	1		
III./JG1	1	2	0			III./JG26	3	1	1		
Total	18	6	1	80	31%	Total	12	8	4	160	38%
Stab/JG2	0	1	0			I./JG27	6	1	0		
I./JG2	9	6	1			II./JG27	1	1	0		
II./JG2	3	1	1			III./JG27	2	0	1		
III./JG2	10	3	2			IV./JG27	2	1	0		
Total	22	11	4	90	31%	Total	11	3	1	85	18%
I./JG3	3	5	0			II./JG53	5	2	1		
III./JG3	3	0	2			III./JG53	0	0	2		
IV./JG3	4	1	0			IV./JG53	5	2	1		
Total	10	6	2	70	26%	Total	10	4	4	50	36%
I./JG4	3	0	0			III./JG54	5	4	1	17	60%
II./JG4	8	3	1			IV./JG54	2	1	0	25	12%
III./JG4	1	0	0			Total	7	5	1		
IV./JG4	6	2	0			I./JG77	2	1	0		
Total	18	5	1	55	42%	II./JG77	1	1	0		
Stab/JG6	0	1	0			III./JG77	3	3	0		
I./JG6	4	1	1			Total	6	5	0	105	10%
II./JG6	5	2	0			ESt/JG104	0	1	0	3	
III./JG6	6	3	0			Total (day)	150	65	19	875	
Total	15	7	1	70	33%	Stab/SG4	1	0	0		
Stab/JG11	2	0	0			III./SG4	2	1	0		
I./JG11	4	0	0			Total	3	1	0		
II./JG11	6	2	0			FlüG1	1	0	0		
III./JG11	9	2	0			NJG1	9	2	0		
Total	21	4	0	65	38%	NJG3	3	1	0		
						NJG101	1	0	0		
						Total	13	3	0		
						KG(J)51	2	0	0		
						Total (other)	19	4	0		
						Grand Total	169	69	19		

Final Reckoning

Germany surrendered to the Allies on 7 May 1945. The Luftwaffe lay destroyed and the German armies were utterly defeated. Germany was to be divided and occupied by the victors.

However, it was a costly struggle. During the course of the air war, the *Luftwaffe* lost completely. By the end of the war, there were few planes and no fuel remaining. Specific figures are unknown; the destruction was complete.

US records

The Americans, on the other hand, kept detailed records. In the air war over Germany, the Americans lost 5548 bombers – 2452 to *Luftwaffe* fighters, 2439 to flak and 657 to 'other causes'; 27,000 aircrew were lost. The Americans dropped over 633,000 tonnes (623,000 tons) of bombs.

For its part, the RAF, mostly at night, destroyed 60 German cities, dropping 980,000 tonnes (964,000 tons) of bombs. The British lost over 55,000 aircrew and over 8300 aircraft in mounting 364,500 combat sorties.

Combined Bomber Offensive

It is estimated that the CBO killed 350,000 to 600,000 German civilians during the war; the numbers are disputed to this day. The CBO was effective in disrupting and destroying German industry, razing cities, annihilating the *Luftwaffe* and burning German oil production. In addition, it maintained pressure on Germany while the Soviets pressed from the east. The CBO was in the end instrumental in the destruction of Germany.

Göring, Hitler and other leaders had much to answer for. While the *Luftwaffe* had begun the war with vast fleets of the latest aircraft, piloted by some of the world's most talented and experienced combat pilots, the German air force ended the war with isolated aircraft, piloted by ill-trained crews, flying virtual suicide missions over the ruins of an utterly devastated country.

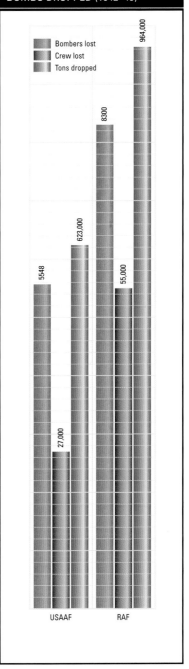

USAAF AND RAF BOMBER AND CREW LOSSES, AND TONS OF BOMBS DROPPED (1942–45)

Legend:
- Bombers lost
- Crew lost
- Tons dropped

USAAF: 5548, 27,000, 623,000
RAF: 8300, 55,000, 964,000

ALLIED BOMBER LOSSES (JANUARY 1944–APRIL 1945)		
Date	RAF Bomber Command	US Eighth Air Force
Jan 1944	314	203
Feb 1944	199	271
Mar 1944	283	345
Apr 1944	214	420
May 1944	274	376
Jun 1944	305	320
Jul 1944	241	352
Aug 1944	221	331
Sep 1944	137	374
Oct 1944	127	177
Nov 1944	139	209
Dec 1944	119	119
Jan 1945	133	314
Feb 1945	173	196
Mar 1945	215	266
Apr 1945	73	190

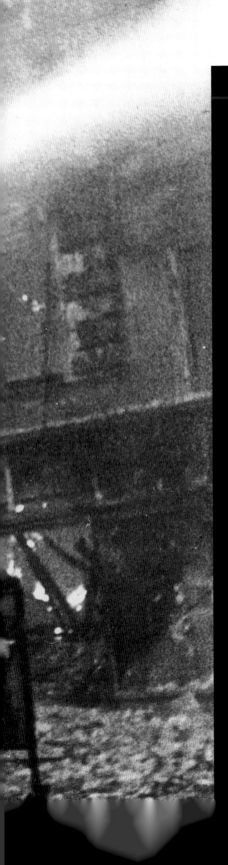

CHAPTER 9

Conclusion: Assessing the Luftwaffe

In the final analysis, the history of the Luftwaffe is the story of an organization that tore itself apart from the inside. The failures of the Luftwaffe ultimately led to the destruction of Germany, and the defeat of the Third Reich. In the modern era of mechanized warfare, the Luftwaffe failed comprehensively, with few successes.

What follows is a summary of the few high points and multiple low points of the history of the Luftwaffe from 1935 to 1945.

■ German firefighters tend to the flames engulfing one of the many thousands of buildings destroyed in Germany's major cities in 1943. The *Luftwaffe* failed to curb the activities of Allied bombers from 1943 onwards, or limit the destruction they wrought on German industry.

Luftwaffe Successes

In the early years of the war, from 1939 to 1941, the Luftwaffe *displayed tactical and operational prowess, introducing the concept of combined arms operations. With the addition of radios to planes (and to tanks on the ground), combined arms evolved into a successful method of operational attack.*

The vaunted German *Blitzkrieg* rolled over unprepared defences in the early years of the war, incorporating the following elements: surprise, initiative and overwhelming force. In early operations, the *Luftwaffe* first achieved air superiority, then led the charge at the point of the mechanized spear. This coordination was so successful that it was emulated by the Soviets, and later the Americans, and remains an important aspect of mechanized warfare to this day. By achieving air superiority early, the *Luftwaffe* could fly and attack at will, which often proved to have a decisive influence on the ground battle. When the *Luftwaffe* failed, specifically in the Battle of Britain, the Germans also failed, and could not achieve strategic result. In the final analysis, air superiority does not necessarily equate to victory, but it remains an important element in warfare.

Technologcial superiority

The *Luftwaffe*'s other success, primarily due to individual aircraft manufacturers, was superior platforms. Throughout the war, and especially at the end, the *Luftwaffe* had access to some of the best machines in the air. The Germans developed the first combat jet aircraft, thanks in no small part to the tenacity of Willi Messerschmitt and Ernst Heinkel. Their efforts, often in defiance of Hitler's wishes, led to the best planes of the war. However, in this technology, there were also failures; not enough emphasis was directed towards maritime aviation

assets, a comprehensive heavy bomber programme, or full production until very late in the war. Thus although the *Luftwaffe* had jets by the middle of 1944, production lagged, manufacturing quality was shoddy and in the end they did not matter. Only a few jets made it into combat, and they were not enough to turn the tide of the war. The Germans had exceptional equipment; in the end, it did not make a significant difference to the war effort. In an aside, the Allies were keenly interested in German wartime advancements and put programmes in place in the waning months of the war to collect German equipment.

The Americans began Operation *Lusty* (for *Luftwaffe* Secret Technology) to collect examples of German high-tech equipment in early 1945. Planes, designers, mechanics and engineers were rounded up and sent to the United States to continue building and improving German designs as the world entered the Cold War. Of particular interest were rockets and jets, technology that was transferred to the United States.

■ **The Messerschmitt Me 323 Gigant was a versatile cargo plane ahead of its time, capable of transporting men, supplies and vehicles. However, it proved prone to numerous technical faults that speeded its demise.**

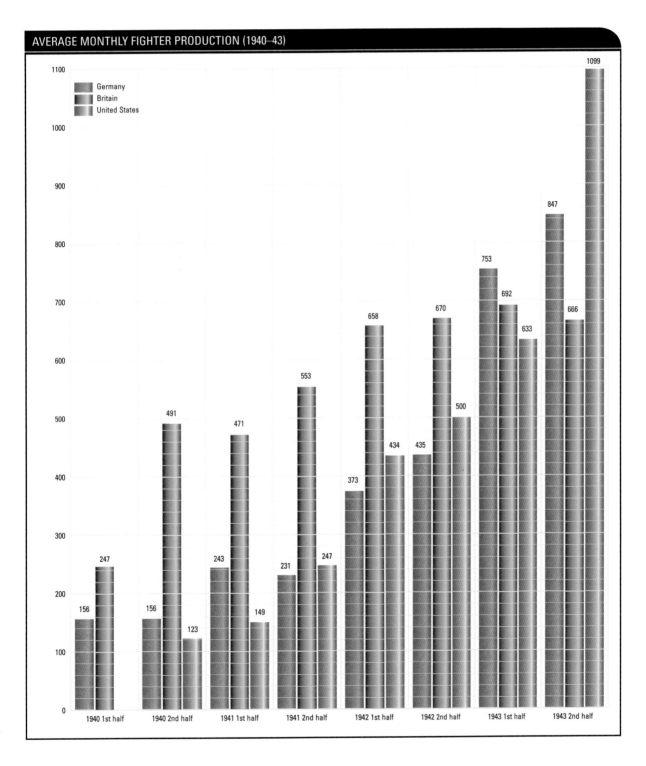

AVERAGE MONTHLY FIGHTER PRODUCTION (1940–43)

Germany
Britain
United States

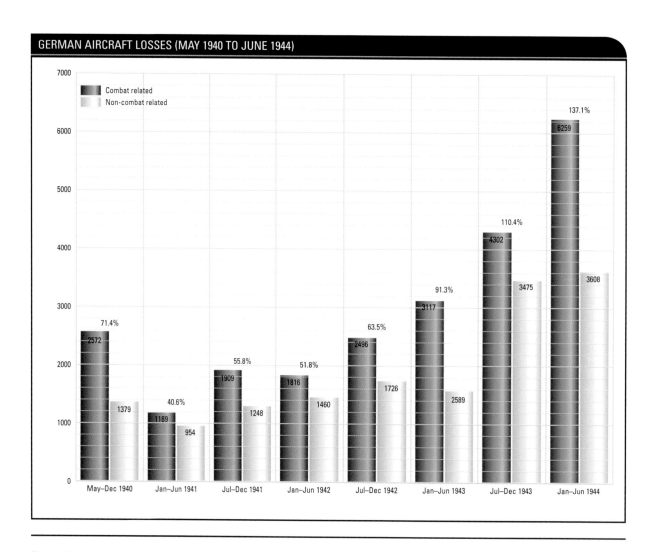

GERMAN AIRCRAFT LOSSES (MAY 1940 TO JUNE 1944)

Luftwaffe Failures

Hermann Göring was especially bad for the Luftwaffe, *and can be blamed for many of the service's failures.*

Although a highly regarded World War I fighter pilot, Göring, who held the unique rank of *Reichsmarschall* from July 1940, had no strategic sense, and failed as a leader. As the supreme commander of Germany's

air effort, he focused too heavily on tactics and fighters, and disregarded the benefits of strategic bombing, maritime operations and logistics. He also made extravagant claims that his service was unable to fulfil;

specific cases include (but are not limited to) his promise that the *Luftwaffe* could defeat the British evacuation at Dunkirk, his word that the *Luftwaffe* could supply the *Afrikakorps* from the air and his

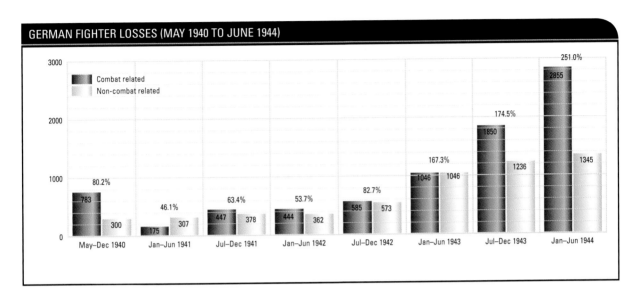

GERMAN FIGHTER LOSSES (MAY 1940 TO JUNE 1944)

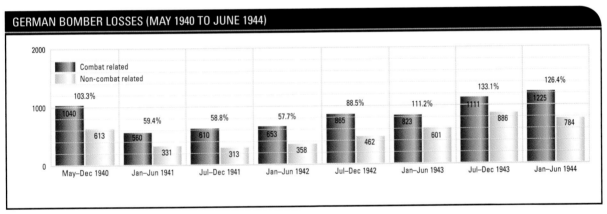

GERMAN BOMBER LOSSES (MAY 1940 TO JUNE 1944)

assurance that the *Luftwaffe* could supply the needs of Paulus' army trapped at Stalingrad. Göring's most spectacular failure was that he assured Hitler that his fighters could defeat the CBO, without providing coherent strategic direction, manpower, or material assistance for the construction or implementation of a successful fighter defence.

Fortunately for the Allies, Göring's spectacular blunders facilitated Allied successes in every theatre of the war as they won the war of attrition against the *Luftwaffe*.

Strategy
The *Luftwaffe* had no coherent strategy from the start of the war to the final collapse. There was little consideration of the strategic importance of air power, only tactical doctrine for combined operations. While this was important, when it came to aerial warfare independent of ground operations, the *Luftwaffe*

failed miserably. Beginning with the decision in the years leading up to the war to forgo strategic bombers, to the little effort put into long-range reconnaissance platforms for the maritime war, the *Luftwaffe* failed to comprehend the importance of aircraft in the strategic role.

With more effort, and better thinkers, the Germans could have produced a fleet of strategic bombers for use against Britain, the Soviet Union or in the Battle of the

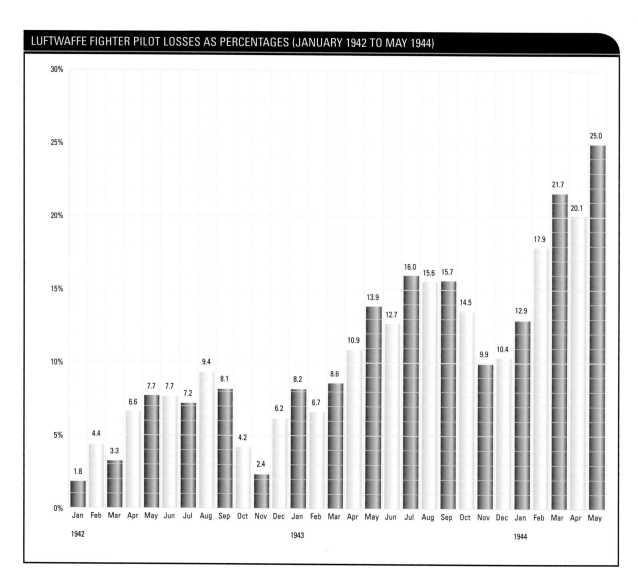

LUFTWAFFE FIGHTER PILOT LOSSES AS PERCENTAGES (JANUARY 1942 TO MAY 1944)

Atlantic; their use in any of these situations may have altered the course of history. Because of the lack of strategic thinking and guidance, the *Luftwaffe* restricted itself to tactical warfare and confined itself to ground support. The lack of strategic guidance resulted in defeat by the strategic-minded air forces of Britain and the United States. Without strategic thinkers, the *Luftwaffe* fought hard and well but in the end lacked direction and coherence.

Production and training
Production was a key failure of the *Luftwaffe* from the start. German aircraft production was good enough (barely) for short, decisive campaigns against inferior enemies; the *Luftwaffe* did well until 1942, with the exception of the Battle of Britain. However, once the Soviets became an enemy after 1941, German production was ill-equipped to face their material superiority, let alone the combined forces of the Soviet Union and the Americans once they joined in.

The Germans increased production and training but could not compete with the production capabilities of the combined Allies. The undefeated British, the massive resources of the Soviet Union and the newly arrived Americans were all immune from or had beaten off *Luftwaffe* (strategic) attack. Even though Germany built 120,000 aircraft during the war – with production figures peaking in 1944 – they were overwhelmed by the combined output of the United States, the USSR and Britain.

For example, the United States alone built over 100,000 fighters, and a total of 300,000 aircraft, during the war. Add 130,000 for Britain and 160,000 for the Soviets, and it is clear why the Germans were eventually doomed in a long war of attrition. Furthermore, German pilot training was hampered by long training cycles, a lack of pilots and a smaller population to draw from. The Allies each were a match for Germany; combined they were overwhelming.

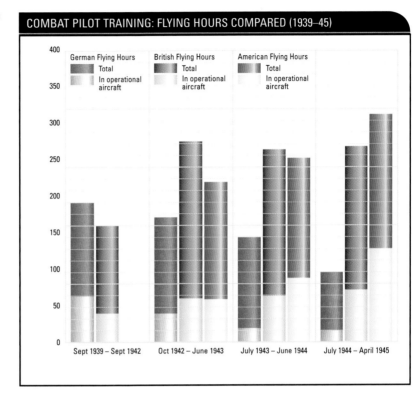

COMBAT PILOT TRAINING: FLYING HOURS COMPARED (1939–45)

German Flying Hours
Total
In operational aircraft

British Flying Hours
Total
In operational aircraft

American Flying Hours
Total
In operational aircraft

Sept 1939 – Sept 1942   Oct 1942 – June 1943   July 1943 – June 1944   July 1944 – April 1945

Geography
In short, the Germans ended up fighting in all directions. German troops and the *Luftwaffe* fought from northern Europe (including the Arctic Ocean, the Baltic and North Seas), to the Mediterranean and North Africa, to the west in the Atlantic and occupied France, and to the east on the Eastern Front against the Soviets. By not defeating Britain, the Germans left a path for British vengeance and American build-up, and left their flank unsecured.

In the south, the choice of a weak ally forced the Germans to expend resources across the Mediterranean and into the Middle East. But Hitler's greatest failure was attacking the Soviet Union, a vast world of determined manpower and resources fighting for its survival. Hitler's attack into the Soviet Union was in itself disastrous; when he launched *Barbarossa* without first securing his flanks, he doomed Germany to a three-front war of attrition. Had Germany faced a one-front war, it may have been substantially different, but with the Allies combined in a death struggle against Germany, the outcome was predictable, if not inevitable.

Ideology
The Nazi ideology of genocide, supported by the *Luftwaffe* in war, was ample motivation for the Allied cause. Hitler's determination to annihilate entire populations gave the Allies just cause and moral purpose for victory. The defeat of the *Luftwaffe* in the air and the German armies on the ground became a crusade for humanity itself and the preservation of civilization.

Summary
The *Luftwaffe* suffered from a number of serious failures, from high command to daily operations. Its successes were outweighed by its failures, and in the end it was defeated by a motivated alliance. The *Luftwaffe*'s role in the war should be studied to learn from this tragic episode in human history.

Maritime Operations

Germany had a long tradition as a belligerent naval power. Although its navy was not as large or important as the British or French maritime forces, the Kriegsmarine *became increasingly important as the war dragged on.*

During World War I, the German *Hochseeflotte* (High Seas Fleet) was a direct competitor to the Royal Navy but took part in only one major surface battle, at Jutland in 1916. At the end of hostilities, the bulk of the surface fleet was captured and scuttled as it sat interned at Scapa Flow. Indeed, the component of the German Navy that had threatened the Allies the most in the Great War was not the High Seas Fleet but the submarine arm. In the post-war period, the make-up of the German Navy was severely limited by the Treaty of Versailles, with submarines forbidden, but once Hitler's Germany began to rearm in the 1930s, so the German Navy concentrated efforts on developing a submarine force to counter enemy shipping in a *guerre de course*. Meanwhile, though, another type of craft had evolved that would have a marked influence on maritime warfare: the aircraft.

Maritime roles

As aircraft evolved, a number of maritime roles emerged for them to fulfil. Aircraft could undertake aerial reconnaissance and anti-shipping missions to assist fleet exercises and for protection. The British used aircraft in coastal patrol and fleet protection (the Fleet Air Arm), and the Americans and Japanese developed aircraft carriers for the same missions. The Germans, who focused on the importance of a submarine (U-boat) fleet, neglected the significance of the air component in naval warfare. Although aircraft could provide an important service in spotting and even attacking shipping, the Germans did not develop adequate resources materially or intellectually for the mission; German submarines went without air cover for most of the war.

When Göring took control of the *Luftwaffe*, he gained power over all air assets, even maritime reconnaissance. As a former fighter pilot, he saw the importance of aircraft as being in offensive ground attack, and dedicated resources and effort to their role in combined operations. Arguably, the *Luftwaffe* performed this role very well, at least until mid-1942. However, Göring neglected air power in maritime warfare throughout the war, leading to decreased effectiveness at sea. His support for maritime operations was lukewarm at best; he often assigned obsolete aircraft for an increasingly crucial mission. The *Luftwaffe*'s maritime mission was seen as a punishment; inadequate resources were committed.

With the opening salvoes of the war, the *Kriegsmarine* was tasked with destroying merchant shipping and the surface fleets of Britain and France. The German high command realized the importance of naval warfare; it had been one of Germany's failures in World War I. In the last war, the Royal Navy had blockaded Germany in a campaign that lasted four years and slowly starved the Germans of food and supplies. In 1939, the *Kriegsmarine* was determined to reverse the roles of the last war and blockade the British instead. German U-boats (*Unterseeboote* – submarines) were

FLIEGERDIVISION LUFT OST (SEPTEMBER 1939)				
Unit	*Base*	*Type*	*Strength*	*Operational*
Stab/KüFlGr506	Pillau/Ostpreussen	?	?	?
1.(M)/506	Pillau/Ostpreussen	He 60	12	10
2.(M)/506	Pillau/Ostpreussen	He 59	10	9
Stab/KüFlGr706	Kamp/Pommern	?	?	?
1.(M)/706	Nest/Pommern	He 60	12	11
1.(M)/306	Nest/Pommern	He 60	12	11
5./BFGr196	Kiel-Holtenau	He 60	10	10

sent out into the North Sea and the Atlantic to sink Royal Navy vessels and merchant ships in an effort to starve the British and force them to capitulate. The Battle of the Atlantic started on the first day of the war and lasted until the final German surrender. Historians have recounted in great detail the Battle of the Atlantic, but it is appropriate to provide some information here on the air component of the battle as fought by the *Luftwaffe*.

On the opening day of the war, the resources allocated by the *Luftwaffe* for naval missions comprised the *Seeluftstreitkräfte* (loosely translated as the Naval Air Arm). The command consisted of 14 *Küstenfliegergruppen* (KüFlGr – coastal aviation groups) and one *Bordfliegergruppe* (BFGr) of ship-based aviation. The 14 coastal aviation groups were divided into *Fliegerdivision Luft West* and *Fliegerdivision Luft Ost*, both under the command of *General der Flieger beim Oberbefehlshaber der Marine*, *Generalmajor* Hans Ritter, who answered to Göring, not to the navy. By the fall of France, when operations began in earnest in the Atlantic, *Fliegerdivision Luft West*, which was responsible for the waters west of Denmark, employed four types of maritime aircraft but had only 100 planes in operation. These aircraft were mostly floatplanes and maritime reconnaissance platforms, mostly for spotting but a few with offensive capabilities.

Battle of the Atlantic

France and Norway had fallen under German control by summer 1940. With the territory, the Germans gained

FLIEGERDIVISION LUFT WEST (AUGUST 1940)

Unit	Base	Type	Strength	Operational
Stab/KüFlGr106	Norderney	?	?	?
1.(M)/106	Norderney	He 60	10	10
2.(F)/106	Norderney	Do 18	12	12
3.(M)/106	Borkum	He 59	10	10
3.(M)/706	Norderney	He 59	12	12
Stab/KüFlGr306	Hörnum/Sylt	?	?	?
2.(F)/306	Hörnum/Sylt	Do 18	12	11
2.(F)/506	Hörnum/Sylt	Do 18	12	11
2.(F)/606	Hörnum/Sylt	Do 18	12	9
Stab/KüFlGr406	List/Sylt	?	?	?
1.(M)/406	List/Sylt	He 115	8	8
2.(F)/406	List/Sylt	Do 18	12	10
3.(M)/406	List/Sylt	He 59	9	9
1./BFGr196	Wilhelmshaven	He 60	12	12

valuable port facilities for U-boats, which extended their range into the Atlantic. It was possible to surround Britain with submarines and effectively cut off any shipping entering and leaving. Subsequently, maritime patrol aircraft took on increased duties as operations extended into the Atlantic. One important operation was rescuing downed pilots during the Battle of Britain. On balance, the Germans were more efficient than the British at rescuing pilots from the Channel; German pilots were confident that if their planes were damaged, they had a good chance of being rescued by German maritime patrols as long as they made it to the Channel.

Other responsibilities for the maritime aircraft included spotting vessels bringing supplies to Britain, including the increased shipping from the United States. After the fall of France, the Americans increased their support for Britain in the form of Lend-Lease; nearly all of the material

came by ship. The *Kriegsmarine* was determined to blockade Britain, in an attempt to starve it into submission. Aircraft assisted in this role not only by spotting ships, and later entire convoys, but also by laying mines, and on occasion bombing and torpedoing surface vessels.

As the war progressed, layers of bureaucracy hindered the effectiveness of German maritime aviation. In one example, *Fliegerführer Atlantik*, in charge of Norwegian and Arctic waters, had in its chain of command *Luftflotte* 3 (based in France) and also had to respond to orders from IV *Fliegerkorps*, while supporting the naval high command and the commander-in-chief of submarines. The convoluted command structure meant that messages went missing and unanswered and response times and actions were delayed; hindrances in a fast-paced maritime war. The main problem was that the *Luftwaffe*, and Göring specifically, did not want to give up jurisdiction over aircraft in any role, especially to another service (the navy). Service rivalries hampered efficient operations. Further, Göring underestimated the importance of the maritime role of aircraft, and frequently took from Peter to pay Paul. Maritime missions suffered

when he thought that planes were better used elsewhere; the Focke-Wulf Condor (Fw 200), an excellent maritime recce platform, was removed from maritime operations when Göring relocated it to relieve Stalingrad in the winter of 1942/43. This move inevitably led to attrition of

the type through operational erosion and combat losses.

Maritime aircraft

When used correctly, the Condor was an excellent maritime patrol platform. With impressive range – over 3500km (2200 miles) – it was an effective reconnaissance aircraft, capable of long missions. In fact, the Fw 200 was the first aircraft to fly non-stop from Berlin to New York City, as an airliner, in 1938. The Condor was used in the Atlantic to spot merchant ships sailing to British ports, directing U-boats to their targets. At the height of the Battle of the Atlantic, Condors were used for bombing ships and, while inaccurate, sank over 330,000 tonnes (325,000 tons) of shipping between June 1940 and February 1941. However, when the Allies countered with ship-launched Hurricane fighters or if Condors strayed too close to Allied airbases, they were vulnerable. The first USAAF victory of the war over a German aircraft was a Condor,

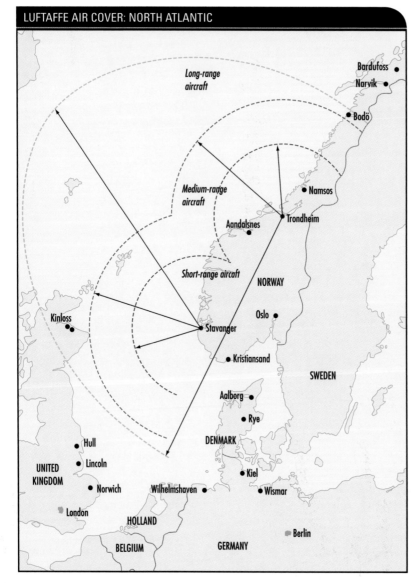

LUFTAFFE AIR COVER: NORTH ATLANTIC

■ **German airbases in Scandinavia provided strike capabilities against Allied shipping in the North Sea and North Atlantic. The map here shows the operational radius of various aircraft types. Short-range aircraft included not only any fighter types tasked for maritime support but also seaplanes such as the Arado Ar 196 and Ar 95. For medium-range sweeps the He 111 and Do 217 were ideal, as was the He 115 seaplane. For operations requiring range in excess of 3350km (2082 miles), there were flying boats like the Bv 138, Bv 222, Do 24 and, of course, the conventional Fw 200 Condor.**

MARITIME AIRCRAFT COMPARED

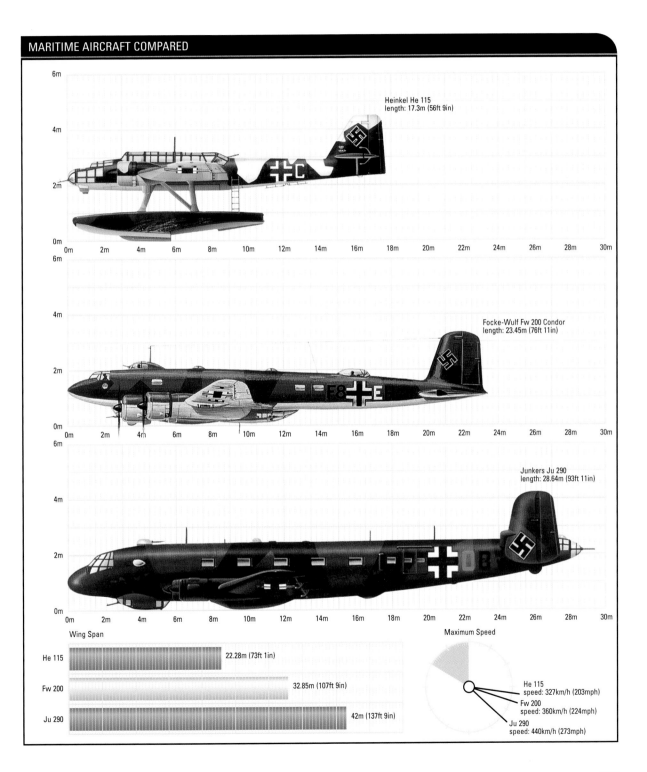

Heinkel He 115
length: 17.3m (56ft 9in)

Focke-Wulf Fw 200 Condor
length: 23.45m (76ft 11in)

Junkers Ju 290
length: 28.64m (93ft 11in)

Wing Span

He 115   22.28m (73ft 1in)

Fw 200   32.85m (107ft 9in)

Ju 290   42m (137ft 9in)

Maximum Speed

He 115
speed: 327km/h (203mph)

Fw 200
speed: 360km/h (224mph)

Ju 290
speed: 440km/h (273mph)

shot down by fighters over Iceland in August 1942. By late 1943, all Condors had been transferred to transport duties and replaced by Junkers Ju 290s. The lack of interest in a maritime patrol platform is shown by the low numbers built; in the entire war, only 276 Fw 200s were produced.

The Ju 290 performed similar tasks to the Condor but was available in only limited numbers. By summer 1944, when the Germans lost French airbases, operations were limited and

by the end of the year ceased entirely. The remaining Ju 290s were shifted to transport roles. A final mission envisaged for the Ju 290 was as a long-range bomber; this never materialized. The German anti-shipping mission suffered from both a lack of interest and a subsequent dearth of aircraft. In the end, the Allies won the Battle of the Atlantic because they were willing to commit the resources that the Germans simply were not.

The story of *Luftwaffe* maritime operations is interesting in that it is another example of too much bureaucracy and not enough interest. There were opportunities for effective use of aircraft in the maritime war which were simply overlooked at best, and ignored at worst. Göring's own ambivalence about the importance of the Battle of the Atlantic and anti-shipping operations resulted in a lost opportunity for the *Luftwaffe* in the grand strategy of the war.

Luftwaffe Ground Units

In addition to the air elements of the Luftwaffe, *there were ground-based* Luftwaffe *commands as well.*

The largest and most active were the anti-air corps, also known as the *Flakkorps*. It made sense to the German high command to have the units responsible for anti-aircraft artillery under *Luftwaffe* command, thus the *Flakkorps* came under the *Luftwaffe* umbrella. In addition to the anti-air units, the paratroopers (*Fallschirmjäger*) were also under *Luftwaffe* control. These specialist soldiers, who jumped from planes or landed in gliders, were integral to the *Luftwaffe*'s vertical envelopment doctrine. They gained recognition in the early battles for Norway and the Low Countries but were best known for their role in the invasion of Crete. Two further specifically ground-based troop types also fell under *Luftwaffe* command, the *Panzerdivision Hermann Göring* and a collection of troops under the command of the

Luftwaffen-Feldkorps (Luftwaffe Field Corps). In all, the *Luftwaffe* ground troops numbered about 1.5 million men by the end of the war; the anti-air troops were the most numerous with approximately 1.2 million.

Luftwaffe Flakkorps
At the start of the war, the role of anti-aircraft defence was assigned to the *Luftwaffe*. Troops were initially ordered to protect airfields, but anti-aircraft assignments were expanded after the initial Allied bombings. Eventually the *Flakkorps* were assigned to protect important industrial targets and major cities, and they took a heavy toll on Allied bombers. Flak units were armed with advanced anti-aircraft technology such as the powerful 88mm (3.45in) *Flugzeugabwehr Kanone* (FlaK, from which 'flak'). The '88' came in three

varieties. The Flak 18 was an 88mm (sometimes referred to as 8.8cm) cannon fixed to a cruciform base that could be folded, attached to wheels and relocated as necessary. The Flak 36 was an improvement, with a two-piece barrel and smaller but heavier base, ostensibly for better mobility. The improved Flak 37 incorporated directional technology for more accurate fire. Other developments followed during the war, but these three weapons were the staples of the *Flakkorps*.

In the early stages of the war, the *Flakkorps* protected airfields and followed the fighting to the front. Many flak gunners learned very early that the cannon could also be used very effectively in an anti-tank role, and the carriages were set up to allow a wider range of targeting, from nearly vertical inclination to attack aerial targets, to nearly horizontal to attack ground targets.

This practice continued with great effect in North Africa and on the Eastern Front, to the point that later in the war the Tiger tank was fitted with an 88mm (3.45in) cannon similar to its anti-aircraft counterpart. As the bombing of Germany intensified after 1943, more personnel were conscripted to the *Flakkorps*, which often employed previously wounded veterans, women and eventually teenagers in the anti-aircraft role. As the war progressed, the defences became more static, but the effectiveness also improved.

Flak batteries were constructed into flak towers around cities, searchlights were added and smoke generators obscured targets. By 1943, new flak guns were employed, with 105mm (4.1in) and 128mm (5in) weapons, using new radar guidance controls, protecting German targets. In painstaking detail, historian Ed Westermann chronicles the myths and legacy of the *Luftwaffe Flakkorps*. He argues that the *Flakkorps* did not take men away from front-line

LUFTWAFFE GROUND UNITS: MOBILE FLAK WEAPONS

3.7-cm Flak auf mittlerer Zugkraftwagen 8t (SdKfz 7/2)

CREW: 7
WEIGHT: 11.16 tonnes (11.06 tons)
LENGTH: 6.55m (21ft 6in)
WIDTH: 2.40m (7ft 10½in)
HEIGHT: 3.20m (10ft 6in)
ENGINE: Maybach HL62TUK 6-cylinder (105kW/140hp)
SPEED: 50km/h (31mph)
RANGE: 250km (156 miles)
ARMAMENT: Twin 37mm (1.5in) Flak 36/37/43 L/89

2-cm Flakvierling auf Fahrgestell Zgkw 8t (SdKfz 7/2)

CREW: 7
WEIGHT: 11.16 tonnes (11.06 tons)
LENGTH: 6.55m (21ft 6in)
WIDTH: 2.40m (7ft 10½in)
HEIGHT: 3.20m (10ft 6in)
ENGINE: Maybach HL62TUK 6-cylinder (105kW/140hp)
SPEED: 50km/h (31mph)
RANGE: 250km (156 miles)
RADIO: None
ARMAMENT: Quad 20mm (0.79in) Flak 38

2-cm Flak 38 auf gepanzerten leichter Zugkraftwagen 1t (SdKfz 10/5)

CREW: 7
WEIGHT: 5.5 tonnes (5 tons)
LENGTH: 4.75m (15ft 7in)
WIDTH: 2.15m (7ft 1in)
HEIGHT: 3.20m (10ft 6in)
ENGINE: Maybach HL42TRKM 6-cylinder (75kW/100hp)
SPEED: 65km/h (40mph)
RANGE: 300km (186 miles)
RADIO: None
ARMAMENT: Twin 20mm (0.79in) Flak 38 L/112.5

fighting, in that the personnel were not fit for field duty in the first place. Nor did the *Flakkorps* employ weapons better used at the front; it was not easy to translate anti-aircraft artillery to other uses, and the Germans had other problems with production of field weapons.

However, the *Flakkorps'* efficiency was impressive: they accounted for over half of the USAAF's losses in the war, forced the bombers to miss targets and caused psychological damage to the aircrews who faced concentrated anti-aircraft artillery. Westermann recounts that 5400 American aircraft were shot down by flak during the war, compared with 4300 shot down by fighters. He goes on to argue that most of the fighters preyed on bombers that had been damaged by flak and strayed from their 'Bomber Boxes'.

In addition, in the British night bombing campaigns, flak brought down 41 per cent of all British losses, or around 1300 aircraft. Most of these planes were shot down by the flak attached to *Luftflotte Reich* under the command of *Generaloberst* Hans-

Jürgen Stumpff, who was ordered to protect the shrinking Reich at the beginning of 1944. In the final defence of the Reich, he employed 10 flak divisions and six flak brigades with 9000 light and 5000 heavy flak guns, 5000 searchlights as well as 774 day-fighters and 381 night-fighters. These were concentrated in the Berlin sector, poised to defend the capital. It was only in the final months of the war, with ordnance shortages and the Allies overrunning German cities, that ground-based anti-aircraft defences finally broke down. However, flak's significance is in its effectiveness; the anti-aircraft arm of the *Luftwaffe* was highly successful in what it was able to accomplish until the very final stages of the war.

Fallschirmjäger

Specialist troops were used by each of the services – the *Luftwaffe* had the *Fallschirmjäger* (paratroopers). These soldiers were attached to *Luftwaffe* units and were the basis for the doctrine of vertical envelopment, a new form of warfare devised during the inter-war period. The Germans

became very adept at the doctrine, and the German *Fallschirmjäger* were among the best in the world until later eclipsed by the Americans. Hitler and Göring both had very high hopes for the paratroopers. They expected them to be game-changing; best employed to overwhelm an enemy force or else in combat in very difficult situations where ground troops were ineffective.

The first test for the *Fallschirmjäger* came during the battle of Norway in April 1940. The airborne assault kicked off the invasion as paratroopers landed at the airports at Oslo and Stavanger and at Aalborg in Denmark. Stavanger and Aalborg were captured quickly; the airfields were only lightly defended. Oslo airport was tougher but was captured with the second wave of troops brought in by transport aircraft – Ju 52s. The only setback in the campaign for the *Fallschirmjäger* was at the railway junction at Dombås, where one company of paratroopers were forced to surrender after holding the junction for five days without

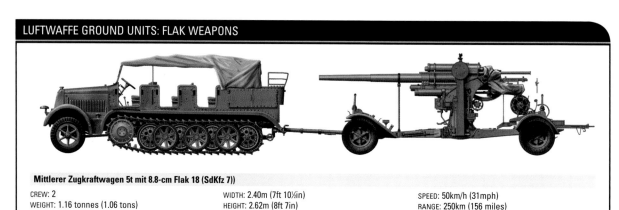

LUFTWAFFE GROUND UNITS: FLAK WEAPONS

Mittlerer Zugkraftwagen 5t mit 8.8-cm Flak 18 (SdKfz 7))

CREW: 2
WEIGHT: 1.16 tonnes (1.06 tons)
LENGTH: 6.85m (20ft 3in)

WIDTH: 2.40m (7ft 10½in)
HEIGHT: 2.62m (8ft 7in)
ENGINE: Maybach HL62 6-cylinder (105kW/140hp)

SPEED: 50km/h (31mph)
RANGE: 250km (156 miles)
RADIO: None

PARATROOPER DIVISIONS
Fallschirmjägerdivisionen
1.Fallschirmjägerdivision
2.Fallschirmjägerdivision
3.Fallschirmjägerdivision
4.Fallschirmjägerdivision
5.Fallschirmjägerdivision
6.Fallschirmjägerdivision
7.Fallschirmjägerdivision
8.Fallschirmjägerdivision
9.Fallschirmjägerdivision
10.Fallschirmjägerdivision
11.Fallschirmjägerdivision
20.Fallschirmjägerdivision
21.Fallschirmjägerdivision
Fallschirmjägerdivision Erdmann
Fallschirmjäger-Ausb.-u.Ersatz-Division

PARATROOPER UNIT ORGANIZATION	
Divisionen	*Divisions*
Lufwaffen-Felddivisionen	Airforce Field Divisions
Division General Göring	Division 'General Göring'
1.Luftwaffe-Ausbildungsdivision	1st Airforce Training Division
Luftwaffedivision Meindl	Airforce Division 'Meindl'
Brigaden	*Brigades*
Brigade General Göring	Brigade 'General Göring'
Luftwaffebrigade Oberrhein	Airforce Brigade 'Upper Rhine'
Regimenter	*Regiments*
Luftlande-Sturmregiment 1	1st Airforce Assault Regiment
Feldregimenter der Luftwaffe	Airforce Field Regiments
Luftwaffen-Jägerregimenter	Airforce Rifle Regiments
Schützenregiment Hermann Göring	Rifle Regiment 'Hermann Göring'
Jägerregiment Hermann Göring	Rifle Regiment 'Hermann Göring'
Grenadierregimenter	Grenadier Regiments
Luftwafferegiment Barenthin	Airforce Regiment 'Barenthin'
Luftwaffe-Infanterieregiment Moskau	Airforce Infantry Regiment 'Moscow'
Feld-Ausbildungsregimenter der Luftwaffe	Airforce Field Training Regiments
Ersatzregiment Hermann Göring	Replacement Regiment 'Hermann Göring'
Luftwaffen-Ausbildungsregimenter	Airforce Training Regiments
Abteilungen/Bataillone	*Battalions*
Luftwaffen-Feldbataillone z.b.V.	Airforce Field Battalions for special use
Luftwaffen-Jägerbataillone z.b.V.	Airforce Rifle Battalions for special use
Infanteriebataillone der Luftwaffe	Airforce Infantry Battalions
Luftwaffen-Schützenbataillone	Airforce Rifle Battalions
Luftwaffebataillon Moskau	Airforce Battalion 'Moscow'
Luftwaffen-Festungsbataillone	Airforce Fortress Battalions
Feldersatzbataillone der Luftwaffe	Airforce Field Replacement Battalions
Feld-Ausbildungsbataillone der Luftwaffe	Airforce Field Replacement Battalions
Ausbildungsbataillone (OB) der Luftwaffe	Airforce Training Battalions

reinforcement. They were later released when Norway surrendered. The Norway campaign was a success for the *Luftwaffe*'s *Fallschirmjäger*, and their exploits continued in the conquest of the Low Countries.

The conquest of Belgium hinged on the 'impregnable' fortress of Eben-Emael. The fort was significant as it overlooked the strategically important Albert Canal and a bridgehead on the German-Belgian border. On the opening day of the campaign, 10 May 1940, 85 *Fallschirmjäger* from 7.*Fliegerdivision* (7th Airborne Division) dropped onto the top of the fortress in gliders. The fort had heavy defences against ground targets but none for aerial targets. The paratroopers, with specially designed shape charges, penetrated the fortress and forced the 1200-man garrison to surrender the next day. The Germans lost only six men in the attack. At the same time, another 400 *Fallschirmjäger*, in three further glider-landed groups, attacked bridges and crossroads. They were equally successful; targets were secured and the Belgians were to capitulate less than three weeks after the invasion began.

The best known *Luftwaffe Fallschirmjäger* action was Operation *Merkur* (Mercury) the German invasion of Crete. The May 1941 invasion was primarily a paratroop operation, with *Luftwaffe Fallschirmjäger* leading the charge against British and Cretan defenders. Ten thousand paratroopers from 7.*Fliegerdivision* were accompanied by 750 glider troops, who landed in three areas of the island to secure airfields and roadways.

Following the vertical envelopment, reinforcements were scheduled to be brought in by air transport and, later, ships. While ultimately successful, the parachute drop was very costly. The Germans ran into strong defences on the island; they had severely underestimated both the British strength and the Cretan will to resist. The landings alone were costly, with around 10 per cent of the forces incapacitated in the initial landings, and additional troops lost in combat to the heavy defences.

By the third day of the fight, the *Fallschirmjäger* had been reinforced but had already suffered heavy casualties – as much as half of their original contingent. Although there is no consensus on the actual numbers, the German official history recounts over 2000 killed, another 2000 missing (and presumed dead) and another 2600 wounded in the battle. However, Crete surrendered on 1 June, and the British were forced to evacuate over 16,000 troops to Egypt.

Nevertheless German losses were atrocious. Hitler was appalled and cancelled a follow-on plan for the vertical envelopment of Malta, and ordered the *Fallschirmjäger* concept shelved. Crete was the final *Fallschirmjäger* operation of the war for the Germans. After Crete, the specialist fighters were used as land-based troops; most went to the Eastern Front to combat the Soviets. They were well respected in combat for their toughness, but they were no longer used for vertical envelopment.

Hermann Göring Division

In 1933, Hermann Göring was appointed Prussian Minister of the Interior, and given control of the police forces. He created a paramilitary group from the police forces that was later renamed and placed under the aegis of the *Luftwaffe* as the *Regiment General Göring*. Parts of the unit received paratrooper training, and the regiment was one of the first units to cross the Austrian border during the *Anschluss*; it also played a role in the Polish campaign and in France. After the fall of France, the regiment returned to Berlin for additional training. When Germany invaded the Soviet Union, the regiment was motorized and participated in Operation *Barbarossa*. Attached to 11th Panzer Division, it was part of the southern advance, frequently turning its heavy guns against Soviet tanks.

In 1942 the regiment was upgraded first to brigade, then to a division and sent to the North African desert to fight with Rommel's *Afrikakorps*. With the loss of North Africa, the remnants of the division were reconstituted as *Panzerdivision Hermann Göring* and sent to Sicily, where the formation fought against the Allied invasion during Operation *Husky*. Sicily was lost, and the division withdrew to Italy, where it fought in retreat against the Allied invasion of the mainland.

In April 1944, the unit was withdrawn from front-line duties, renamed the *Fallschirm-Panzerdivision 1 Hermann Göring* and sent to the Eastern Front to fight the

COMMANDERS: H-GÖRING DIV

Name	Date
Generalmajor Paul Conrath	May 1943
Generalmajor Erich Walther	September 1944
Oberst Wilhelm Söth	November 1944
Oberst Georg Seegers	February 1945
Oberst Helmut Hufenbach	March 1945
Generalmajor Erich Walther	March 1945

HERMANN GÖRING DIVISION INSIGNIA

The Göring Division's association with paratroopers is evident in its divisional symbol, which incorporates the diving eagle insignia of the *Fallschirmjäger*.

The basic *Fallschirm-Panzerkorps Hermann Göring* symbol was a diamond. This is the vehicle insignia of the corps staff.

Other units in the corps used the diamond with different interior designs. This is the symbol of the HQ Company of *Fallschirm-Pz.Art.Rgt 2 HG*.

The flag of the Hermann Göring Panzer Corps carried the *Luftwaffe* Eagle on the pink *Waffenfarbe* of the *Panzertruppen*.

Soviet advance. By the autumn, parts of the division had been hived off to form a sister formation, the *Fallschirm-Panzergrenadierdivision 2 Hermann Göring*. By the end of the year, both divisions had been all but destroyed by the Soviet advance, although they were successful in defending against the Soviets north of Warsaw. The divisions, amalgamated as the *Fallschirm-Panzerkorps Hermann Göring*, ended the war around Dresden, battling the Soviets.

The wartime exploits of the Hermann Göring formation were legendary, and a number of commanders were brought to trial in absentia for war crimes, specifically instances in Italy and during the Polish Uprising, where the unit was accused of civilian massacres. The members of the unit still alive at the end of the war were captured by the Soviets and sent to post-war prison camps; there were few survivors.

Luftwaffen-Feldkorps

The last of the *Luftwaffe* units who fought on the ground were the *Luftwaffen-Feldkorps*, *Luftwaffe* personnel pressed into infantry service. Without aircraft to fly, or unrequired in other roles, these men were handed rifles and sent to the Eastern Front. Men were pulled from construction units, the *Luftwaffe* forestry service, aviation administration services, air traffic control and similar roles to fight the Soviet tide. Their first action was in support of Manstein's relief of Stalingrad late in 1942, but the poorly trained soldiers were ineffective in combat. Overall, according to the historian Martin Windrow, 22 field divisions were raised and put under the command of four *Feldkorps*, numbered I to IV. However, these divisions were mostly undermanned: none had a full complement; all numbered between 4000 and 12,000 strong. Thrown into the fight on the Eastern Front, the poorly equipped, badly trained and unmotivated troops withered in the face of late-war Soviet power. Their record was unremarkable, as was to be expected.

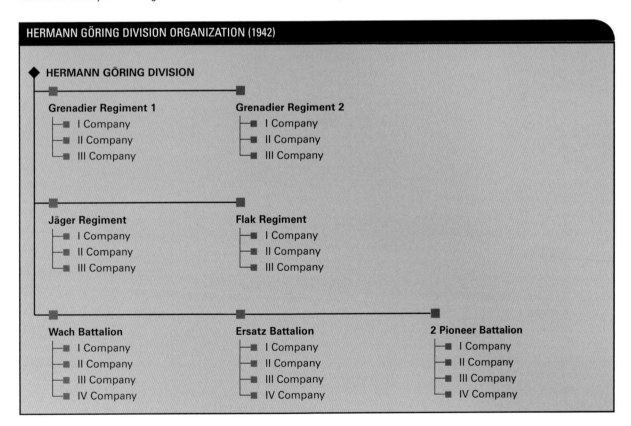

HERMANN GÖRING DIVISION ORGANIZATION (1942)

◆ **HERMANN GÖRING DIVISION**

Grenadier Regiment 1
- I Company
- II Company
- III Company

Grenadier Regiment 2
- I Company
- II Company
- III Company

Jäger Regiment
- I Company
- II Company
- III Company

Flak Regiment
- I Company
- II Company
- III Company

Wach Battalion
- I Company
- II Company
- III Company
- IV Company

Ersatz Battalion
- I Company
- II Company
- III Company
- IV Company

2 Pioneer Battalion
- I Company
- II Company
- III Company
- IV Company

Recruitment

The table below shows all Luftwaffe *personnel, including ground troops, compared to total* Wehrmacht *personnel during World War II.*

Generally, the Luftwaffe *made up between 10 and 20 percent of total armed forces numbers at any one time, reaching a peak in the key years of offensive operations during 1941, 1942 and 1943.*

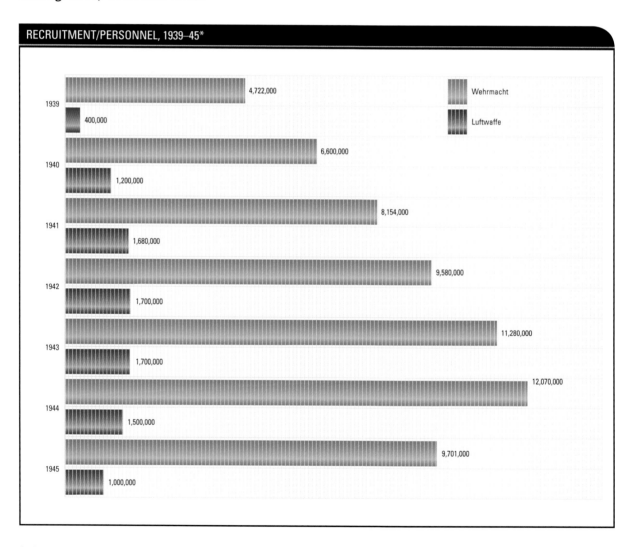

RECRUITMENT/PERSONNEL, 1939–45*

	Wehrmacht	Luftwaffe
1939	4,722,000	400,000
1940	6,600,000	1,200,000
1941	8,154,000	1,680,000
1942	9,580,000	1,700,000
1943	11,280,000	1,700,000
1944	12,070,000	1,500,000
1945	9,701,000	1,000,000

(* Courtesy http://www.feldgrau.com/stats.html. A word of caution regarding these numbers: there is no one single source for statistics and data on German service totals during WWII, and sources vary.)

Messerschmitt Bf 109 Production

The Messerschmitt Bf 109 was probably Germany's most important fighter in World War II, making up the backbone of the Luftwaffe *in almost every theatre. Although replaced by the Focke Wulf Fw 190 from 1941 onwards, Bf 109s were still on frontline service at the war's end.*

Originally conceived as an interceptor, later models were developed to carry out multiple tasks, serving as bomber escorts, fighter bombers, night fighters, bomber interceptors, ground-attack aircraft and also as reconnaissance aircraft.

The Bf 109 was the most produced warplane during World War II, with 30,573 examples built during the war, as well as being the most produced fighter aircraft in aviation history, with a total of 33,984 units built up to April 1945. Fighter production totalled 47 percent of all German aircraft built, and the Bf 109 accounted for 57 percent of all German fighter types made.

After the war, Bf 109s were still being operated by air forces in Romania, Yugoslavia and Finland in the 1950s and as late as the 1960s in Spain, well into the era of the jet.

■ **Bf 109G-6s from JG 27 patrol over the Adriatic Sea from their base in Greece. The nearest aircraft is unmodified, but the two furthest from the camera have tropical filters and underwing gondolas for the MG 151/20 cannon, known as the 'Kanonenboote' (gunboat).**

Factory, Location	Up to 1939	1939	1940	1941	1942	1943	1944	1945	Total
MESSERSCHMITT BF 109 FIGHTER PRODUCTION (1936–45)									
Messerschmitt, Regensburg	–	–	–	203	486	2,164	6,329	1,241	10,423
Arado, Warnemünde	–	–	–	370	–	–	–	–	370
Erla, Leipzig	–	–	–	683	875	2,015	4,472	1,018	9,063
Fieseler, Kassel	–	–	–	155	–	–	–	–	155
W.N.F., Wiener Neustadt	–	–	–	836	1,297	2,200	3,081	541	7,892
Györi Wagon-és Gépgyár, Györ	–	–	–	–	–	39	270	–	309
Ago, Oschersleben	–	–	–	381	–	–	–	–	381
Totals	**1,860**	**1,540**	**1,868**	**2,628**	**2,658**	**6,418**	**14,152**	**2,800**	**33,984**

Bibliography

BOOKS

Bekker, Cajus. *The Luftwaffe Diaries*. Da Capo Press, 1994.

Bishop, Patrick. *Battle of Britain: Day-to-Day Chronicle 10 July – 31 October*. Quercus Publications, 2009.

Boyne, Walter. *Messerschmitt Me 262, Arrow to the Future*. Schiffer Military History, 1992.

Caldwell, Donald and Richard Muller. *The Luftwaffe over Germany, Defense of the Reich*. Greenhill Books, 2007.

Classen, Adam. *Hitler's Northern War*. University Press of Kansas, 2001.

Corum, James and Richard Muller. *The Luftwaffe's Way of War, 1911–1945*. Nautical and Aviation Publishing, 1998.

Corum, James. *The Luftwaffe: Creating the Operational Air War, 1918–1940*. University Press of Kansas, 1997.

Held, Werner and Ernst Obermaier. *The Luftwaffe in the North African Campaign, 1941–1943*. Schiffer Military History, 2004.

Hootan, E.R. *The Rise and Rise of the Luftwaffe*. Brockhampton Press, 1999.

Mason, Herbert Malloy. *The Rise of the Luftwaffe*. Ballentine Books, 1975.

McNab, Chris. *Order of Battle: German Luftwaffe in World War II*. Amber Books, 2009.

Muller, Richard. *The German Air War in Russia*. Nautical and Aviation Publishing, 1992.

Murray, Williamson *The Luftwaffe 1933–1945, Strategy for Defeat*. Brassey's Press, 1996.

Overy, R.J. *The Air War 1939–1945*. Potomac Books, 2005.

Overy, R.J. *The Battle of Britain*. W.W. Norton and Company, 2002.

Pavelec, Sterling M. *The Jet Race and the Second World War*. Praeger, 2007.

Perret, Geoffrey. *Winged Victory, the Army Air Forces in World War II*. Random House 1997.

Westermann, Edward. *Flak*. University Press of Kansas, 2005.

USEFUL WEBSITES

The Luftwaffe 1933–45 Michael Holm
– *http://www.ww2.dk/*

Axis History Factbook Marcus Wendel
– *http://www.axishistory.com/*

Sturmvogel Jason Long
– *http://www.geocities.com/CapeCanaveral/2072/index.html*

Luftwaffe Resource Center
– *http://www.warbirdsresourcegroup.org/LRG/index.html*

Feldgrau.com Jason Pipes – *http://www.feldgrau.com/*

Glossary of Key Abbreviations

AG	Aufklärungsgruppe (reconnaissance group)
BF	Bordflieger (ship-based aviation)
F	Fern- (long-range strategic aviation)
JaFü	Jagdfliegerführer (fighter command)
JG	Jagdgeschwader (fighter group)
KG	Kampfgeschwader (bomber group)
KGzbV	Kampfgeschwader zur besonderen Verwendung (lit. 'Bomber groups for special purpose'; transport group)
KüFl	Küsten Flieger (coastal aviation)
KüFlGr	Küstenfliegergruppe (coastal aviation group)
LG	Lehrgeschwader (demonstration/operational development group)
NG	Nahaufklärungsgruppe (short-range reconnaissance group)
NJG	Nachtjagdgeschwader (night-fighter group)
NSGr	Nachtschlachtgruppe (night attack group)
OKL	Oberkommando der Luftwaffe
OKW	Oberkommando der Wehrmacht
SAGr	Seeaufklärungsgruppe (maritime reconnaissance group)
SG	Schlachtgeschwader (close-support/assault group)
StG	Sturzkampfgeschwader (dive bomber group)
TG	Transportgeschwader (transport group)
ZG	Zerstörergeschwader (twin-engined fighter group; lit. 'destroyer group')

SAYVILLE LIBRARY
88 GREENE AVENUE
SAYVILLE, NY 11782

FEB 0 3 2011